Lecture Notes in Computer Science   12475

More information about this subseries at http://www.springer.com/series/7408

Gustavo Carvalho · Volker Stolz (Eds.)

Formal Methods: Foundations and Applications

23rd Brazilian Symposium, SBMF 2020
Ouro Preto, Brazil, November 25–27, 2020
Proceedings

 Springer

Editors
Gustavo Carvalho ⓘ
Federal University of Pernambuco
Recife, Brazil

Volker Stolz ⓘ
Western Norway University
of Applied Sciences
Bergen, Norway

ISSN 0302-9743 ISSN 1611-3349 (electronic)
Lecture Notes in Computer Science
ISBN 978-3-030-63881-8 ISBN 978-3-030-63882-5 (eBook)
https://doi.org/10.1007/978-3-030-63882-5

LNCS Sublibrary: SL2 – Programming and Software Engineering

This Springer imprint is published by the registered company Springer Nature Switzerland AG
The registered company address is: Gewerbestrasse 11, 6330 Cham, Switzerland

Preface

This volume contains the papers presented at the 23rd Brazilian Symposium on Formal Methods (SBMF 2020). The conference was supposed to be held in Ouro Preto, Brazil, during November 25–27, 2020. However, in light of the COVID-19 pandemic, it was replaced by a virtual event only on the same dates.

SBMF is an event devoted to the development, dissemination, and use of formal methods for the construction of high-quality computational systems, aiming to promote opportunities for researchers and practitioners with an interest in formal methods to discuss the recent advances in this area. SBMF is a consolidated scientific-technical event in the software area. Its first edition took place in 1998, reaching the 23rd edition in 2020. The proceedings of the last editions have been published mostly in Springer's *Lecture Notes in Computer Science* series as volumes 5902 (2009), 6527 (2010), 7021 (2011), 7498 (2012), 8195 (2013), 8941 (2014), 9526 (2015), 10090 (2016), 10623 (2017), and 11254 (2018).

The conference included three invited talks, given by Nikolaj Bjørner (Microsoft Research, USA), Rohit Gheyi (Universidade Federal de Campina Grande, Brazil), and Martin Leucker (University of Lübeck, Germany). A total of 10 papers were presented at the conference and are included in this volume. They were selected from 17 submissions that came from 7 different countries: Brazil, France, Israel, Norway, Portugal, the UK, and the USA. The Program Committee comprised 44 members from the national and international community of formal methods. Each submission was reviewed by three Program Committee members (single-blind review). Submissions, reviews, deliberations, and decisions were handled via EasyChair, which provided good support throughout this process.

We are grateful to the Program Committee and to the additional reviewers for their hard work in evaluating submissions and suggesting improvements. We are very thankful to the general chair of SBMF 2020, Rodrigo Ribeiro (Universidade Federal de Ouro Preto, Brazil), who made everything possible for the conference to run smoothly. SBMF 2020 was organized by the Universidade Federal de Ouro Preto (UFOP) and promoted by the Brazilian Computer Society (SBC). We would like to thank Formal Methods Europe (FME) for their sponsorship and Springer for agreeing to publish the proceedings as a volume of *Lecture Notes in Computer Science*. Volker Stolz is grateful to the Norwegian Agency for International Cooperation and Quality Enhancement in Higher Education (DIKU) for support through grant UTF-2018-CAPES-Diku/10001 "Modern Refactoring."

November 2020

Gustavo Carvalho
Volker Stolz

Organization

General Chair

Rodrigo Ribeiro   Universidade Federal de Ouro Preto, Brazil

Program Committee Chairs

Gustavo Carvalho   Universidade Federal de Pernambuco, Brazil
Volker Stolz   Western Norway University of Applied Sciences, Norway

Steering Committee

Simone Cavalheiro   Universidade Federal de Pelotas, Brazil
Adolfo Duran   Universidade Federal da Bahia, Brazil
José Fiadeiro   University of Dundee, UK
Tiago Massoni   Universidade Federal de Campina Grande, Brazil
Mohammad Mousavi   University of Leicester, UK
Phillip Wadler   The University of Edinburgh, UK

Program Committee

Aline Andrade   Universidade Federal da Bahia, Brazil
Luis Barbosa   Universidade do Minho, Portugal
Christiano Braga   Universidade Federal Fluminense, Brazil
Manfred Broy   Technische Universität München, Germany
Sérgio Campos   Universidade Federal de Minas Gerais, Brazil
Gustavo Carvalho   Universidade Federal de Pernambuco, Brazil
Ana Cavalcanti   University of York, UK
Simone Cavalheiro   Universidade Federal de Pelotas, Brazil
Márcio Cornélio   Universidade Federal de Pernambuco, Brazil
Andrea Corradini   Università di Pisa, Italy
Jim Davies   University of Oxford, UK
Leonardo de Moura   Microsoft Research, USA
David Déharbe   CLEARSY Systems Engineering, France
Clare Dixon   The University of Liverpool, UK
José Fiadeiro   University of Dundee, UK
Rohit Gheyi   Universidade Federal de Campina Grande, Brazil
Arnd Hartmanns   University of Twente, The Netherlands
Robert Hierons   Brunel University London, UK
Juliano Iyoda   Universidade Federal de Pernambuco, Brazil
Thierry Lecomte   CLEARSY Systems Engineering, France

Michael Leuschel	Universität Düsseldorf, Germany
Giovanny Lucero	Universidade Federal de Sergipe, Brazil
Patrícia Machado	Universidade Federal de Campina Grande, Brazil
Tiago Massoni	Universidade Federal de Campina Grande, Brazil
Ana Melo	Universidade de São Paulo, Brazil
Álvaro Moreira	Universidade Federal do Rio Grande do Sul, Brazil
Anamaria Moreira	Universidade Federal do Rio de Janeiro, Brazil
Alexandre Mota	Universidade Federal de Pernambuco, Brazil
Mohammad Mousavi	University of Leicester, UK
David Naumann	Stevens Institute of Technology, USA
Sidney Nogueira	Universidade Federal Rural de Pernambuco, Brazil
José Oliveira	Universidade do Minho, Portugal
Marcel Oliveira	Universidade Federal do Rio Grande do Norte, Brazil
Leila Ribeiro	Universidade Federal do Rio Grande do Sul, Brazil
Augusto Sampaio	Universidade Federal de Pernambuco, Brazil
Adenilso Simão	Universidade de São Paulo, Brazil
Colin Snook	University of Southampton, UK
Volker Stolz	Western Norway University of Applied Sciences, Norway
Sofiène Tahar	Concordia University, Canada
Leopoldo Teixeira	Universidade Federal de Pernambuco, Brazil
Maurice ter Beek	Istituto di Scienza e Tecnologie dell'Informazione, Italy
Nils Timm	University of Pretoria, South Africa
Philip Wadler	The University of Edinburgh, UK
Jim Woodcock	University of York, UK

Additional Reviewers

Yassmeen Elderhalli
Jaakko Järvi
Breno Miranda
Raúl Monti
Renata Reiser
Mohsen Safari

Contents

Software Product Lines

Invited Talks

Formal Verification of Neural Networks?

Martin Leucker[(✉)]

Institute for Software Engineering and Programming Languages,
University of Lübeck, Lübeck, Germany
leucker@isp.uni-luebeck.de

Abstract. Machine learning is a popular tool for building state of the
art software systems. It is more and more used also in safety critical
areas. This demands for verification techniques ensuring the safety and
security of machine learning based solutions. However, we argue that
the popularity of machine learning comes from the fact that no formal
specification exists which renders traditional verification inappropriate.
Instead, validation is typically demanded, but formalization of so far
informal requirements is necessary to give formal evidence that the right
system is build. Moreover, we present a recent technique that allows to
check certain properties for an underlying recurrent neural network and
which may be uses as a tool to identify whether the system learned is
right.

1 Introduction

When developing a program, one of the main fundamental problems in practice
is to get it *correct*. Especially for safety-critical systems, lives may depend on the
correct functioning of the software, for example, software controlling a car. But
also in less safety-critical areas, the verification of systems plays an important
economical role. Since its first days, it has been a challenge to get software systems correct, and a plethora of different methods have been developed ranging
from debugging and testing to formal verification techniques. More generally,
formal methods have been developed over the past decades to support the rigorous development of software systems. See [6] for an expert survey on formal
methods, giving insight to the past, present, and future of formal methods.

On the other hand, artificial intelligence and as part of it machine learning
is currently en vogue for developing software based systems. Especially deep
learning methods turned out to be successful when developing applications for
speech or image recognition, see for example [4,10,11], although it seems unclear,
why such methods actually perform well in practice [14]. In general, deep learning methods may play one fundamental approach for synthesizing programs [7]
rather than programming them manually.

As such, one may come up with the fundamental question of how to verify
such networks for being sure that they adhere to what they are suppose to
achieve. The latter question, however, has to be made precise. Let us first recall
the common definition of verification:

© Springer Nature Switzerland AG 2020
G. Carvalho and V. Stolz (Eds.): SBMF 2020, LNCS 12475, pp. 3–7, 2020.
https://doi.org/10.1007/978-3-030-63882-5_1

> *Verification is a method for showing whether a system adheres to its specification.*

Let us elaborate on this definition more carefully. The definition contains the notion of a *system* which is considered to be the system under test, the artefact that we are going to check. In our case it would be something like a (deep) neural network. Another ingredient of the definition is the notion of a *specification*. The specification defines the anticipated, correct behavior of the system to build. A huge variety of specification formalisms especially for specifying intended, correct behaviour have been developed in the past decade. A prominent example is Linear-time Temporal Logic (LTL), as suggested by Pnueli [13]. It has been noted that specifying the intended behaviour is inherently complex and approaches like specification patterns [5] or enriching temporal specification languages with syntactic sugar [3] have been developed to lower the burden of formulating specifications, just to name a two examples.

However, in machine learning applications (for which for example deep learning is employed), there is typically no specification on what the system is supposed to do. Instead, a neural network is *trained* on typical examples resulting in the final network.

We claim that it is crucial that machine learning works *without* a specification. We believe that its success—and its main application area—is in domains where a specification is ultimately complicated, nearly as complicated as programming a program itself. To illustrate our statement, think of specifying how a cat or a malignant tumor looks exactly. While it is easy for every human or a trained medical doctor to decide case by case whether a cat or a tumor is shown on a given image, respectively, a formalization seems extremely complicated.

So, in machine learning, we are facing the problem that we do not have a formal specification, that we only have examples of the intended behaviour of our system, but at the same time, we want assurance that the system works well in practice.

2   Verification vs. Validation vs. Trustworthy AI

Software engineering research has well understood the need for distinguishing the two questions:

- what a program is supposed to do according to its specification, and
- what a program is supposed to do according to the clients needs

where the client here reflects the stakeholder ordering a piece of software. While dealing with the first question is called *verification*, the methods for answering the second question are studied under the term *validation*. It is said that Barry Boehm memorably characterized the difference as follows[1]

---

[1] "In short, Boehm (3) expressed the difference between the software verification and software validation as follows: Verification: "Are we building the product right?" Validation: "Are we building the right product?" [12].

- Verification is building the system right.
- Validation is building the right system.

So, if at all, the quest for getting a safe system is first of all validation rather than verification. What does *right* mean, when the system is (only) given by means of examples but at the same time used in critical domains?

A quite elaborated notion that—as we claim—could be an interpretation of *right* is *trustworthy*. This term has been coined by a European expert group in the context of AI[2]. Rather than correctness, trustworthiness covers a broader understanding for building the system right. "'Trustworthy AI should be

1. lawful - respecting all applicable laws and regulations,
2. ethical - respecting ethical principles and values, and
3. robust - both from a technical perspective while taking into account its social environment."

To this extent, seven key requirements have been formulated that any trustworthy AI system should meet at least:[3]

- *Human agency and oversight* aiming for AI systems being human centric.
- *Technical Robustness and safety* aiming for AI systems to be resilient and secure, ensuring "that also unintentional harm can be minimized and prevented".
- *Privacy and data governance* including adequate data governance mechanisms.
- *Transparency* requesting that the data, system and AI business models should be transparent.
- *Diversity, non-discrimination and fairness* requiring that "unfair bias must be avoided".
- *Accountability* asking for measures ensuring responsibility and accountability.

The above key requirements are not exhaustive but give a clear perspective on what should be expected from the "right" AI-based system, also those based on neural networks.

As stated in [8], these requirements may be realized by technical and non-technical methods, and we consider it to be an important research topic to work on formal methods ensuring especially the above requirements.

3   Property-Directed Verification of Recurrent Neural Networks

Now, does the above discussion mean that formal verification such as model checking [2] is unimportant in the setting of AI and especially neural networks?

---

[2] https://ec.europa.eu/digital-single-market/en/news/ethics-guidelines-trustworthy-ai.

[3] The requirements are listed here in a very brief form. Please consult the original article for an elaborate explanation.

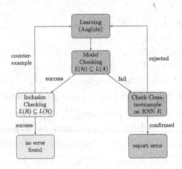

Fig. 1. Property-directed verification of RNNs

We think that this is by no means the case but verification has to be under-stood differently. A (formal) specification may represent (a formalisation) of one of the requirements above and verification may be understood as a parameter-ized analysis algorithm showing a property of the underlying system. In simple words, research on verifying deep neural networks has to incorporate verification methods but especially formalization on what to check.

A recent approach for verifying properties of recurrent neural networks is given in [9]. It is observed that a recurrent neural network can be understood as an infinite-state machine, whenever it is used as a finite classifier. For such an infinite state system a finite-state automaton may be learned using automata learning techniques such as Angluin's L* [1] as a surrogate model approximating the system at hand. The surrogate model may then be used to check whether it meets its specification, for example using model checking techniques.

A surrogate model is a substitute model acting often in a specific role. [9] intertwines the task of verification and of learning the surrogate model in the form that a model is learned driven by the property to verify. While precise answers are obtained for checking the property on the *surrogate model* and an explicit counter example is provided if the underlying RNN does not satisfy the property at hand, a successful verification in terms of the *RNN* is only given up-to a given error probability. The latter is due to the fact that the infinite-state RNN is only statistically compared with the surrogate model. The procedure is sketched in Fig. 1, where the specification to check is denoted by a language $L(A)$ of an automaton, the RNN is denoted by R and the surrogate model to be learned is denoted by $\mathcal{H}$ as it acts as hypothesis in the setting of Angluin's L*.

[9] shows that the method is indeed beneficial in identifying both violations of a specification as well as the successful verification of properties (up-to a given error probability).

4　Conclusion

In this extended abstract we have discussed the role of verification in the setting of learning-based systems, which are derived by generalizing example behaviors.

We recalled that the success of such machine learning based approaches lies especially in application scenarios where no formal specification is given, when formalizing a specification is a challenge on its own.

We recalled key requirements developed by a European expert group on AI and posed their formalization and support by formal methods as a research agenda for forthcoming years.

Finally, we presented the gist of a novel verification approach for recurrent neural networks that is one example of an analysis algorithm rather than a verification algorithm parameterized by a given property. We suggest such algorithms as starting point for developing further formal methods for checking requirements on neural networks.

References

1. Angluin, D.: Learning regular sets from queries and counterexamples. Inf. Comput. **75**(2), 87–106 (1987). https://doi.org/10.1016/0890-5401(87)90052-6
2. Baier, C., Katoen, J.: Principles of Model Checking. MIT Press, Cambridge (2008)
3. Bauer, A., Leucker, M.: The theory and practice of SALT. In: Bobaru, M., Havelund, K., Holzmann, G.J., Joshi, R. (eds.) NFM 2011. LNCS, vol. 6617, pp. 13–40. Springer, Heidelberg (2011). https://doi.org/10.1007/978-3-642-20398-5_3
4. Deng, L., Hinton, G., Kingsbury, B.: New types of deep neural network learning for speech recognition and related applications: an overview. In: 2013 IEEE International Conference on Acoustics, Speech and Signal Processing, pp. 8599–8603 (2013)
5. Dwyer, M.B., Avrunin, G.S., Corbett, J.C.: Patterns in property specifications for finite-state verification. In: Boehm, B.W., Garlan, D., Kramer, J. (eds.) International Conference on Software Engineering, ICSE 1999, pp. 411–420. ACM (1999)
6. Garavel, H., Beek, M.H., Pol, J.: The 2020 expert survey on formal methods. In: ter Beek, M.H., Ničković, D. (eds.) FMICS 2020. LNCS, vol. 12327, pp. 3–69. Springer, Cham (2020). https://doi.org/10.1007/978-3-030-58298-2_1
7. Gulwani, S., Polozov, O., Singh, R.: Program synthesis. Found. Trends®in Program. Lang. 4(1–2), 1–119 (2017). https://doi.org/10.1561/2500000010
8. High-Level Expert Group on AI: Ethics guidelines for trustworthy AI. Report, European Commission, Brussels, April 2019. https://ec.europa.eu/digital-single-market/en/news/ethics-guidelines-trustworthy-ai
9. Khmelnitsky, I., et al.: Property-directed verification of recurrent neural networks (2020). Preprint https://arxiv.org/abs/2009.10610
10. Liu, J., et al.: Applications of deep learning to MRI images: a survey. Big Data Min. Anal. **1**(1), 1–18 (2018)
11. Mahmud, M., Kaiser, M.S., Hussain, A., Vassanelli, S.: Applications of deep learning and reinforcement learning to biological data. IEEE Trans. Neural Netw. Learn. Syst. **29**(6), 2063–2079 (2018)
12. Kopetz, H.: Automatic Error Detection. Software Reliability, pp. 68–80. Macmillan Education UK, London (1976). https://doi.org/10.1007/978-1-349-86129-3_9
13. Pnueli, A.: The temporal logic of programs. In: Proceedings of the 18th IEEE Symposium on the Foundations of Computer Science (FOCS 1977), Providence, Rhode Island, 31 October–2 November 1977, pp. 46–57. IEEE Computer Society Press (1977)
14. Sejnowski, T.J.: The unreasonable effectiveness of deep learning in artificial intelligence. CoRR abs/2002.04806 (2020). https://arxiv.org/abs/2002.04806

Navigating the Universe of Z3 Theory Solvers

Nikolaj Bjørner[✉] and Lev Nachmanson

Microsoft Research, Washington, D.C., USA
nbjorner@microsoft.com

Abstract. Modular combination of theory solvers is an integral theme in engineering modern SMT solvers. The CDCL(T) architecture provides an overall setting for how theory solvers may cooperate around a SAT solver based on conflict driven clause learning. The Nelson-Oppen framework provides the interface contracts between theory solvers for disjoint signatures. This paper provides an update on theories integrated in Z3. We briefly review principles of theory integration in CDCL(T) and then examine the theory solvers available in Z3, with special emphasis on two recent solvers: a new solver for arithmetic and a pluggable user solver that allows callbacks to invoke propagations and detect conflicts.

1 Introduction

The aim of this paper is to provide an up-to-date overview of Z3's core solver engines. While some of the engines date back quite some time, other engines have been replaced over time, added, and even some have been removed; and then re-added in different guise. A recent addition has been a theory solver for arithmetic developed from the ground up. We give an overview of the main features of this new engine and explain selected new approaches used in the solver. A recent addition includes a mechanism for pluggable propagation. We also provide an introduction to this engine.

We will apply the following taxonomy when discussing the theory solvers. It extends the reduction approach to decision procedures [17] as explained in the context of Z3 in [12].

- Boolean theories
  - Domains that are inherently finite domain and can be solved by reducing to an underlying CDCL engine.
  - Instances: Bit-vectors, Cardinality and Pseudo-Boolean constraints.
- Base theories
  - Theories that form a basis for all other theories.
  - Instances: the theory of uninterpreted functions and the theory of arithmetic.
- Reducible theories
  - Theories that can be solved by reducing into base theories.

© Springer Nature Switzerland AG 2020
G. Carvalho and V. Stolz (Eds.): SBMF 2020, LNCS 12475, pp. 8–24, 2020.
https://doi.org/10.1007/978-3-030-63882-5_2

- Instances: Arrays, IEEE floating points, algebraic datatypes, recursive functions.
- Hybrid theories
  - Theories that combine non-disjoint signatures from different theories.
  - Instances: Sequences, Model-based quantifier instantiation.
- External theories
  - Theories that may be developed externally by propagating consequences and identifying conflicts.
  - Instance: an external propagator plugin.

1.1 Present and Future

Z3 now has two CDCL(T) solvers. For main SMT workloads it offers a CDCL(T) core that integrates all the theories that we mention here. This core is a continuation of the main solver of Z3 since its inception. A core with near up-to-date advances in SAT solving has been used so far for workloads originating from bit-vector and Pseudo-Boolean constraints. This core is currently being updated to handle most if not all the SMT workloads of the legacy core with the intent of modernizing Z3's core and allowing integration of new techniques around in-processing, logging of clausal proofs, model repair, and other goodies. From the perspective of this paper, we do not distinguish these cores. Z3 exposes several other core solvers that either build on top of the SMT solver or entirely bypass it. For Horn clauses, Z3 contains dedicated engines for finite domain Horn clauses using finite hash-tables, and for Constrained Horn Clauses (CHC) it uses the SPACER [18] solver; for quantifier-free formulas over Tarski's fragment of polynomial arithmetic it exposes a self-contained solver; and for quantified formulas for theories that admit quantifier-elimination it exposes self-contained solvers.

2 CDCL(T) - In the Light of Theory Solvers

In this section, we recall the main mechanisms used in mainstream modern SAT solvers in the light of theory solving. When SAT solving, as implemented using conflict driven clause learning, CDCL, is combined with theory solving it augments propositional satisfiability with theory reasoning. The CDCL solver maintains a set of formulas F and a partial assignment to literals in F that we refer to as M.

The solver starts in a state $\langle M, F \rangle$, where M is initially empty. It then attempts to complete M to a full model of F to show that F is satisfiable and at the same time adds consequences to F to establish that F is unsatisfiable. The transition between the search for a satisfying solution and a consequence is handled by a *conflict resolution* phase. The state during conflict resolution is a triple $\langle M; F; C \rangle$, where, besides the partial model M and formula F, there is also a conflict clause C false under M. The auxiliary function *Theory* is used to advance decisions, propagations and identify conflicts. If *Theory* determines that S is conflicting with respect to the literals in M it produces a conflict clause

C, that contains a subset of conflicting literals from M. It can also produce a trail assignment A, which is either a propagation or decision and finally, if it determines that S is satisfiable under trail M it produces SAT.

From the point of view of the CDCL(T) solver theory reasoning is a module that can take a state during search and produce verdicts on how search should progress. We use the following verdicts of a theory invocation $Theory(M; F)$:

- SAT. The theory solver may determine that the assignment M extends to a model of F.
- Conflict C. The theory solver may determine that a subset M is inconsistent relative to F. In the propositional case an inconsistent clause C is a member of F, such that each literal in C is false in M. With theory reasoning, C does not need to correspond to a clause in F, but be assignments in M that are inconsistent modulo theories.
- A propagation ℓ^C. The theory solver propagates a literal ℓ.
- A decision ℓ^δ.

Thus, the verdict determes whether the partial model extends to a model of the theories, can identify a subset of M as an unsatisfiable core, propagate the truth assignment of a literal ℓ, or create a new case split ℓ^δ for a literal ℓ that has not already been assigned in M. We write $SAT = Theory(M, F)$ when the verdict is that M extends to a valid theory model of F, we write $C = Theory(M, F)$ when C is a conflict clause, based on negated literals from M and $A = Theory(M, F)$, when the verdict A is either a propagation or decision.

$$\langle M; F \rangle \qquad \Rightarrow SAT \qquad\qquad\qquad\qquad SAT = Theory(M, F)$$

$$\langle M; F \rangle \qquad \Rightarrow \langle M; F; C \rangle \qquad\qquad\qquad C = Theory(M, F)$$

$$\langle M; F \rangle \qquad \Rightarrow \langle M, A; F \rangle \qquad\qquad\quad A = Theory(M, F)$$

$$\langle M; \emptyset, F \rangle \qquad \Rightarrow UNSAT$$

$$\langle M, \overline{\ell}^\delta; F; C \rangle \Rightarrow \langle M, \ell^C; F \rangle \qquad\qquad\qquad \ell \in C$$

$$\langle M, \ell^{C'}; F; C \rangle \Rightarrow \langle M; F; (C \setminus \{\overline{\ell}\}) \cup (C' \setminus \{\ell\}) \rangle \; \overline{\ell} \in C$$

$$\langle M, A; F; C \rangle \quad \Rightarrow \langle M; F; C \rangle \qquad\qquad\qquad otherwise$$

Example 1

Consider the formula $(x > 0 \vee y > 0) \wedge x + y < 0$. The initial state of search is

$$\langle \epsilon; (x > 0 \vee y > 0) \wedge x + y < 0 \rangle$$

based on the empty partial assignment ϵ and the original formula. A possible next state is to propagate on the unit literal $x + y < 0$, producing

$$\langle x + y < 0^{x+y<0}; (x > 0 \vee y > 0) \wedge x + y < 0 \rangle$$

This step may be followed by a case split setting $x > 0$.

$$\langle x + y < 0^{x+y<0}, \neg(x > 0)^\delta; (x > 0 \vee y > 0) \wedge x + y < 0\rangle$$

which triggers a propagation

$$\langle x + y < 0^{x+y<0}, \neg(x > 0)^\delta, y > 0^{x>0\vee y>0}; (x > 0 \vee y > 0) \wedge x + y < 0\rangle$$

The resulting state is satisfiable in the theory of arithmetic. On the other hand, if we had made the case split on $x > 0$ instead of $\neg(x > 0)$, and then guess the assignment $y > 0$, we would have encountered a conflicting state with conflict clause $\neg(x > 0) \vee \neg(y > 0)$[1]:

$$\langle x+y < 0^{x+y<0}, x > 0^\delta, y > 0^\delta; (x > 0 \vee y > 0) \wedge x+y < 0; \neg(x > 0)\vee\neg(y > 0)\rangle$$

The last decision is then reverted to produce the satisfiable state

$$\langle x + y < 0^{x+y<0}, x > 0^\delta, \neg(y > 0)^{\neg(x>0)\vee\neg(y>0)}; (x > 0 \vee y > 0) \wedge x + y < 0\rangle$$

A third scenario uses theory propagation. In this scenario, the decision $x > 0$ is made, but instead of making a decision $y > 0$, the theory solver for arithmetic is given a chance to find opportunities for propagation. It deduces that $x + y < 0, x > 0$ implies $\neg(y > 0)$, and therefore establishes the theory propagation

$$\langle x + y < 0^{x+y<0}, x > 0^\delta, \neg(y > 0)^{\neg(y>0)\vee\neg(x>0)}; (x > 0 \vee y > 0) \wedge x + y < 0\rangle$$

We are again eliding the unit literal $x+y < 0$ from the explanation for $\neg(y > 0)$.

2.1 Invariants

To be well-behaved we expect *Theory* to produce propagations on literals that don't already appear in M, and crucially enforce the main invariants:

- The conflict clause C is false in M and a consequence of F. Thus, for state $\langle M; F, C\rangle$ we have $F \models_T \bigvee_{\ell \in C} \neg\ell$, as well as $\overline{C} \in M$.
- A propagated literal is justified by the current partial model M. Thus, for state $\langle M\ell^C, F\rangle$ we have $F \models_T C$, $\ell \in C$, and for each $\ell' \in C \setminus \{\ell\} : \overline{\ell'} \in M$.

That is, each conflict clause is a consequence of F and each propagation is also a consequence of F, and the premises of a propagation is justified by T.

---

[1] To keep the formula short we have applied a shortcut and removed the literal $\neg(x + y < 0)$ from the conflict clause. In practice, solvers automatically remove unit literals that are false from conflict clauses.

3   Boolean Theories

Bit-vectors are in the current solver treated as tuples of Boolean variables and all bit-vector operations are translated to Boolean SAT. The approach is called bit-blasting. Only mild equational reasoning is performed over bit-vectors. The benefits of the CDCL SAT engine have been mostly enjoyed for applications in symbolic execution of 32-bit arithmetic instructions. Bit-blasting has its limitations: applications that use quantifiers and applications around smart contracts that use 256 bits per word are stressing this approach. A revised bit-vector solver that integrates algebraic reasoning and lazy bit-blasting is therefore currently being developed.

Cardinality and Pseudo-Boolean inequalities can also be translated into CNF clauses. It is often an advantage when there are very few variables in the summations, but the overhead of translation can quickly become impractical. Z3 therefore contains dedicated solvers for cardinality and Pseudo-Boolean constraints.

4   Base Theories

A first base theory is the theory of uninterpreted functions. This theory captures a shared property of all theory: that equality is a congruence relation. The theory is described many places, including in [5].

4.1   Arithmetic

There are several alternate engines for arithmetical constraints in Z3. Some of the engines are engineered for fragments of arithmetic, such as difference arithmetic, where all inequalities are of the form $x - y \leq k$, for k a constant, and unit-two-variable-per-inequality (UTVPI), where all inequalities are of the form $\pm x \pm y \leq k$. A new main solver for general arithmetic formulas has emerged recently, with the longer term objective of entirely replacing Z3's legacy arithmetic solver. We will here describe internals of the newer solver in more detail.

In overview, the arithmetic solver uses a waterfall model for solving arithmetic constraints.

- First it establishes feasibility with respect to linear inequalities. Variables are solved over the rationals.
- Second, it establishes feasibility with respect to mixed integer linear constraints. Integer variables are solved if they are assigned integer values.
- Finally, it establishes feasibility with respect to non-linear polynomial constraints.

4.1.1 Rational Linear Arithmetic

The solver for rational linear inequalities uses a dual simplex solver as explained in [14]. It maintains a global set of equalities of the form $Ax = 0$, and each variable x_j is assigned lower and upper bounds during search. The solver then checks for feasibility of the resulting system $Ax = 0, lo_j \leq x_j \leq hi_j, \forall j$ for dynamically changing bounds lo_j, hi_j. The bounds are *justified* by assignments in M.

Finding Equal Variables - Cheaply. The new arithmetic solver contains a novel, efficient, method for finding pairs of variables that are forced equal. By finding such variable, the arithmetic solver can then propagate equalities to other theories. Such equality propagation can make a big difference for efficiently integrating arithmetic in hybrid theories, such as the theory of sequences. We will in the following outline the new idea.

A starting point is a tableau with bounds $Ax = 0, lo_j \leq x_j \leq hi_j, \forall j$. The tableau contains a sub-tableau of equalities where at most two variables are non-fixed in every equation, such that the coefficients of the non-fixed variables have the same absolute value. That is, let S be a system of linear equations of the form $e_i := a_i x_i + b_i y_i = c_i$, where x_i, y_i are variables and c_i is a constant, and $a_i, b_i \in \{-1, 1\}$ for $0 \leq i < n$. It is relatively cheap to detect whether a row in a tableau corresponds to such an equation: it can have at most two non-fixed variables whose coefficients must have the same absolute values. We assume that the variable values and the constants are rational numbers. For bounds propagation it is only relevant to consider feasible tableaux. So S has a solution V, so we have $a_i V(x_i) + b_i V(y_i) = c_i$ for every i. Let us call variables u and v equivalent if in every solution of S they have the same values.

Given S and V, we provide an efficient algorithm for finding pairs of variables (u, t) such that u is equivalent to t.

Let us start from an example. Consider the following system

$$x - y = 3, \qquad y - w = 2, \qquad w + t = 4$$
$$y + z = 3, \qquad z + u = 4, \qquad v - z = 2, t - s = 1$$

and solution

$$V: \quad x \to 5, \ y \to 2, \ z \to 1, \ u \to 3, \ w \to 0, \ s \to 3, \ t \to 4, \ v \to 3$$

By examining V, we might suspect that the u, v, and s are pairwise equivalent. However, if we increase x by one we have another solution

$$V': \quad x \to 6, \ y \to 3, \ z \to 0, \ u \to 4, \ w \to 1, \ s \to 2, \ t \to 3, \ v \to 2$$

Since $V'(u) \neq V'(v)$, we can conclude that u is not equivalent to either s or v. But we can prove that v and s are equivalent. Another observation is that each variable changed its value by ± 1: changing as x or as $-x$.

We introduce our algorithm by recalling which inference rules it simulates, without actually literally performing the inferences. The inferences are

$$\frac{x - y = c_1 \qquad y - z = c_2}{x - z = c_1 + c_2} \qquad \frac{x + y = c_1 \qquad z - y = c_2}{x + z = c_1 + c_2} \qquad \frac{x + y = c_1 \qquad z + y = c_2}{x - z = c_1 - c_2}$$

The goal of deriving implied equalities is achieved if we can infer an equality $x - y = 0$ using the above inference rules. Now, the crucial observation is that there is no need to perform arithmetic on the constant offsets c_i because we have a valuation V and the property for every derived equation $x - y = c$:

$$c = 0 \Leftrightarrow V(x) = V(y)$$

So it is enough to look at the variables x, y and check if their values are the same for a derived equality. The benefit of avoiding arithmetic on the coefficients can be significant when the coefficients cannot be represented using ordinary 64-bit registers, but require arbitrary precision arithmetic. Note that the same method also detects fixed variables; whenever deriving $x + x = c$, we have proved x to be fixed at value $c/2$. In this case, the method needs to calculate c. All other variables connected to x through binary equalities are naturally also fixed.

To implement search over the derivation rules efficiently, we build a depth-first search forest where the nodes are annotated by variables annotated by signs and their values from V. Edges are annotated by octagon equations. The forest is built by picking a so-far unprocessed variable and growing a tree under it by traversing all equations involving the variable. During the tree expansion the algorithm checks if two nodes with the same *value* and same *signs* are connected. To propagate a new equality we trace back the path that was used to derive the equality and assemble the justifications from each row.

Example 2

Let us show how the procedure works on the example from above and valuation V. Starting with the node $\langle +t, 4 \rangle$, the equation $t - s = 1$ produces the children $\langle +s, 3 \rangle$ and $\langle -w, 0 \rangle$. The second child can be expanded in turn into $\langle -y, -2 \rangle$, $\langle z, 1 \rangle$, $\langle v, 3 \rangle$. This establishes a path from $\langle s, 3 \rangle$ to $\langle v, 3 \rangle$. The two nodes are labeled by the same values and same signs.

4.1.2   Integer Linear Arithmetic

The mixed integer linear solver comprises of several layers. It contains several substantial improvements over Z3's original arithmetic solver and currently outperforms the legacy solver on the main SMTLIB benchmark sets, and to our knowledge mostly on user scenarios.

GCD Consistency. Each row is first normalized by multiplying it with the least common multiple of the denominators of each coefficient. For each row it assembles a value from the fixed variables. A variable x_j is fixed if the current values lo_j, hi_j are equal. Then it checks that the gcd of the coefficients to variables divide the fixed value. If they don't the row has no integer solution.

Patching. Following [11], the integer solver moves non-basic variables away from their bounds in order to ensure that basic, integer, variables are assigned integer values. The process examines each non-basic variable and checks every row where it occurs to estimate a safe zone where its value can be changed without breaking any bounds. If the safe zone is sufficiently large to patch a basic integer variable it performs an update. This heuristic is highly incomplete, but is able to locally patch several variables without resorting to more expensive analyses.

Cubes. One of the deciding factors in leapfrogging the previous solver relied on a method by Bromberger and Weidenbach [7,8]. It allows to detect feasible inequalities over integer variables by solving a stronger linear system. In addition, we observed that the default strengthening proposed by Bromberger and Weidenbach can often be avoided: integer solutions can be guaranteed from weaker systems.

We will here recall the main method and our twist. In the following we let A, A' range over integer matrices and a, b, c over integer vectors. The 1-norm $\|A\|_1$ of a matrix is a column vector, such that each entry i is the sum of the absolute values of the elements in the corresponding row A_i. We write $\|A_i\|_1$ to directly access the 1-norm of a row.

A (unit) *cube* is a polyhedron that is a Cartesian product of intervals of length one for each variable. Since each variable therefore contains an integer point, the interior of the polyhedron contains an integer point. The condition for a convex polyhedron to contain a cube can be recast as follows:

Example 3
Suppose we have $3x + y \leq 9 \wedge -3y \leq -2$ and wish to find an integer solution. By solving $3x + y \leq 9 - \frac{1}{2}(3 + 1) = 7, -3y \leq -2 - \frac{1}{2}3 = -3.5$ we find a model where $y = \frac{7}{6}, x = 0$. After rounding y to 1 and maintaining x at 0 we obtain an integer solution to the original inequalities.

Our twist on Bromberger and Weidenbach's method is to avoid strengthening on selected inequalities. First we note that *difference* inequalities of the form $x - y \leq k$, where x, y are integer variables and k is an integer offset need not be strengthened. For octagon constraints $\pm x \pm y \leq k$ there is a boundary condition: they need only require strengthening if x, y are assigned at mid-points between integral solutions. For example, if $V(x) = \frac{1}{2}$ and $V(y) = \frac{3}{2}$, for $x + y \leq 2$. Our approach is described in detail in [4].

Branching. Similar to traditional MIP branch-and-bound methods, the solver creates somewhat eagerly case splits on bounds of integer variables if the dual simplex solver fails to assign them integer values.

Gomory and Hermite Cuts. The arithmetic solver produces Gomory cuts from rows where the basic variables are non-integers after the non-basic variables have been pushed to the bounds. It also incorporates algorithms from [9,13] to generate cuts after the linear systems have been transformed into Hermite matrices.

4.1.3   Non-linear Arithmetic
Similar to solving for integer feasibility, the arithmetic solver solves constraints over polynomials using a waterfall model for non-linear constraints. At the basis

it maintains for every monomial term $x \cdot x \cdot y$ an equation $m = x \cdot x \cdot y$, where m is a variable that represents the monomial $x \cdot x \cdot y$. The module for non-linear arithmetic then attempts to establish a valuation V where $V(m) = V(x) \cdot V(x) \cdot V(y)$, or derive a consequence that no such valuation exists. The stages in the waterfall model are summarized as follows:

Bounds Propagation on Monomials. A relatively inexpensive step is to propagate and check bounds based on on non-linear constraints. For example, for $y \geq 3$, then $m = x \cdot x \cdot y \geq 3$, if furthermore $x \leq -2$, we have the strengthened bound $m \geq 12$. Bounds propagation can also flow from bounds on m to bounds on the variables that make up the monomial, such that when $m \geq 8, 1 \leq y \leq 2, x \leq 0$, then we learn the stronger bound $x \leq -2$ on x.

Bounds Propagation with Horner Expansions. If $x \geq 2, y \geq -1, z \geq 2$, then $y + z \geq 1$ and therefore $x \cdot (y + z) \geq 2$, but we would not be able to deduce this fact if combining bounds individually for $x \cdot y$ and $x \cdot z$ because no bounds can be inferred for $x \cdot y$ in isolation. The solver therefore attempts different re-distribution of multiplication in an effort to find stronger bounds.

Gröbner Reduction. We use an adaptation of ZDD (Zero suppressed decision diagrams [19,20]) to represent polynomials. The representation has the advantage that polynomials are stored in a shared data-structure and operations over polynomials are memoized. A polynomial over the real is represented as an acyclic graph where nodes are labeled by variables and edges are labeled by coefficients. For example, the polynomial $5x^2y + xy + y + x + 1$ is represented by the acyclic graph shown below.

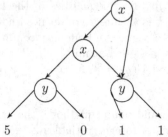

The root node labeled by x represents the polynomial $x \cdot l + r$, where l is the polynomial of the left sub-graph and r the polynomial of the right sub-graph. The left sub-graph is allowed to be labeled again by x, but the right sub-graph may only have nodes labeled by variables that are smaller in a fixed ordering. The fixed ordering used in this example sets x above y. Then the polynomial for the right sub-graph is $y + 1$, and the polynomial with the left sub-graph is $5xy + (y + 1)$.

The Gröbner module performs a set of partial completion steps, preferring to eliminate variables that can be isolated, and expanding a bounded number of super-position steps.

Incremental Linearization. Following [10] we incrementally linearize monomial constraints. For example, we include lemmas of the form $x = 0 \rightarrow m = 0$ and $x = 1 \rightarrow m = y$, for $m = x^2 y$.

NLSat. As an end-game attempt, the solver attempts to solver the non-linear constraints using a complete solver for Tarski's fragment supported by the NLSat solver [16].

5   Reducible Theories

5.1   Refinement Types

Let us illustrate a use of *reduction* from richer theories to base theories based on a simple example based on refinement types. It encodes refinement types using auxiliary functions as explained in [15]. Abstractly, a refinement type of sort S uses a predicate p over S. At least one element of S must satisfy p for the construction to make sense. The refinement type $S \mid p$ represents the elements of S that satisfy p. The properties we need to know about elements of $S \mid p$ can be encoded using two auxiliary functions that form a surjection *restrict* from $S \mid p$ into S with a partial inverse *restrict* that maps elements from S into $S \mid p$. The properties of these functions are summarized as follows:

$p : S \rightarrow Bool$
$relax : S \mid p \rightarrow S$
$restrict : S \rightarrow S \mid p$
$\forall x : S \mid p . restrict(relax(x)) = x$
$\forall s : S . p(s) \rightarrow relax(restrict(s)) = s$
$\forall x : S \mid p . p(relax(x))$

Let us illustrate the sort of natural numbers as a refinement type of integers:

Example 4

$sort\ Nat = Int \mid \lambda x . x \geq 0$
$\forall n : Nat . restrict(relax(n)) = n \wedge relax(n) \geq 0$
$\forall i : Int . i \geq 0 \rightarrow relax(restrict(i)) = i$

We obtain a theory solver for formulas with refinement types by instantiating these axioms whenever there is a term t introduced of sort $S \mid p$ introduced as part of the input or during search (from instantiating quantifiers). The main challenge with supporting this theory is to ensure that the new terms introduced from axiom instantiation is bounded. We don't want the solver to create terms $relax(restrict(relax(restrict(\ldots))))$.

- For every sub-term of the form $restrict(t)$, where t is not $relax(t')$ instantiate the axiom:

- $p(t) \Rightarrow relax(restrict(t)) = t$
– For every term t of sort $S \mid p$ instantiate the axioms:
  - $restrict(relax(t)) = t$
  - $p(relax(t))$

5.2   Reducible Theories in Z3

5.2.1   Arrays

Z3 reduces the theory of arrays to reasoning about uninterpreted functions. It furthermore treats arrays as function spaces. The first-order theory of arrays enjoys compactness and so the following formula is satisfiable[2]

$$\forall a : Array(Int, Int) . \exists k . \forall i \geq k . a[i] = 0.$$

The same formula is not satisfiable when arrays range over function spaces. The distinction is only relevant for formulas that contain quantifiers over arrays.

The central functionality of the decision procedure for arrays is to ensure that a satisfying model under the theory of EUF translates to a satisfying model in the theory of arrays. To this end, the main service of the theory solver is to saturate the search state with β reduction axioms for array terms that admit beta-reduction. We call these terms λ terms and they are defined by the beta-reduction axioms:

$$
\begin{aligned}
\beta(Store(A, j, v)[i]) \quad &= \quad if\ i\ =\ j\ then\ v\ else\ A[i] \\
\beta(Map(f, A, B)[i]) \quad &= \quad f(A[i], B[i]) \\
\beta(AsArray(f)[i]) \quad &= \quad f(i) \\
\beta(Const(v)[i]) \quad &= \quad v \\
\beta((\lambda x\ .\ M)[i]) \quad &= \quad M[i/x]
\end{aligned}
$$

The reduction into EUF, is then in a nutshell an application of the following inference rule:

$$\frac{b\text{ is a lambda term} \qquad a[j]\text{ is a term} \qquad b \sim a\ (a, b\text{ are equal under EUF})}{b[j] = \beta(b[j])}$$

5.2.2   Floating Points

Floating point semantics can be defined in terms of bit-vector operations. The solver for floating points uses this connection to reduce the theory of floating points to bit-vectors.

---

[2] Thanks to Jasmin Blanchette for drawing attention to this distinction.

5.2.3   Algebraic Datatypes

The theory of algebraic datatypes is compiled into uninterpreted functions. In this theory, constructors are injective functions. Injectivity is ensured by adding axioms for partial inverses. For the example of LISP S-expressions these axioms are:

$$car(cons(x, y)) = x, cdr(cons(x, y)) = y$$

The main functionality provided by the theory solver that cannot be reduced to EUF is the *occurs check*.

6   Hybrid Theories

A prime example of a hybrid theory in Z3 is the theory of strings, regular expressions and sequences.

The theory of strings and regular expressions has entered mainstream SMT solving thanks to community efforts around standardization and solvers. The SMTLIB2 format for unicode strings [1]. It integrates operations that mix equational solving over the free monoid with integer arithmetic (for string lengths and extracting sub-strings). Regular expression constraints furthermore effectively introduce constraints that require unfolding recursive relations. Z3 uses symbolic derivatives [21] to handle regular expressions, noteworthy, with complementation and intersection handled by derivatives.

A second prolific example of a hybrid theory is Z3's model-based quantifier instantiation engine (MBQI). Here, a theory is encoded using a quantifier. The MBQI engine supports extensions of Bradley-Manna-Sipma's array property fragment [6] that effectively combines arithmetic with uninterpreted functions.

7   External Theories

The universe of theories is in principle unbounded. Many theories can be captured using a set of quantified axioms and therefore be handled by machinery for quantifiers. But encodings have their own limitations, noteworthy it might not be possible to encode a theory using a small number of axioms. Users can of course encode theory solvers directly themselves within Z3's core. This has been accomplished in the case of Z3Str3 [2], but it is a significant engineering effort and ties a theory to a fixed signature. A more flexible approach was exposed around 2010 in the format of user theories. A user theory plugin could be encoded outside of Z3 and it integrated with the main CDCL(T) engine. Some examples of the user theory were presented in [3]. The user theories were subsequently removed from Z3 as it was not possible to properly integrate them in model construction. Recent experiences with solving constraint satisfaction problems suggested that a restricted version of user theories would be instrumental. A variant of user theories have therefore been resurrected under the banner of a *user propagator* to capture its main functionality: it allows client code participate in propagation and creating conflicts in response to variable assignments.

We will illustrate the user propagator by a simple example. The example illustrates as a Pseudo-Boolean constraint that when encoded directly would be quadratic in the number of variables. The user propagator, though, does not require quadratic space overhead. We encode the constraint that

$$3 \, |\{ \, (i,j) \mid i < j \wedge x_i + x_j = 42 \wedge (x_i > 30 \vee x_j > 30) \, \}|$$
$$+ \, |\{ \, (i,j) \mid i < j \wedge x_i + x_j = 42 \wedge x_i \leq 30 \wedge x_j \leq 30 \, \}| \qquad \leq 100$$

and every subset (i,j) that contributes to the sum and contains at least half of the variables must add up to at least 10. We first define the variables used in the problem:

```
from z3 import *
```

```
xs = BitVecs(["x%d" % i for i in range(8)], 10)
```

Then a user-propagator can be initialized by sub-classing to the `UserPropagateBase` class that implements the main interface to Z3's user propagation functionality.

```
class UserPropagate(UserPropagateBase):
    def __init__(self, s):
        super(self.__class__, self).__init__(s)
        self.add_fixed(self.myfix)
        self.add_final(self.myfinal)
        self.xvalues = {}
        self.id2x = {self.add(x) : x for x in xs}
        self.x2id = { self.id2x[id] : id for id in self.id2x }
        self.trail = []
        self.lim = []
        self.sum = 0
```

The map `xvalues` tracks the values of assigned variables and `id2x` and `x2id` maps tracks the identifiers that Z3 uses for variables with the original variables. The `sum` maintains the running sum of according to our unusual constraint.

The class must implement methods for pushing and popping backtrackable scopes. We use a `trail` to record closures that are invoked to restore the previous state and `lim` to maintain the the size of the trail for the current scope.

```
    # overrides a base class method
    def push(self):
        self.lim.append(len(self.trail))

    # overrides a base class method
    def pop(self, num_scopes):
        lim_sz = len(self.lim)-num_scopes
        trail_sz = self.lim[lim_sz]
        while len(self.trail) > trail_sz:
```

```
        fn = self.trail.pop()
        fn()
    self.lim = self.lim[0:lim_sz]
```

We can then define the main callback used when a variable tracked by identifier id is fixed to a value e. The identifier is returned by the solver when calling the function self.add(x) on term x. It uses this identifier to communicate the state of the term x. When terms range over bit-vectors and Booleans (but not integers or other types), the a client can register a callback with self.add_fixed to pick up a state where the variable is given a full assignment. For our example, the value is going to be a bit-vector constant, from which we can extract an unsigned integer into v. The trail is augmented with a restore point to the old state and the summation is then updated and the Pseudo-Boolean inequalities are then enforced.

```
    def myfix(self, id, e):
        x = self.id2x[id]
        v = e.as_long()
        old_sum = self.sum
        self.trail.append(lambda : self.undo(old_sum, x))
        for w in self.xvalues.values():
            if v + w == 42:
                if v > 30 or w > 30:
                    self.sum += 3
                else:
                    self.sum += 1
        self.xvalues[x] = v
        if self.sum > 100:
            self.conflict([self.x2id[x] for x in self.xvalues])
        elif self.sum < 10 and len(self.xvalues) > len(xs)/2:
            self.conflict([self.x2id[x] for x in self.xvalues])
```

It remains to define the last auxiliary methods for backtracking and testing.

```
    def undo(self, s, x):
        self.sum = s
        del self.xvalues[x]


    def myfinal(self):
        print(self.xvalues)


s = SimpleSolver()
for x in xs:
    s.add(x % 2 == 1)
```

```
p = UserPropagate(s)
s.check()
print(s.model())
```

In this example, it takes relatively few conflicts to establish a satisfying assignment, one where 9 out of 10 variables are set to 1 and the last variable is set to 41. The solver is only as good as the propagation strength and the quality of the conflicts it can generate. For instance, if we change the condition $v > 30 \lor w > 30$ to $v < 30 \land w < 30$ the constraints are not solved with the same ease.

The user propagator also allows to register callbacks when two added terms are known to be equal to the solver, and when two variables are known to be distinct. Note again that the use-case for the user propagator is for Bit-vector and Boolean variables.

8   Conclusion

We provided an overview of solver integration in Z3 with special emphasis on a newly revised arithmetic solver and a user propagator. While most applications use a small combination of mainstream theories, there is plenty of room for expanding theory solvers both in depth, in terms of capabilities and efficiency; and expand the repertoire of solvers to new theories. While applications have been enabled by current SMT solvers, they also introduce new challenges by highlighting bottlenecks and shortcomings. Current efforts center around modernizing Z3's entire core engine around up-to-date SAT solving techniques. Among many potential advantages it would allow Z3 to apply in-processing simplifications for quantifiers and SMT theories, and for instance, handle large bit-vectors by integrating algebraic methods, incremental bit-blasting, local search and leverage other recent advances in bit-vector reasoning. The universe (of solvers) is still expanding.

References

1. Barrett, C., Fontaine, P., Tinelli, C.: The Satisfiability Modulo Theories Library (SMT-LIB) (2016). www.SMT-LIB.org
2. Berzish, M., Ganesh, V., Zheng, Y.: Z3str3: a string solver with theory-aware heuristics. In: Daryl Stewart and Georg Weissenbacher, editors, 2017 Formal Methods in Computer Aided Design, FMCAD 2017, Vienna, Austria, 2–6 October 2017, pp. 55–59. IEEE (2017). ISBN 978-0-9835678-7-5. https://doi.org/10.23919/FMCAD.2017.8102241
3. Bjørner, N.: Engineering theories with Z3. In: Yang, H. (ed.) APLAS 2011. LNCS, vol. 7078, pp. 4–16. Springer, Heidelberg (2011). https://doi.org/10.1007/978-3-642-25318-8_3
4. Bjørner, N., Nachmanson, L.: Theorem recycling for theorem proving. In: Kovács, L., Voronkov, A. (eds.) Vampire 2017. Proceedings of the 4th Vampire Workshop, EPiC Series in Computing, vol. 53, pp. 1–8. EasyChair (2018). https://doi.org/10.29007/r58f. https://easychair.org/publications/paper/qGfG

5. Bjørner, N., de Moura, L., Nachmanson, L., Wintersteiger, C.M.: Programming Z3. In: Bowen, J.P., Liu, Z., Zhang, Z. (eds.) SETSS 2018. LNCS, vol. 11430, pp. 148–201. Springer, Cham (2019). https://doi.org/10.1007/978-3-030-17601-3_4

6. Bradley, A.R., Manna, Z., Sipma, H.B.: What's decidable about arrays? In: Emerson, E.A., Namjoshi, K.S. (eds.) VMCAI 2006. LNCS, vol. 3855, pp. 427–442. Springer, Heidelberg (2005). https://doi.org/10.1007/11609773_28

7. Bromberger, M., Weidenbach, C.: Fast cube tests for LIA constraint solving. In: Olivetti, N., Tiwari, A. (eds.) IJCAR 2016. LNCS (LNAI), vol. 9706, pp. 116–132. Springer, Cham (2016). https://doi.org/10.1007/978-3-319-40229-1_9

8. Bromberger, M., Weidenbach, C.: New techniques for linear arithmetic: cubes and equalities. Formal Methods Syst. Design 51(3), 433–461 (2017). https://doi.org/10.1007/s10703-017-0278-7

9. Christ, J., Hoenicke, J.: Cutting the mix. In: Kroening, D., Păsăreanu, C.S. (eds.) CAV 2015. LNCS, vol. 9207, pp. 37–52. Springer, Cham (2015). https://doi.org/10.1007/978-3-319-21668-3_3

10. Cimatti, A., Griggio, A., Irfan, A., Roveri, M., Sebastiani, R.: Experimenting on solving nonlinear integer arithmetic with incremental linearization. In: Beyersdorff, O., Wintersteiger, C.M. (eds.) SAT 2018. LNCS, vol. 10929, pp. 383–398. Springer, Cham (2018). https://doi.org/10.1007/978-3-319-94144-8_23

11. de Moura, L.M., Bjørner, N.: Model-based theory combination. Electron. Notes Theor. Comput. Sci. 198(2), 37–49 (2008). https://doi.org/10.1016/j.entcs.2008.04.079

12. de Moura, L.M., Bjørner, N.: Generalized, efficient array decision procedures. In: Proceedings of 9th International Conference on Formal Methods in Computer-Aided Design, FMCAD 2009, Austin, Texas, USA, 15–18 November 2009, pp. 45–52 (2009). https://doi.org/10.1109/FMCAD.2009.5351142

13. Dillig, I., Dillig, T., Aiken, A.: Cuts from proofs: a complete and practical technique for solving linear inequalities over integers. In: Bouajjani, A., Maler, O. (eds.) CAV 2009. LNCS, vol. 5643, pp. 233–247. Springer, Heidelberg (2009). https://doi.org/10.1007/978-3-642-02658-4_20

14. Dutertre, B., de Moura, L.: A fast linear-arithmetic solver for DPLL(T). In: Ball, T., Jones, R.B. (eds.) CAV 2006. LNCS, vol. 4144, pp. 81–94. Springer, Heidelberg (2006). https://doi.org/10.1007/11817963_11

15. Jacobs, B.: Categorical Logic and Type Theory. Studies in Logic and the Foundations of Mathematics, vol. 141. North Holland, Elsevier (1999)

16. Jovanovic, D., de Moura, L.M.: Solving non-linear arithmetic. In: Automated Reasoning - 6th International Joint Conference, IJCAR 2012, Manchester, UK, 26–29 June 2012. Proceedings, pp. 339–354 (2012). https://doi.org/10.1007/978-3-642-31365-3_27

17. Kapur, D., Zarba, C.: A reduction approach to decision procedures. Technical report, University of New Mexico (2006). https://www.cs.unm.edu/~kapur/mypapers/reduction.pdf

18. Komuravelli, A., Gurfinkel, A., Chaki, S., Clarke, E.M.: Automatic abstraction in SMT-based unbounded software model checking. In: Sharygina, N., Veith, H. (eds.) CAV 2013. LNCS, vol. 8044, pp. 846–862. Springer, Heidelberg (2013). https://doi.org/10.1007/978-3-642-39799-8_59

19. Minato, S.: Zero-suppressed BDDs for set manipulation in combinatorial problems. In: Dunlop, A.E. (ed.) Proceedings of the 30th Design Automation Conference, Dallas, Texas, USA, 14–18 June 1993, pp. 272–277. ACM Press (1993). https://doi.org/10.1145/157485.164890

20. Nishino, M., Yasuda, N., Minato, S., Nagata, M.: Zero-suppressed sentential decision diagrams. In: Schuurmans, D., Wellman, M.P. (ed.) Proceedings of the Thirtieth AAAI Conference on Artificial Intelligence, Phoenix, Arizona, USA, February 12–17 2016, pp. 1058–1066. AAAI Press (2016). http://www.aaai.org/ocs/index.php/AAAI/AAAI16/paper/view/12434
21. Stanford, C., Veanes, M., Bjørner, N.: Symbolic Boolean derivatives for efficiently solving extended regular expression constraints. Technical Report MSR-TR-2020-25, Microsoft, August 2020. https://www.microsoft.com/en-us/research/publication/symbolic-boolean-derivatives-for-efficiently-solving-extended-regular-expression-constraints/

Revisiting Refactoring Mechanics from Tool Developers' Perspective

Jonhnanthan Oliveira[1], Rohit Gheyi[1(✉)], Felipe Pontes[1], Melina Mongiovi[1], Márcio Ribeiro[2], and Alessandro Garcia[3]

[1] Federal University of Campina Grande, Campina Grande, Brazil
{jonhnanthan,felipe}@copin.ufcg.edu.br, rohit@dsc.ufcg.edu.br,
melina@computacao.ufcg.edu.br
[2] Federal University of Alagoas, Maceió, Brazil
marcio@ic.ufal.br
[3] Pontifical Catholic University of Rio de Janeiro, Rio de Janeiro, Brazil
afgarcia@inf.puc-rio.br

Abstract. Refactoring is a widely used development practice, available in mainstream IDEs. A previous work conducted a survey with developers, and finds that most of them use their experience to define refactoring mechanics for each refactoring type. However, we do not know whether a similar scenario happens in the context of refactoring tool developers. In this work, we conduct a study to compare refactoring mechanics implemented by tool developers. We apply 10 types of refactorings to 157,339 programs using 27 refactoring implementations from three tools, and compare the outputs. The refactoring implementations of Eclipse, NetBeans, and JRRT have different mechanics in all refactoring types.

Keywords: Refactoring mechanics · Tool developers

1 Introduction

Refactoring [6,15,23] is the process of changing a program to improve its internal structure while preserving its observable behavior. Over the years refactoring has become a central part of software development processes, such as eXtreme Programming [1]. In addition, IDEs (Eclipse [3], NetBeans [24], IntelliJ [11]) have automated a number of refactorings, such as Rename Class, Pull Up Method, and Encapsulate Field.

Oliveira et al. conduct a survey with 107 developers [22]. They ask developers the refactoring output (the resulting program after applying a refactoring) of 7 refactoring types applied to small programs [22]. There is no consensus about the refactoring output in five out of seven questions in their survey. Although some works explain refactoring mechanics [6,15,23], which is a concise, step-by-step description of how to carry out the refactoring, most developers (71.02%) use their experience to define refactoring mechanics for each refactoring type. The refactoring names are used to have an intuition about what to expect after a refactoring

© Springer Nature Switzerland AG 2020
G. Carvalho and V. Stolz (Eds.): SBMF 2020, LNCS 12475, pp. 25–42, 2020.
https://doi.org/10.1007/978-3-030-63882-5_3

application. However, Vakilian et al. [34] find that the names of some automated refactorings are confusing, and developers cannot predict the outcomes of complex tools. Murphy-Hill et al. [20] find that the names of the refactoring types are a distraction to the developer because it can vary from one environment to another. Oliveira et al. [22] conclude there is no ground truth refactoring mechanics specification widely accepted by developers. However, we do not know whether a similar problem happens in the context of refactoring tool developers.

In this work, we conduct a study to compare refactoring mechanics used by tool developers of refactoring implementations. Our goal is to compare the refactoring implementations' mechanics. To evaluate it, we use a number of small Java programs using JDOLLY as input to Eclipse, NetBeans, and JastAdd Refactoring Tools (JRRT [27]). JDOLLY is an automated and bounded-exhaustive Java program generator [16,18,28] based on Alloy, a formal specification language [9]. Eclipse and NetBeans are popular IDEs that allow developers to apply refactorings. JRRT improves the correctness and applicability of refactorings by using formal techniques [27]. We apply the same refactoring type with the same input program and parameters to the different implementations. We perform a pairwise comparison (Eclipse × NetBeans, Eclipse × JRRT, and NetBeans × JRRT) to identify differences using an Abstract Syntax Tree (AST) differencing algorithm distance [4]. We applied 10 types of refactorings (Pull Up Method/Field, Push Down Method/Field, Rename Class/Method/Field, Add Parameter, Encapsulate Field, and Move Method) using 27 refactoring implementations of Eclipse, NetBeans, and JRRT to 157,339 programs. The refactoring implementations of Eclipse, NetBeans, and JRRT have different mechanics in 17.8% of the analyzed transformations in all refactoring types. Although we use small Java programs, we also corroborate that the same differences appear when applying the same refactorings to real programs. Furthermore, we also investigate the parameters used by popular IDEs when applying refactorings. We find that they have different refactoring parameters for some refactoring types. Some of them also have different default values.

The main contributions of this work are the following:

- A technique to detect differences in refactoring implementations (Sect. 3);
- A comparison of the mechanics of 27 refactoring implementations of Eclipse, NetBeans, and JRRT (Sect. 4).

We organize this paper as follows. We present a motivating example in Sect. 2. Section 3 presents our technique to detect differences in refactoring implementations. We evaluate it in Sect. 4. Finally, we relate our approach to others (Sect. 5), and present concluding remarks (Sect. 6).

2   Motivating Example

Consider applying the Inline Method refactoring to the method `foo` in class `A` in the Java input program of Fig. 1, which is an example of a program generated by JDOLLY. The Inline Method refactoring puts the method's body into the body of its callers and removes the method. The code presented in Fig. 1(A) shows the first step concluded but it does not remove the method. Moreover, in this example, the implementation of the refactoring adds more statements in the body of the refactored method. By using the default parameters of Eclipse JDT 4.5 to apply this refactoring type, it yields the program described in Fig. 1(A). This example is a test case from the Eclipse test suite. However, if we provide the same input program to NetBeans 8.2 considering the default parameters to apply the Inline Method refactoring, the tool yields the output program presented in Fig. 1(B). A similar scenario happens when we apply the Inline Method refactoring to real programs, such as Fescar[1], Apollo[2], and Druid.[3]

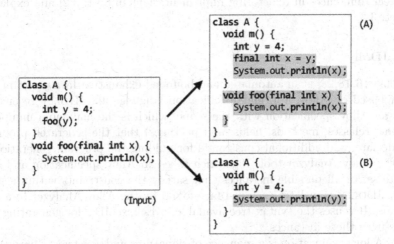

Fig. 1. The Inline Method refactoring applied to a Java input program using the Eclipse JDT 4.5 (A) and NetBeans 8.2 (B) refactoring implementations.

A previous study [22] conducted a survey with 107 developers. Most of them (84.11%) prefer to remove `foo` (Fig. 1(B)), which is the output of NetBeans and IntelliJ. However, 13.08% of developers prefer maintaining `foo` (Fig. 1(A)), and also adding a declaration of a final field, which is the output of Eclipse. The survey also shows that developers do not agree with refactoring mechanics of five out of seven refactoring types applied to small programs [22]. Different outcomes from tools show different points of view among tool developers, and may impact developers that use those tools to apply refactorings. This may be a barrier to use refactoring tools [32].

---

[1] It is a distributed transaction solution with high performance and ease of use for microservices architecture.

[2] It is a reliable distributed configuration system to manage applications' configurations in different environments and different clusters.

[3] It is a database connection pool written in Java that provides monitoring functionalities.

Although some works explain refactoring mechanics [6,15,23], most developers use their experience to define refactoring mechanics for each refactoring type [22]. There is no ground truth refactoring mechanics specification widely accepted by developers [22]. However, we do not know whether a similar condition occurs in the context of refactoring tool developers. In this work, we conduct a study to better understand refactoring mechanics used by tool developers.

3 Technique

In this section, we overview JDOLLY [16] in Sect. 3.1. We overview our technique to detect differences in refactoring implementations in Sect. 3.2, and explain it in Sect. 3.3.

3.1 JDolly

JDOLLY [16,18,28] is an automated and bounded-exhaustive Java program generator based on Alloy, a formal specification language [9]. JDOLLY receives as input an Alloy specification with the scope, which is the maximum number of elements (classes, methods, fields, and packages) that the generated programs may declare, and additional constraints for guiding the program generation. It uses the Alloy Analyzer tool [10], which takes an Alloy specification and finds a finite set of all possible instances that satisfy the constraints within a given scope. JDOLLY translates each instance found by the Alloy Analyzer to a Java program. It reuses the syntax tree available in Eclipse JDT for generating programs from those instances.

An Alloy specification is a sequence of signatures and constraints paragraphs declarations. A signature introduces a type and can declare a set of relations. Alloy relations specify multiplicity using qualifiers, such as **one** (exactly one), **lone** (zero or one), and **set** (zero or more). In Alloy, a signature can extend another, establishing that the extended signature is a subset of the parent signature. For example, the following Alloy fragment specifies part of the Java metamodel of JDOLLY encoded in Alloy. A Java class is a type, and may extend another class. Additionally, it may declare fields and methods.

```
sig Type {}
sig Class extends Type {
    extend: lone Class,
    methods: set Method,
    fields: set Field
}
sig Method {}
sig Field {}
```

A number of well-formed constraints can be specified for Java. For instance, a class cannot extend itself. In Alloy, we can declare facts, which encapsulate formulas that always hold. The ClassCannotExtendItself fact specifies this constraint. The **all**, **some**, and **no** keywords denote the universal, existential, and non-existential quantifiers respectively. The ^ and ! operators represent the transitive closure and negation operators respectively. The dot operator (.) is a generalized definition of the relational join operator.

fact ClassCannotExtendItself {
  all c: Class | c ! **in** c.^extend
}

The Alloy model is used to generate Java programs using the **run** command, which is applied to a predicate, specifying a scope for all declared signatures in the context of a specific Alloy model. Predicates (**pred**) are used to encapsulate reusable formulas and specify operations. For example, the following Alloy fragment specifies that we should run the **generate** predicate using a scope of 3. The user can also specify different scopes for each signature.

pred generate[] {···}
run generate **for** 3

The user can guide JDOLLY to generate more specific programs. For example, to generate programs to test the Pull Up Method refactoring, JDOLLY uses the following additional constraints. It specifies that a program must have at least one class (C2) extending another class (C1), and that C2 declares at least a method (M1).

one sig C1, C2 **extends** Class {}
one sig M1 **extends** Method {}
pred generate[] {
  C1 = C2.extend
  M1 **in** C2.methods
}

Furthermore, developers can specify a skip number to jump some of the Alloy instances. For a skip of size **n** such that **n** > 1, JDOLLY generates one program from an Alloy instance, and jumps the following **n** − 1 Alloy instances. Consecutive programs generated by JDOLLY tend to be very similar, potentially detecting the same kind of bug [9,18]. Thus, developers can set a parameter to skip some of the generated programs to reduce the time needed to test the refactoring implementations. It avoids generating an impracticable number of Alloy instances by the Alloy Analyzer.

3.2 Overview

The main steps of our approach are the following. First, it automatically generates programs using JDOLLY, which are used as inputs for a refactoring (Step 1). The refactoring implementations under test are applied to each generated program (Step 2), and yield refactoring outputs. Finally, we use an AST differencing algorithm to compare the refactoring outputs (Step 3). If the algorithm finds a difference, we show it to the user. Figure 2 illustrates the main steps.

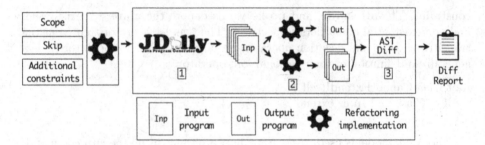

Fig. 2. An approach to detect differences in refactoring implementations. First, JDOLLY automatically generates programs (Step 1). For each generated program, each refactoring implementation under test applies the transformation (Step 2). Finally, it identifies differences by using an AST differencing algorithm (Step 3).

3.3 Detecting Differences in Refactoring Implementations

Our approach compares the application of two refactoring implementations of the same refactoring type on the same input program. We use an AST differencing algorithm (GUMTREE [4]) to compare the outputs of the refactoring implementations. It performs a per-file comparison, and has an improved detection of move actions over the previous work [5]. The approach receives two compilable programs as input, and yields a list of actions for each class indicating the differences. We call one program as the source, and the other one as the target. The goal is to detect all possible actions that could be performed in the source to yield the target program. For each file, GUMTREE yields a list of actions to change the AST of the source program to yield the AST of the target program. GUMTREE detects four kinds of actions: insert, delete, update, and move. The order of declarations (fields and methods) does not change the Java semantics. Therefore, we discard lists that contain only move actions. We manually inspect some differences to analyze whether there is a difference in both refactoring implementations, in one of them, or it is a false positive. Even GUMTREE having an improved detection of move actions, it may yield lists with other actions (for example, update actions) from a comparison composed only by move actions. We consider this scenario as a false positive.

For example, consider the input program presented in Fig. 3. Suppose we would like to apply the Pull Up Method refactoring to m. First, we apply it using the refactoring implementation in Eclipse. It yields the program presented in Fig. 3(A). Then we apply the same refactoring using JRRT, and it yields the program presented in Fig. 3(B). The approach performs a per-file analysis to the output programs presented in Figs. 3(A) and (B). GUMTREE yields a non-empty list of actions for this pair of files. GUMTREE reports one *insert* action and two *delete* actions related to switching `protected` and `abstract` keywords on class A, one *delete* action related to removing the `public` modifier of class B, one *update* action related to changing the modifier of class C from `public` to abstract, and ten *delete* actions related to removing the m method. As a result, we conclude that Eclipse and JRRT perform different transformations.

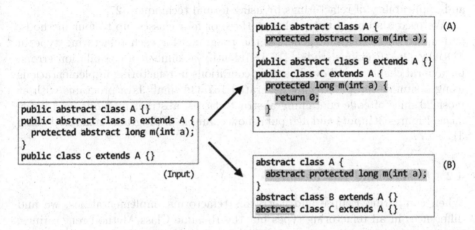

Fig. 3. Differences of Pull Up Method refactoring in implementations of Eclipse (A) and JRRT (B).

4   Evaluation

In this section, we present the experiment definition (Sect. 4.1). Section 4.2 presents and discusses the results. Section 4.3 describes some threats to validity.

4.1   Experiment Definition

The goal of our experiment is to use our proposed approach to observe the extent of differences in refactoring implementations for the purpose of evaluating it with respect to refactoring mechanics in tool developers' perspective. For this goal, we address the following research questions.

- RQ$_1$. What refactoring types have differences when comparing Eclipse and NetBeans refactoring implementations?
- RQ$_2$. What refactoring types have differences when comparing Eclipse and JRRT refactoring implementations?
- RQ$_3$. What refactoring types have differences when comparing NetBeans and JRRT refactoring implementations?

To answer our research questions, we use our approach to count the number of refactoring types that have differences.

We ran the experiment on a Desktop computer 3.6 GHz core i7 with 16 GB RAM running Ubuntu 12.04 and Oracle JDK 1.7. We evaluated 27 refactoring implementations of Eclipse JDT 4.5, NetBeans 8.2, and JRRT (02/mar/13) of 10 refactoring types. Eclipse JDT and NetBeans are popular IDEs that allow developers to apply refactorings. JRRT was proposed to improve the correctness and applicability of refactorings by using formal techniques [27].

We used a scope of two packages, three or four classes, up to four methods, and up to three fields to generate the programs for each refactoring type in JDOLLY [28]. Previous studies [16,18] identify a number of compilation errors, behavioral changes, and overly strong conditions in refactoring implementations using a similar setup. JDOLLY generated 157,339 small Java programs with at most 20 lines of code containing abstract classes, abstract methods, and interfaces. Figures 3(Input) and 4(Input) show example of programs generated using JDOLLY.

4.2 Results and Discussion

When comparing Eclipse and NetBeans refactoring implementations, we find differences in all refactoring types but the Rename Class/Method refactorings. By dividing the total number of differences found in all refactoring types and the total number of input programs considered in each analyzed refactoring type, they have differences in 16.3% of the transformations considered in our study. In addition, we identify differences in all refactoring types but the Rename Class refactoring when comparing NetBeans and JRRT refactoring implementations. They differ in 20.1% of the transformations considered in our study. Moreover, when comparing Eclipse and JRRT refactoring implementations, our approach detects differences in all refactoring types (Rename Field/Method, Move Method, Add Parameter, Push Down Field/Method, Encapsulate Field, Pull Up Field/Method). They have differences in 17.3% of the transformations considered in our study. Table 1 summarizes the number of differences found.

For example, consider the input program presented in Fig. 4(Input). Suppose we would like to apply the Push Down Method refactoring to m. First, we apply it using the refactoring implementation in Eclipse JDT 4.5. It yields the program presented in Fig. 4(A). Then we apply the same refactoring using NetBeans 8.2, and it yields the program presented in Fig. 4(B).

Oliveira et al. [22] show both transformations presented in Fig. 4 to developers, and ask them which one they prefer. Most developers (80.37%) prefer to move the method to its direct subclass. However, others (15.89%) expect to move the method not only to its direct subclass, but also to a subclass of its direct subclass. Others (1.87%) expect the tool to yield a warning in both options. Over 50% of the time, developers select an option in a question but if he/she uses the preferred tool to apply the refactoring, the tool yields a different option [22]. This may be a barrier for developers to use refactoring tools [32].

We present small programs to make it easier to explain, but a similar scenario also occurs in real projects. For instance, if we apply the Push Down Method refactoring to the AbstractDecoder.getDecodableMimeTypes method in the

Table 1. Number of differences found by our approach. Programs = number of programs; Differences = number of transformations applied by both implementations that have different output programs; - = we did not evaluate some NetBeans implementations.

Refactoring Types	Programs	Differences		
		Eclipse x NetBeans	Eclipse x JRRT	NetBeans x JRRT
Pull Up Method	12,927	-	7,871	-
Pull Up Field	42,051	-	41	-
Push Down Method	3,462	449	554	449
Push Down Field	23,528	32	200	245
Add Parameter	13,319	3,823	5,698	9,170
Encapsulate Field	13,956	7,752	1,302	2,418
Rename Field	6,267	374	2,642	1,752
Rename Class	11,842	0	1,711	0
Rename Method	21,568	0	6,521	13,712
Move Method	8,419	4,327	749	1,122
Total Percentage		16.3%	17.3%	20.1%

Spring Framework[4] project using Eclipse and NetBeans, we get differences of the same type. In the real examples mentioned in this study, they contain method calls, non-empty method bodies, field accesses, and so on.

As another example, consider the input program presented in Fig. 5(Input). Suppose we would like to apply the Encapsulate Field refactoring to f. First, we apply it using the refactoring implementation in Eclipse JDT 4.5. It yields the program presented in Fig. 5(A). Then we apply the same refactoring using NetBeans, and it yields the program presented in Fig. 5(B). We can have a similar result in real projects declaring private fields. Oliveira et al. [22] show both transformations presented in Fig. 5 to developers, and ask them which one they prefer. Only 4.67% of developers prefer not to apply the refactoring. In addition, 28.04% of developers expect to apply the refactoring and generate private accessors methods, and 58.88% of them expect to apply the refactoring and generate public accessors methods. In this question, we do not have a consensus. This may impact not only users using tools to apply refactorings, but also researchers building refactoring tool detectors.

Our approach also finds differences in the Rename Method refactoring when comparing Eclipse and JRRT, and when comparing NetBeans and JRRT. We cluster pair of programs with the same list of actions yielded by GUMTREE in each refactoring type in Step 3, and manually analyzed some pair of programs in

---

[4] The Spring Framework is an open source application framework for building web Java applications.

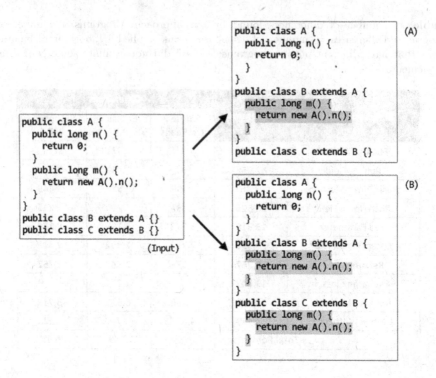

Fig. 4. Differences of Push Down Method refactoring in implementations of Eclipse (A) and NetBeans (B).

each cluster to better understand the difference. As a result, we classified some of the differences found in categories presented in Table 2. Some differences are minor, such as the order of modifiers when applying the Encapsulate Field refactoring. The refactoring implementation may introduce coding style issues. However, in some cases, one refactoring implementation increases the method or field accessibility while another implementation maintains it when applying the Add Parameter refactoring. The refactoring implementation may increase coupling in some cases. As another example, a refactoring implementation removes a method, while the other refactoring implementation keeps it when applying the Inline Method refactoring. Furthermore, there are categories that represent incorrect transformations: (i) the resulting program incorrectly implements the set method after applying the Encapsulate Field refactoring; (ii) the field is not added to the target after applying the Push Down Field refactoring; (iii) the method is not added to all subclasses when applying the Push Down Method refactoring. It is important to mention that we also identify transformations applied to real projects exposing most of the major changes (87.5%) presented in Table 2.

Previous studies [13,32] state that developers do not care whether refactorings change the observable behavior. We do not filter out behavioral changes in

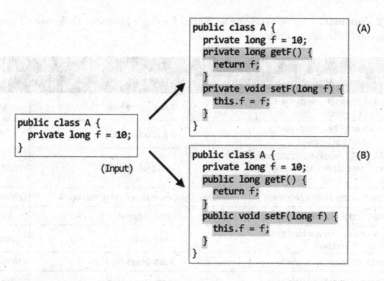

```
public class A {                        (A)
    private long f = 10;
    private long getF() {
        return f;
    }
    private void setF(long f) {
        this.f = f;
    }
}
```

```
public class A {
    private long f = 10;
}
          (Input)
```

```
public class A {                        (B)
    private long f = 10;
    public long getF() {
        return f;
    }
    public void setF(long f) {
        this.f = f;
    }
}
```

Fig. 5. Differences of Encapsulate Field refactoring in implementations of Eclipse and NetBeans.

our current approach, but we can improve it by using SAFEREFACTOR [29] before Step 3 in Fig. 2. SAFEREFACTOR automatically evaluates whether two versions of a program have the same behavior by automatically generating test cases only for the common methods impacted by the change. It identified a number of bugs in refactorings implementations of Eclipse JDT, JRRT, and NetBeans [28]. We use SAFEREFACTOR to analyze some program transformations that our approach identifies differences. Most of them are classified by SAFEREFACTOR as behavior preserving transformations.

Parameters. To better understand refactoring mechanics considered by each implementation, we analyze the parameters of 12 refactorings of Eclipse JDT 4.5, and NetBeans 8.2, and 11 refactorings of IntelliJ Ultimate 2018.3. The Add Parameter refactoring is not supported by IntelliJ. In this investigation, notice we also include IntelliJ. We prefer to investigate popular IDEs. So, we do not include JRRT. For each refactoring, we identify a list of parameter options in each refactoring implementation. Based on their labels, we classify parameters that are declared in more than one implementation. We do not find any tool with the same refactoring parameters. Figure 6 shows the percentage of parameters shared by Eclipse, NetBeans, and IntelliJ. Eclipse&NetBeans indicates the percentage of parameters in common in Eclipse and NetBeans implementations. IntelliJ indicates the percentage of parameters only in IntelliJ implementation.

We do not find any refactoring with exactly the same parameter options for all refactoring implementations considered in our study. Considering refactorings implementations of Eclipse JDT 4.5, NetBeans 8.2, and IntelliJ Ultimate 2018.3, the Encapsulate Field, Push Down Field/Method, and

Table 2. Summary of some differences found by our approach. Difference Type = it specifies the difference found.

Difference Type	Refactoring	Tool(s)
It incorrectly implements the SET method	Encapsulate Field	JRRT
The GET or SET methods have a private accessibility	Encapsulate Field	JRRT
The GET or SET methods should have the same accessibility of the original field	Encapsulate Field	NetBeans
It increases the field accessibility	Rename Field, Push Down Field, Pull Up Field	Eclipse, JRRT
It decreases the method accessibility	Add Parameter	JRRT
The parameter is not added to the method	Add Parameter	Eclipse
The field is not added to the target	Push Down Field	NetBeans
It does not update all field calls	Push Down Field	Eclipse
It makes a class or method abstract	Pull Up Method	Eclipse, JRRT
It increases the method accessibility	Push Down Method, Move Method	JRRT
It does not remove the source class method	Pull Up Method	Eclipse, NetBeans, JRRT
The method is not added to all subclasses	Push Down Method	NetBeans
Minor Changes		
It includes a this when accessing a field	Move Method	Eclipse
It creates a local variable	Move Method	JRRT
The order of the abstract modifier is different	Encapsulate Field, Rename Field, Rename Method, Add Parameter, Push Down Field, Pull Up Method, Push Down Method, Move Method	JRRT
It does not add the import to create the new object	Push Down Method	JRRT
It includes a ClassName.this when accessing an object	Move Method	Eclipse

Rename Method/Class/Field refactorings have most parameters in common (50%), while the Inline Method refactoring has the least commonality (13%). For instance, all implementations of the Rename Class refactoring require the user to specify the new class name. As another example, when you apply the Add Parameter refactoring using NetBeans, it is possible to declare it final. However, the Eclipse implementation does not provide an option to declare a method parameter as final.

In some cases, tools have the same parameter, but they have different default values. For example, the Inline Method refactoring in Eclipse has a default value

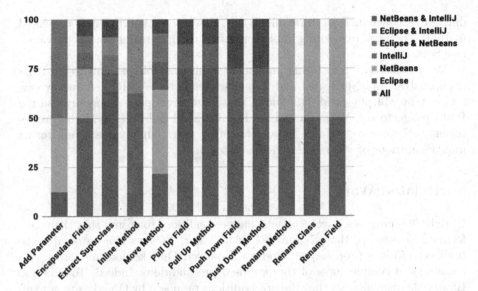

Fig. 6. Summary of the percentage of parameters shared by Eclipse, NetBeans, and IntelliJ.

to maintain the inlined method, while it is the opposite in NetBeans. Developers using different tools may face different results if they use different parameter options. We also find different results when using the same values for some parameter options (see Table 2).

4.3 Threats to Validity

There is no consensus among refactoring tool developers about refactoring mechanics in a number of refactoring types. The diversity of the generated programs may be related to the number of detected differences. The higher the diversity, more differences our approach may find. So, the scope, constraints, and skip used by JDOLLY control the number of generated programs, and consequently may also hide possible differences. We manually analyze the differences in Step 3 to identify false positives.

We manually compare the default values of all refactoring implementations of Eclipse, NetBeans, and JRRT used in this study. The Encapsulate Field and Move Method refactorings in Eclipse and NetBeans are the only ones that have different default values. In the Encapsulate Field refactoring implementation of Eclipse, the default value for accessibility modifier in the getter and setter methods depends on the field accessibility. In NetBeans, the default value is `public`. A similar difference occurs in the refactoring implementations of the Move Method refactoring in Eclipse and NetBeans. The default values for the moved method accessibility is `package-private` and *Escalate* in Eclipse and NetBeans, respectively. NetBeans automatically raises the accessibility to a necessary level. Some differences shown in Table 1 are due to this. However, most differences presented in Table 2 occur in refactoring implementations using the same parameter values (see Sect. 4.2).

We evaluated 27 refactoring implementations available in mainstream IDEs (Eclipse JDT and NetBeans) and in one academic tool (JRRT). A survey carried out by Murphy et al. [19] shows that Java developers commonly use the Pull Up refactoring. We evaluated the Pull Up Field and Pull Up Method refactorings. We plan to evaluate more refactoring types, and evaluate refactoring implementations of other IDEs, such as IntelliJ.

5   Related Work

Opdyke [23] proposes a set of refactoring preconditions to ensure that the transformations preserve the program behavior. Later, Roberts [25] automates the basic refactorings proposed by Opdyke. However, Opdyke does not prove correctness and completeness of the proposed preconditions. Indeed, Tokuda and Batory [33] demonstrate that the preconditions proposed by Opdyke are not sufficient to guarantee behavior preservation after applying transformations. Moreover, proving refactorings with respect to a formal semantics considering all language constructs constitutes a challenge [26]. In our work, we analyze whether tool developers use a widely accepted ground truth refactoring mechanics specification when implementing refactoring.

Murphy-Hill et al. [20] find that the names of the refactoring tools are a distraction to the developer because it can vary from one environment to another. For example, Fowler's Introduce Explaining Variable [6] is called Extract Local Variable in Eclipse. Vakilian et al. [34] study 26 developers working in their natural settings on their code for a total of 1,268 programming hours over three months to understand how they interact with automated refactorings. They identify factors that affect the appropriate and inappropriate uses of automated refactorings. Some coarse-grained refactorings are ambiguous, and developers cannot predict the outcome of the refactoring implementation. We find that even refactorings applied to small programs containing few lines of code may be useful to identify differences in refactoring tools.

Kim et al. [14] perform a field study of refactoring benefits and challenges at Microsoft through three complementary study methods: a survey, semi-structured interviews with professional software engineers, and quantitative analysis of version history data. With an exception of the Rename refactoring, more than a half of the participants said that they apply those refactorings manually. Murphy-Hill et al. [21] present an analysis of four sets of data that provides new insight into how developers refactor in practice. Refactoring implementations themselves are underused, particularly when we consider refactorings that have a method-level granularity or above. Tempero et al. [32] conduct a survey with 3,785 developers to see the barriers of applying refactorings. They found that the decision of whether or not to refactor was due to non-design considerations. They mentioned inadequate tool support as a reason for not refactoring. In our work, we find that refactoring mechanics in mainstream IDEs are different. This may be one of the reasons why developers prefer to manually apply refactorings [32].

Steimann and Thies [31] identify that mainstreams IDEs such as Eclipse, NetBeans, and IntelliJ are flawed when it comes to maintaining accessibility. They identify scenarios where the application of existing refactorings such as Pull Up Members causes unexpected changes to program behavior. Schäfer et al. [27] present a number of Java refactoring implementations. They translate a Java program to an enriched language that is easier to specify and check preconditions, and apply the transformation. They aim to improve correctness and applicability of the Eclipse refactoring implementations. In our work, we compare JRRT to mainstreams IDEs to identify differences in refactoring implementations.

Daniel et al. [2] propose an approach for automated testing refactoring engines. The technique is based on ASTGen, a Java program generator, and a set of programmatic oracles. To evaluate the refactoring correctness, they implemented six oracles that evaluate the output of each transformation. They used the oracles DT, Inverse Transformations, and Custom Oracles to identify incorrect transformations. The Inverse oracle checks whether applying a refactoring to a program, its inverse refactoring to the target program yields the same initial program. If they are syntactically different, the refactoring engine developer has to manually check whether they have the same behavior. They evaluated the technique by testing 42 refactoring implementations, and found three transformation issues using Differential Testing and Inverse oracles in 2 refactoring implementations of Eclipse and NetBeans of the Encapsulate Field refactoring, and only one bug using the Custom oracle. Gligoric et al. [7] use real systems to reduce the effort for writing test generators using the same oracles [8]. They found 141 bugs related to compilation errors in refactoring implementations for Java and C in 285 h. Our goal is to evaluate whether refactoring tools have the same refactoring mechanics. We use JDOLLY [28] to automatically generate programs.

There are some techniques to identify overly weak (compilation errors and behavioral changes) [28] and overly strong conditions [16, 30] in refactoring implementations. Mongiovi et al. [18] improve the Alloy specification to include more Java constructs in JDOLLY and to skip some instances. Soares et al. [29] propose SAFEREFACTOR to check whether two programs have the same observable behavior. Mongiovi et al. [17] improve SAFEREFACTOR by including change impact analysis. Oliveira et al. [22] conduct a survey with 107 developers to understand refactoring mechanics used by developers. Most developers use their experience to define refactoring mechanics for each refactoring type. In this paper, our goal is to revisit refactoring mechanics from tool developers' perspective. We analyze refactoring mechanics used by refactoring implementations of Eclipse, NetBeans, and JRRT.

6   Conclusion

In this work, we conduct a study to review the refactoring mechanics used by refactoring tools. We compare the refactoring implementations of some implementations. We automatically generate 157,339 small Java programs using JDOLLY. Our approach attempts to apply ·a refactoring type using the refactoring implementations of mainstreams IDEs (Eclipse and NetBeans) and an academic tool (JRRT) to each generated program. For each output, we perform a pairwise comparison between two refactoring implementations. We evaluate 10 types of refactorings in 27 refactoring implementations. The refactoring implementations of Eclipse, NetBeans, and JRRT have differences in all refactoring types. The results give evidences that refactoring types have different mechanics in the context of refactoring implementation' developers. We also find that popular IDEs have different parameters available to apply refactorings. Some default values of refactoring parameters are also different.

We conclude there is no ground truth refactoring mechanics specification widely accepted by refactoring tool developers. This can make the implementation and maintenance of refactoring tools a non-trivial task since each developer can have a different opinion on how to implement a refactoring. For instance, a developer can change the result of a refactoring implemented by another developer of the same team while fixing a bug. Furthermore, this may be a barrier for developers to use automated support to apply refactorings [32]. They may prefer to perform a manual refactoring, which is a time-consuming and error-prone activity. Moreover, this problem may impact developers that use refactoring implementations and do not carefully review the refactoring output. After a while, developers may have to undo, improve, or correct some changes.

To improve this scenario, it is important for the refactoring community to discuss about the ground truth refactoring mechanics specification that should be used. Some works explaining the refactoring mechanics [6,12,15,23] can be considered in the discussion. This specification must state the refactoring mechanics, pre- and post-conditions, and the minimum set of parameters accepted by each refactoring type. It must be a complete and precise specification. The specification will help IDE refactoring engine developers, and refactoring researchers to create better tools, derive more accurate insights from studies. Moreover, it may also help refactoring practitioners to have more confidence in tools.

As future work, we intend to evaluate more tools (such as IntelliJ), and more refactoring types to detect and study more differences. Furthermore, we aim at using SAFEREFACTOR [17,29] before Step 3 in Fig. 2 to only consider behavior preserving transformations. Moreover, we intend to investigate why popular IDEs use different default values for some refactoring parameters (Fig. 6).

Acknowledgments. We would like to thank the anonymous reviewers, Gustavo Soares, Augusto Sampaio, Paulo Borba, and Leopoldo Teixeira for their insightful suggestions. This work was partially supported by CNPq (426005/2018-0 and 311442/2019-6) and CAPES (117875 and 175956) grants.

References

1. Beck, K.: Extreme Programming Explained: Embrace Change. Addison-Wesley Longman Publishing Company Inc., Boston (2000)
2. Daniel, B., Dig, D., Garcia, K., Marinov, D.: Automated testing of refactoring engines. In: Proceedings of the Foundations of Software Engineering, pp. 185–194. ACM (2007)
3. Eclipse.org.: Eclipse Project (2018). http://www.eclipse.org
4. Falleri, J., Morandat, F., Blanc, X., Martinez, M., Monperrus, M.: Fine-grained and accurate source code differencing. In: Proceedings of the Automated Software Engineering, ASE, pp. 313–324 (2014)
5. Fluri, B., Wuersch, M., PInzger, M., Gall, H.: Change distilling: tree differencing for fine-grained source code change extraction. IEEE Trans. Softw. Eng. **33**(11), 725–743 (2007)
6. Fowler, M., Beck, K., Brant, J., Opdyke, W., Roberts, D.: Refactoring: Improving the Design of Existing Code. Addison-Wesley Professional, Boston (1999)
7. Gligoric, M., Behrang, F., Li, Y., Overbey, J., Hafiz, M., Marinov, D.: Systematic testing of refactoring engines on real software projects. In: Castagna, G. (ed.) ECOOP 2013. LNCS, vol. 7920, pp. 629–653. Springer, Heidelberg (2013). https://doi.org/10.1007/978-3-642-39038-8_26
8. Gligoric, M., Gvero, T., Jagannath, V., Khurshid, S., Kuncak, V., Marinov, D.: Test generation through programming in UDITA. In: Proceedings of the International Conference on Software Engineering, ICSE, pp. 225–234. ACM (2010)
9. Jackson, D.: Software Abstractions: Logic, Language, and Analysis. The MIT Press, Cambridge (2012)
10. Jackson, D., Schechter, I., Shlyahter, H.: Alcoa: the alloy constraint analyzer. In: Proceedings of the International Conference on Software Engineering, pp. 730–733. ICSE (2000)
11. JetBrains: IntelliJ IDEA (2018). https://www.jetbrains.com/idea/
12. Kerievsky, J.: Refactoring to Patterns. Pearson Higher Education, London (2004)
13. Kim, M., Zimmermann, T., Nagappan, N.: A field study of refactoring challenges and benefits. In: Proceedings of the International Symposium on the Foundations of Software Engineering, pp. 50:1–50:11. FSE (2012)
14. Kim, M., Zimmermann, T., Nagappan, N.: An empirical study of refactoring challenges and benefits at microsoft. IEEE Trans. Software Eng. **40**(7), 633–649 (2014)
15. Mens, T., Tourwé, T.: A survey of software refactoring. IEEE Trans. Software Eng. **30**(2), 126–139 (2004)
16. Mongiovi, M., Gheyi, R., Soares, G., Ribeiro, M., Borba, P., Teixeira, L.: Detecting overly strong preconditions in refactoring engines. IEEE Trans. Software Eng. **44**(5), 429–452 (2018)
17. Mongiovi, M., Gheyi, R., Soares, G., Teixeira, L., Borba, P.: Making refactoring safer through impact analysis. Sci. Comput. Program. **93**, 39–64 (2014)
18. Mongiovi, M., Mendes, G., Gheyi, R., Soares, G., Ribeiro, M.: Scaling testing of refactoring engines. In: Proceedings of the International Conference on Software Maintenance and Evolution, ICSME, pp. 371–380 (2014)
19. Murphy, G., Kersten, M., Findlater, L.: How are java software developers using the eclipse IDE? IEEE Softw. **23**(4), 76–83 (2006)
20. Murphy-Hill, E., Ayazifar, M., Black, A.P.: Restructuring software with gestures. In: Proceedings of the Symposium on Visual Languages and Human-Centric Computing, VL/HCC, pp. 165–172 (2011)

21. Murphy-Hill, E., Parnin, C., Black, A.P.: How we refactor, and how we know it. IEEE Trans. Software Eng. **38**(1), 5–18 (2012)
22. Oliveira, J., Gheyi, R., Mongiovi, M., Soares, G., Ribeiro, M., Garcia, A.: Revisiting the refactoring mechanics. Inf. Softw. Technol. **110**, 136–138 (2019)
23. Opdyke, W.: Refactoring object-oriented frameworks. Ph.D. thesis, University of Illinois at Urbana-Champaign (1992)
24. Oracle: Netbeans IDE (2018). http://www.netbeans.org
25. Roberts, D.: Practical analysis for refactoring. Ph.D. thesis, University of Illinois at Urbana-Champaign (1999)
26. Schäfer, M., Ekman, T., Moor, O.: Challenge proposal: verification of refactorings. In: Proceedings of the 3rd Workshop on Programming Languages Meets Program Verification, pp. 67–72. ACM (2008)
27. Schäfer, M., de Moor, O.: Specifying and implementing refactorings. In: Proceedings of the International Conference on Object-Oriented Programming, Systems, Languages, and Applications, OOPSLA, pp. 286–301 (2010)
28. Soares, G., Gheyi, R., Massoni, T.: Automated behavioral testing of refactoring engines. IEEE Trans. Software Eng. **39**(2), 147–162 (2013)
29. Soares, G., Gheyi, R., Serey, D., Massoni, T.: Making program refactoring safer. IEEE Softw. **27**(4), 52–57 (2010)
30. Soares, G., Mongiovi, M., Gheyi, R.: Identifying overly strong conditions in refactoring implementations. In: Proceedings of the International Conference on Software Maintenance, ICSM, pp. 173–182 (2011)
31. Steimann, F., Thies, A.: From public to private to absent: refactoring java programs under constrained accessibility. In: Proceedings of the European Conference on Object-Oriented Programming, ECOOP, pp. 419–443 (2009)
32. Tempero, E., Gorschek, T., Angelis, L.: Barriers to refactoring. Commun. ACM **60**(10), 54–61 (2017)
33. Tokuda, L., Batory, D.: Evolving object-oriented designs with refactorings. Autom. Softw. Eng. **8**, 89–120 (2001)
34. Vakilian, M., Chen, N., Negara, S., Rajkumar, B.A., Bailey, B.P., Johnson, R.E.: Use, disuse, and misuse of automated refactorings. In: Proceedings of the International Conference on Software Engineering, ICSE, pp. 233–243 (2012)

Experience Reports

Safety Assurance of a High Voltage Controller for an Industrial Robotic System

Yvonne Murray[1(✉)], David A. Anisi[1,2], Martin Sirevåg[1], Pedro Ribeiro[3] ,
and Rabah Saleh Hagag[1]

[1] Department of Mechatronics, Faculty of Engineering and Science,
University of Agder (UiA), Grimstad, Norway
{yvonne.murray,david.anisi}@uia.no, {martsi18,rabahh18}@student.uia.no
[2] Robotics Group, Faculty of Science and Technology,
Norwegian University of Life Sciences (NMBU), Ås, Norway
david.anisi@nmbu.no
[3] Department of Computer Science, University of York, York, UK
pedro.ribeiro@york.ac.uk

Abstract. Due to the risk of discharge sparks and ignition, there are strict rules concerning the safety of high voltage electrostatic systems used in industrial painting robots. In order to assure that the system fulfils its safety requirements, formal verification is an important tool to supplement traditional testing and quality assurance procedures. The work in this paper presents formal verification of the most important safety functions of a high voltage controller. The controller has been modelled as a finite state machine, which was formally verified using two different model checking software tools; Simulink Design Verifier and RoboTool. Five safety critical properties were specified and formally verified using the two tools. Simulink was chosen as a low-threshold entry point since Math-Works products are well known to most practitioners. RoboTool serves as a software tool targeted towards model checking, thus providing more advanced options for the more experienced user. The comparative study and results show that all properties were successfully verified. The verification times in both tools were in the order of a few minutes, which was within the acceptable time limit for this particular application.

Keywords: Formal verification · Model checking · High Voltage Controller (HVC) · Industrial robots

1 Introduction

Formal verification provides an extra level of assurance by verifying the logic of a system and making sure that it works in accordance to its specifications in every situation. This will ideally help identify potential pitfalls in a much earlier phase of the development cycle [1]. The two main approaches are model checking [2]

© The Author(s) 2020
G. Carvalho and V. Stolz (Eds.): SBMF 2020, LNCS 12475, pp. 45–63, 2020.
https://doi.org/10.1007/978-3-030-63882-5_4

and theorem proving [3]. Application of formal methods in industrial use cases is an important supplement to the traditional testing and safety risk identification and mitigation actions which are already taking place [4]. Obtaining sufficiently high testing coverage in complex industrial systems may be very time consuming and tedious. In practice, it may even be impossible to test for every scenario or situation, which means that testing could possibly fail to reveal potential safety critical bugs and errors. As a testimony of this, Sect. 2 outlines some previous errors that went by undetected by traditional testing methods.

Industrial paint robots use High Voltage (HV) to perform electrostatic painting, where particles are electrically charged and attracted to the grounded paint object, as seen in Fig. 1. In this way, painting quality is ensured while paint consumption and costs are minimized. However, HV also poses certain risks, particularly in explosive atmospheres where potential discharge sparks may cause ignition. Fire in the painting cell will result in costly production delays, as well as damage to the equipment. Therefore, it is of great importance that the High Voltage Controller (HVC) is working as intended, and there are strict rules to ensure the safety of the system and personnel. These include both software-based safety layers such as over current- and max current detection, as well as physical safety layers based on (optical) fencing, minimum clearance distances, and use of safety clothes such as anti-static shoes and gloves.

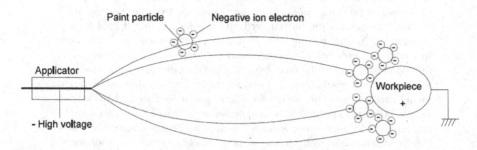

Fig. 1. In electrostatic painting, high voltage (approximately 50–100 kV) charges the paint particles at the applicator. The particles follow the lines of the electrostatic field from the applicator (cathode) to the earthed object (anode).

An HVC used in an industrial paint robot has been provided for this case study. After passing the traditional quality assurance and testing procedures, some undesired system behavior was discovered. Thus, even though risk mitigation plans were identified systematically (e.g., using HAZID/HAZOP), and thorough testing on both component and system level had been conducted, some errors still managed to go undetected. The undetected errors had in common that they happened when certain conditions and situations happened in a very specific order, and that specific series of events had not been tested. This gave a strong motivation for performing a formal verification of the HVC, in order to ensure both that the found errors had been fixed and that there were no other situations where the same errors could occur.

The logic of the C++ code of the HVC can be modelled as a finite state machine, which means that model checking is an appropriate method for the formal verification of the properties. The methodology of model checking has some apparent advantages that fits industrial applications very well; it is a rather general verification approach which has some commercial-grade, high-performance model checkers available. It provides diagnostic information (counter-example) that can be used for debugging purposes, is easier to integrate with existing development and engineering practices and last but not least; is more intuitive and familiar to most practitioners than theorem proving [2].

In this work, two different software tools have been used to model and verify the HVC system. The first is Simulink Design Verifier (SDV) by MathWorks [5] and the second is RoboTool [6,7], developed by the RoboStar group at University of York. Here-within, Simulink was chosen as a low-threshold entry point since MathWorks products are well known to most practitioners. RoboTool serves as a software tool targeted towards model checking, thus providing more advanced options for the more experienced user. In addition to presenting and analyzing an interesting industrial use case considering formal verification of the safety aspects of the HVC unit of a paint robot, the main objective of this work is to do a comparative study of the software tools with regards to functionality, usability and effectiveness, e.g., modelling, validation and analysis time.

Application of formal verification methodology within the control and robotics community have mainly adopted the hybrid system and automata framework of Alur *et al.* [8,9]. In this setting, finite- and infinite-time reachability constitute the main verification tools, but unfortunately turn out to be an undecidable problem in general, leaving conservative set approximation as the only viable approach [10,11]. Hybrid automata theory also assumes having infinite accuracy and instantaneous reaction which serves as a noticeable discrepancy to the real system and implementation; potentially invalidating the formal verification results [12]. Narrowing down to industrial paint robots, [13] considers formal verification of the paint spraying use case using ARIADNE tool for reachability analysis. The focus here is solely on parametric design verification. To the best of our knowledge, there is no prior art considering formal verification of the safety aspects of the HVC unit of an industrial paint robot, which is the focus of the paper at hand.

The remaining of this paper is structured as follows. Section 2 details the HVC system and previous errors that were not found by traditional testing methods. It also contains formulation of the properties to be formally verified. Section 3 presents a simplified finite state machine of the HVC. Section 4 explains how the state machine was modelled in RoboTool and SDV, and how these tools were used to verify the properties. Finally, Sect. 5 provides some discussion and conclusions, as well as a comparison between the two tools. Additionally, suggestions for further research is presented.

2   HVC and Previously Detected Errors

A simplified block diagram of the part of the paint robot that contains the HVC can be seen in Fig. 2. Here, the $r(t) = HV\_SetPoint$ signal is used as reference for the desired voltage level on the HVC, while the 24 V power signal provides the HVC with electrical power. The HVC module runs the control loop and associated control logic. The $u(t) = PWM\_Output$ signal shows the calculated value for the high voltage regulator, from 0 to 100%, which is then increased in the transformer. In the Cockcroft–Walton (CW) generator, there are several voltage doubling circuits, and the voltage is rectified and further increased, before arriving to the applicator. Here, $y(t) = [IM, \quad HV\_Actual]^T$ denote current and voltage measurements, respectively, which are fed back into the HVC.

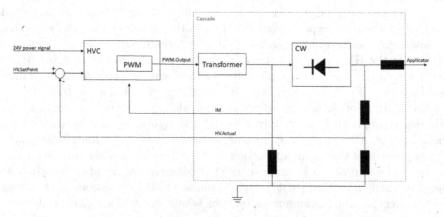

Fig. 2. Block diagram of one part of the paint robot, containing the HVC.

Referring to Fig. 3, the previous version of the HVC had two main issues, containing several variations:

1. Issues with the actual voltage level on the HVC, HV_Actual:
   (a) Both the set-point and HV_Actual had a non-zero value, but they differed from each other. The HVC board did not respond to any further set-point changes, and had a constant actual value.
   (b) There was no set-point, but HV_Actual had a non-zero value.
   (c) There was a set-point, but HV_Actual was still zero.
2. Issues with the 24 V power signal:
   (a) The HVC sometimes reported the 24 V power signal missing, even though it was actually present, resulting in a deadlock.
   (b) Sometimes, an additional bug also occurred, where the HVC froze when the 24 V power signal failed. In that case, the HVC limit supervision did not disable PWM, and the HVC continued to set out high voltage until it was reset or powered off. This can be seen graphically in Fig. 3(b).

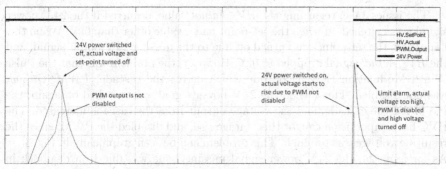

(a) Error concerning *HV_Actual* value.

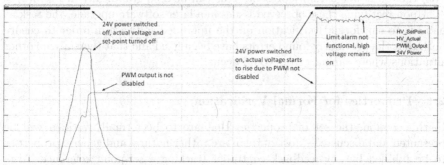

(b) Error when the 24V power signal failed and the HVC froze.

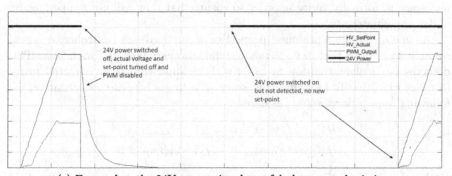

(c) Error when the 24V power signal was falsely reported missing.

Fig. 3. Some errors that were not discovered through traditional testing of a previous version of the HVC software. These shed light on the need for the industry to adopt formal verification methodology when developing safety critical systems. The x-axis unit is time, while the y-axis units are kV for the high-voltage signals, percent for the PWM and binary on/off for the 24 V power signal. Here, the schematic representation and inter-relation between the signals are in focus, not the exact values.

The issues 1a–c, regarding the HV_Actual value, occurred if the 24 V power signal was switched off when the set-point had a value other than 0kV. When this happened, the set-point was turned off due to the missing 24 V power signal, and the HV_Actual signal dropped to 0kV. However, the problem was that the Pulse Width Modulation (PWM) output which drives the cascade, PWM_Output, was not disabled. Thus, when the 24 V power signal was switched on again, the PWM fed the cascade, and the voltage output from the cascade increased. The HVC limit supervision caught this voltage rise, and disabled the PWM, since the resulting voltage was too high. This problem can be seen graphically in Fig. 3(a). As for issue 2a, the 24 V power signal missing issue was due to a deadlock in the HVC that resulted in the controller reporting the 24 V power signal missing, even though it was actually present. This can be seen graphically in Fig. 3(c).

Upon rectifying these observed issues in a later software upgrade, the task at hand is to run formal verification on the upgraded software in order to ensure both that the previously found errors have been fixed and that there are no other situations where similar errors could occur.

2.1   Properties for Formal Verification

In this section, the set of properties that are to be formally verified will be presented and discussed. Most of them are rather natural and generic properties to be fulfilled by any feedback controller tracking a set-point reference. Also, the previously detected errors provide a testimony of which properties that are necessary to formally verify in order to ensure that they will not happen again, under any circumstances.

As one of the most profound properties of any feedback controller, it is reasonable to require that HV_Actual should always follow $HV\_SetPoint$. This deserves particular attention in cases with residual voltage as depicted in for instance Fig. 3(b). To formalize this, since all voltages here are non-negative, the following implications were considered:

$$\begin{aligned} HV\_SetPoint = 0 &\rightarrow HV\_Actual = 0 \\ HV\_SetPoint > 0 &\rightarrow HV\_Actual > 0 \end{aligned} \tag{1}$$

Notice that by logical transposition of (1), the following implications also hold true:

$$HV\_Actual > 0 \rightarrow HV\_SetPoint > 0$$
$$HV\_Actual = 0 \rightarrow HV\_SetPoint = 0$$

As a result, the first property boils down to verification of:

$$HV\_SetPoint = 0 \longleftrightarrow HV\_Actual = 0.$$

To avoid residual effects and windup type of behavior in the HVC, it is also reasonable to verify that both PWM_Output and $HV\_SetPoint$ are set to 0 whenever the 24 V power signal, and thereby the HVC-module, is switched off. Additionally, in order to increase the confidence in the correctness of the model, it is customary to verify that the HVC state machine is not able to go into deadlock, and that all the states in the finite state machine are reachable, *i.e.*, the state machine has no dead logic.

To sum up, the properties chosen for the formal verification are:

P1: That the actual system voltage always follows the set-point:

$$HV\_SetPoint = 0 \longleftrightarrow HV\_Actual = 0$$

P2: That *PWM_ Output* is set to 0 whenever the 24 V power signal is off:

$$24\,V\_Power = 0 \to PWM\_Output = 0$$

P3: That *HV_ SetPoint* is set to 0 when the 24 V power signal is switched off:

$$24\,V\_Power = 0 \to HV\_SetPoint = 0$$

P4: That the state machine is not able to go into deadlock
P5: That all states in the state machine are reachable.

3 Finite State Machine Modelling

In order to perform model checking on the HVC, its functionalities were modeled as a finite state machine. This section presents the general finite state machine, which was directly derived from the implemented C++ code and depicted in Fig. 4. This state machine was then modelled and verified in RoboTool and Simulink. This is the topic of Sect. 4.

In the state GateDriverRamping, which is the state the HVC first enters when it is switched on, the PWM duty-cycle is ramped up gradually to ensure stability and gradual increasing of current and voltage. Then, in the Initialization state, initial parameters are set, as well as upper and lower limits for the high voltage.

After the GateDriverRamping and Initialization steps are successfully finished, the state machine enters the Wait24VPower state. When the HVC has 24 V power switched on and stable, the system enters the ClosedLoop state. This is the ideal state for operation, and is where the controller is regulating the voltage in relation to the set-point. In case the voltage is breaching the upper or lower limits, the state machine moves from ClosedLoop to ErrorMode.

There is also a possibility to go straight to ErrorMode from any of the other states, if certain variables are set or any watchdogs or interrupts are triggered. For instance, an interrupt is triggered if the supply voltage is below a certain threshold, and another is triggered if *HV_ Actual* is above or below the upper and lower limits, respectively. Getting out of ErrorMode requires manual acknowledgement of the occurred errors.

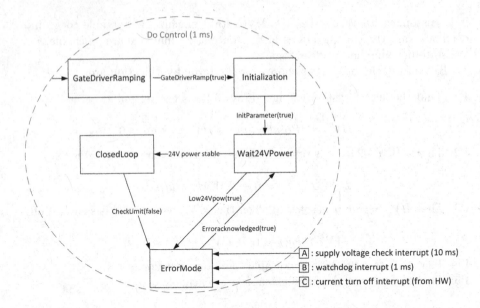

Fig. 4. Finite state diagram of the High Voltage Controller (HVC).

4   Model Checking

The finite state machine created from the C++ code of the HVC has to be modelled in a model checking tool in order to verify the selected properties. To this end, two different tools are adopted, in order to compare and evaluate their functionality and effectiveness. In this work, the finite state machine has been modelled in RoboTool [6] using the modelling language RoboChart, and in SDV [5] using the modelling language Stateflow. This is done in Sect. 4.1 and 4.2 respectively.

4.1   Model Checking in RoboTool

RoboTool and its modelling language RoboChart are specifically designed to model robotic systems for formal verification [6]. The tool automatically generates Communicating Sequential Processes (CSP) [14] proof models, which are verified using the Failures-Divergences Refinement (FDR) model-checker [15,16].

When using RoboChart for modelling, it is important to be aware that the model has to be of a higher abstraction level than models used for dynamic simulation. Capturing the behaviour from the C++ code in an abstract modelling paradigm like RoboChart can be challenging, especially for practitioners who are used to work with input-driven, dynamic simulations. Instead, the model is analyzed by the verification tool by only assuming bounded data-types and going through all possible transitions in order to verify or disprove a property. Specific values for variables or inputs could be used, but this would restrict the range of values provided by the bounded data type. Thus, keeping a high level of abstraction during the modelling process is essential for getting a meaningful result from the model checking.

Simplifications to Reduce Verification Time. State-space explosion is a well-known issue for model checkers. For this reason, some lower level functionalities from the C++ code were simplified. As an example, the ramping function in GateDriverRamping was modelled simply by staying in the state for a certain number of time steps, representing the ramping time. This simplification, justified by the fact that GateDriverRamping occurs before the initialization state and therefore does not influence neither the verification properties nor results, greatly reduced the verification time.

The Model. For modelling the state machine as closely as possible to Fig. 4, the software operations (IOps), variables (IVars), events (IEvents), external events (IEvents_ext) and a robotic platform (RP1), were specified as shown in Fig. 5. The robotic platform (RP1) is an abstraction of the physical system, and only uses events that require communication with the system (IEvents_ext), whereas the other events and variables are internal to the software. For more details about the language structure and semantics used in RoboTool, please consult [6,17].

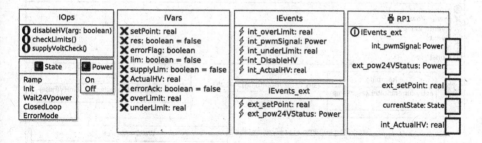

Fig. 5. Components and enumerated types used in the RoboChart model.

Figure 6 shows the RoboChart module mod_sys, which defines the connections between the controllers (ctrl0-3), and the robotic platform (RP1). In RoboChart, connections with the platform are asynchronous, indicated by the keyword async, as interactions with the hardware cannot be refused, only ignored [7, p. 3110].

Using the components from Fig. 5, a state machine model was created using the graphical user interface in RoboTool. An overview of the states and the transitions between them can be seen in Fig. 7.

All of the top-level states have an entry action, which indicates the current state via the typed event currentState. This is useful for analysis of properties that are only applicable in certain states. The detailed view of the two most important states (ClosedLoop and ErrorMode) can be seen in Fig. 8 and 9.

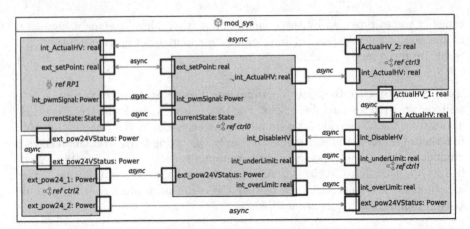

Fig. 6. RoboChart module mod_sys defining the connections between controllers and the robotic platform. Controller ctrl0 contains the main State_machine, a recast in RoboChart of the state machine presented in Fig. 4. The watchdogs have been combined into one state machine, defined inside controller ctrl1. Controllers ctrl2 and ctrl3 are used purely for relaying events int_ActualHV and ext_pow24VStatus to other controllers.

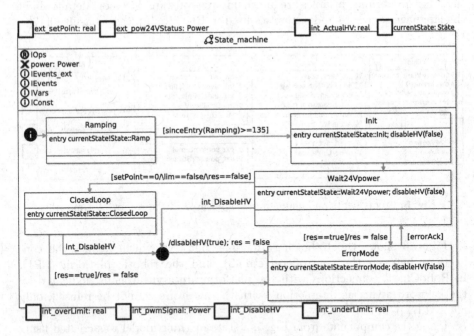

Fig. 7. Main State_machine corresponding to that of Fig. 4 recast in RoboChart, with the internal behaviour of composite states (other than Ramping) elided.

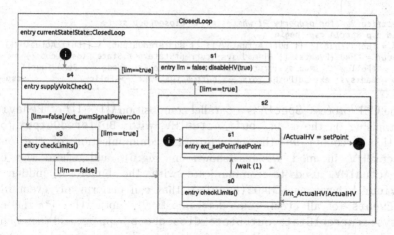

Fig. 8. ClosedLoop state of State_machine.

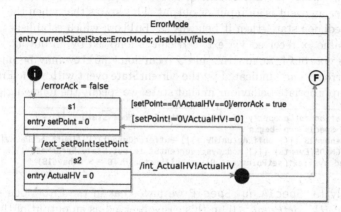

Fig. 9. ErrorMode state of State_machine.

Verification of Selected Properties. In order to verify the properties from Sect. 2 in FDR, the properties had to be formally written in CSP. To specify simple assertions, such as deadlock freedom, RoboTool provides a simple textual domain-specific language. More complex properties, however, have to be specified directly in CSP_M, the machine-readable version of CSP. A full account of the CSP specifications for all properties discussed in what follows can be found online[1].

The first property to verify, P1 as described in Sect. 2, is that *HV_Actual* follows *HV_SetPoint*. Due to the necessary simplifications that were made when modelling *HV_Actual* and *HV_SetPoint*, a binary version of property P1 had to be considered, where the signals *HV_Actual* and *HV_SetPoint* are considered to be either on or off. Notice that this modification is without loss of generality.

---

[1] https://github.com/robo-star/hvc-case-study.

```
// Specification for property P1 while in the ClosedLoop state
untimed csp Spec1A csp—begin
Spec1A = (Behaviour [| {| buff_ActualHV |} |] BufferedOutput) \ {|buff_ActualHV|}
Behaviour = CHAOS(Events) [| {| mod_sys::currentState.out.State_ClosedLoop |} |>
        (Follow /\ (mod_sys::currentState.out.State_ErrorMode —> Behaviour))
Follow = mod_sys::ext_setPoint.in?x —> buff_ActualHV!x —> Follow          csp—end
```

The CSP process `Spec1A` is a parallel composition ($[|\cdots|]$) of `Behaviour`, synchronising on the event `buff_ActualHV`, with `BufferedOutput` (omitted) that accounts for the asynchronous communication of the output `int_ActualHV` in `mod_sys` (as shown in Fig. 6), and where the event `buff_ActualHV`, used to communicate with the buffer, is hidden (\). `Behaviour` behaves as `CHAOS(Events)`, that can perform any event in the set `Events` (of all events) non-deterministically until ($[|\cdots|>$) the event `mod_sys::currentState.out.State_ClosedLoop` happens, and then behaves as `Follow`. Events in the CSP semantics of RoboChart are named according to the hierarchy, where `::` is a delimiter, and have a parameter `in` or `out` to indicate whether an event is an input or output. This states that when the system is in the ClosedLoop state, then it behaves as `Follow`, which establishes that the input ($?$) value `x` received via ext_setPoint is followed by an output ($!$) of the same value via `buff_ActualHV`, and a recursion. `Follow` may be interrupted ($/\backslash$) if an error occurs, indicated by the currentState event with value ErrorMode. To ensure appropriate behaviour in that state, we specify the following property.

```
// Specification for property P1 while in the ErrorMode state
untimed csp Spec1B csp—begin
Spec1B = (Behave1B [|{| buff_ActualHV |}|] BufferedOutput) \ {|buff_ActualHV|}
Behave1B = CHAOS(Events) [|{| mod_sys::currentState.out.State_ErrorMode |}|>
        (mod_sys::ext_setPoint.out.0 —> buff_ActualHV!0 —> Behave1B)          csp—end
```

Similarly to `Spec1A`, in `Spec1B` we have that in the ErrorMode state the value of the *HV_SetPoint* is 0, in this case observed as an output of the system via ext_setPoint, and that the value of int_ActualHV should also follow.

The specification for verifying P1 is written as two **assertions**, reproduced below, which were verified in FDR. Here, `mod_sys_noppwm` is a version of `mod_sys` where the unrelated events ext_pow24VStatus and int_pwmSignal are hidden, to ensure that the verification with respect to `Spec1A` and `Spec1B` is meaningful. It is verified **in the traces model** that ensures safety [14, p. 36], that is, an implementation `P` **refines** Spec if, and only if, every behaviour of `P` is also a behaviour of `Spec`. Both of the assertions passed, thus successfully verifying property P1.

```
untimed csp mod_sys_noppwm associated to mod_sys csp—begin
mod_sys_noppwm = mod_sys::O__(0)\{|mod_sys::int_pwmSignal,mod_sys::ext_pow24VStatus|}
csp—end // Assertions for property P1
assertion A1A : mod_sys_noppwm refines Spec1A in the traces model
assertion A1B : mod_sys_noppwm refines Spec1B in the traces model
```

The second property (P2) requires that *PWM_Output* should be set to 0 when the 24 V power signal switches off. The CSP specification is shown below.

```
// Specification for property P2
untimed csp PWM csp—begin
PWM = mod_sys::ext_pow24VStatus.in.Power_Off —> PWM
  [] mod_sys::int_pwmSignal.out.Power_Off —> PWM
  [] mod_sys::int_pwmSignal.out.Power_On —> PWM_on
PWM_on = (mod_sys::ext_pow24VStatus.in.Power_Off —>
        (RUN({|mod_sys::ext_pow24VStatus.in.Power_Off|})
          /\ mod_sys::int_pwmSignal.out.Power_Off —> PWM)
  [] mod_sys::int_pwmSignal.out.Power_Off —> PWM
  [] mod_sys::int_pwmSignal.out.Power_On —> PWM_on)          csp—end
```

In PWM, there is an external choice ([]) where the power status can be switched off via ext_pow24VStatus, or the int_pwmSignal may be switched Off. Once the int_pwmSignal becomes On, then the process behaves as PWM_on, where there is another choice: if the power status changes to Off via ext_pow24VStatus, then the output int_pwmSignal should follow as Off, while allowing further readings of the power status, specified using RUN, via ext_pow24VStatus, to take place. Observe that *P2* is specified by tracking the changes of int_pwmSignal relative to the input value of ext_pow24VStatus.

The assertion to verify the specification in FDR, as seen below, also passed, thus successfully verifying property P2, where mod_sys_pwm is a constrained form of mod_sys where other events are hidden similarly to previous assertions.

```
//Assertion for property P2
assertion A2 : mod_sys_pwm refines PWM in the traces model
```

The third property to verify, P3, is that *HV_SetPoint* is set to 0 when the 24 power signal switches off. The specification in CSP is as follows.

```
//Specification for property P3
untimed csp Spec3 csp—begin
Spec3 = CHAOS(Events) [| {|mod_sys::ext_pow24VStatus.in.Power_Off|} |>
        (RUN({|mod_sys::ext_pow24VStatus.in.Power_Off|})
          /\ mod_sys::ext_setPoint.out.0 —> Spec3)          csp—end
```

The assertion to verify P3 in FDR was written similarly to the ones for P1 and P2, as seen below. It passed in FDR, thus successfully verifying P3.

```
//Assertion for property P3
assertion A3 : mod_sys_setpoint refines Spec3 in the traces model
```

The assertion-specific language in RoboTool was used to specify and validate P4 and P5, which are that the state machine should be deadlock free and that all states should be reachable. The assertions written in RoboTool can be seen in the code below.

```
//P4: Checks if the model is deadlock free
assertion A4 : mod_sys is deadlock-free
//P5: Checks for reachability of states:
assertion A5 : State_machine::Ramping is reachable in State_machine
assertion A6 : State_machine::Init is reachable in State_machine
assertion A7 : State_machine::Wait24Vpower is reachable in State_machine
assertion A8 : State_machine::ClosedLoop is reachable in State_machine
assertion A9 : State_machine::ErrorMode is reachable in State_machine
```

All these assertions passed in FDR, which implies that the state machine is in fact deadlock free, and all the states are reachable. Thus, also P4 and P5 were verified successfully.

4.2   Model Checking in Simulink Design Verifier (SDV)

Simulink is a popular tool for traditional, input-driven simulation, and the modelling in SDV is similar to regular modelling used for simulation [5]. Thus, it requires less abstraction than in RoboTool, and it is more straightforward to translate the C++ code directly to the modelling language. The graphical language Stateflow, which is specifically created to model state machines, can be used with SDV, and was chosen to model the finite state machine from Sect. 3. SDV uses Prover Plug-In® products from Prover® Technology to do the model checking and prove the model properties [18]. It is built upon Gunnar Stålmarck's proof procedure, which uses tautology checks to prove that an assertion holds true in every possible interpretation [19].

Simplifications to Reduce Verification Time. Also in the Simulink Design Verifier model, some simplifications had to be made in order to keep verification times reasonable. For example when modelling the transformer and CW generator from Fig. 2. The transformer is modelled as a simple transfer function, with non model-fitted values, poles and zeroes. The CW block is simply modelled with a gain block from the Simulink library, also this with an arbitrary value.

Additionally, the 24 V power signal and the PWM output signal have been simplified to being modelled binary, so they can be either on or off. Knowing if the signal is on or off is sufficient for verifying the properties listed for this use case.

The Model. An overview of the Simulink model can be seen in Fig. 10.

The main state machine from Fig. 4 can be found within the purple box, while variables, inputs and outputs are connected to it as seen in the figure. The grey box to the right contains the model of the transformer and CW block from Fig. 2. The green boxes are the verification subsystems containing the code for verifying the selected properties.

As seen in Fig. 10, the model used in SDV allows for defining inputs and outputs, similarly to a traditional simulation model. This made it possible to model the finite state machine very closely to the C++ code. However, some extra variables were introduced in order to model the ramping function.

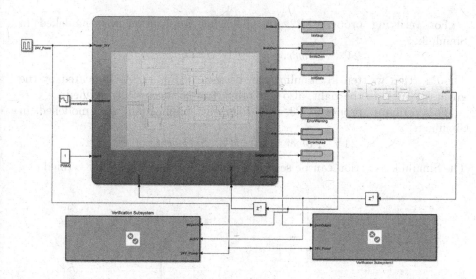

Fig. 10. Overview of the Simulink model. (Color figure online)

Verification of Selected Properties. In order to verify the properties from Sect. 2, the properties had to be formally modelled in SDV, using logical operator blocks. For verifying property P1, the following implications were considered and modelled in Simulink, as seen in Fig. 11:

$$HV\_SetPoint = 0 \rightarrow HV\_Actual = 0,$$
$$HV\_SetPoint > 0 \rightarrow HV\_Actual > 0.$$

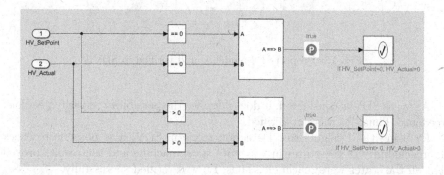

Fig. 11. Property P1 modelled and verified in SDV. It is checked that whenever the value of *HV_SetPoint* is 0 or above 0, it implies the same for *HV_Actual*. The green rectangles to the right indicate that the properties were successfully verified. (Color figure online)

For verifying property P2, the following implication was modelled in Simulink:

$$24\,V\_Power = 0 \rightarrow PWM\_Output = 0.$$

The assertion written in Simulink can be seen in Fig. 12. As indicated by the green rectangle to the right, also this property was successfully verified.

For verifying property P3, the following implication was modelled in Simulink:

$$24\,V\_Power = 0 \rightarrow HV\_SetPoint = 0.$$

The Simulink assertion can be seen in Fig. 13, and was successfully verified.

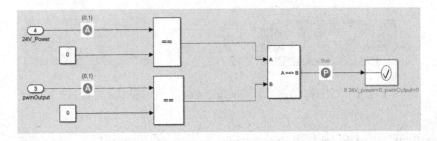

Fig. 12. Property P2 modelled and verified in SDV. The assumption blocks assume the values of $24\,V\_Power$ and PWM_Output to be either 0 or 1, which is reasonable since they are modelled as binary. (Color figure online)

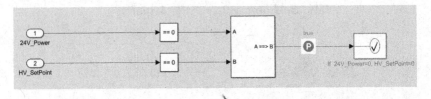

Fig. 13. Property P3 modelled and verified in SDV.

As far as SDV is considered, it does not offer the possibility to verify deadlock freedom[2]. Thus, P4 was not verified.

By using the Design Error Detection mode in SDV, it is possible to check the reachability of the states in the finite state machine and the results proved that all the states were reachable. Thus, P5 was verified successfully.

---

[2] Deadlock detection is instead provided by MathWorks Polyspace toolbox.

5   Concluding Remarks and Future Work

As detailed in Sect. 4, some simplifications had to be made to the models used in RoboTool and SDV. In RoboTool, all properties were verified. Since SDV is not able to verify deadlock freedom, P4 was not verified in this tool.

The collective results formally show that all five specifications as listed in Sect. 2.1 are fulfilled, and thus the previously detected errors from Sect. 2 have been corrected. As these errors went undetected by traditional testing methods in an earlier version of the software, the results in this paper also serve as a testimony of the strength and suitability of using formal verification methods for industrial safety critical systems.

Both tool-chains offered the necessary functionality to model the HVC state machine and perform model checking. The verification times in both tools were typically about 2–3 min when running on a Windows laptop with Intel® Core© i5 CPU @ 2.71 GHz. These computation times are well within acceptable limits for offline, one-time verification purposes. However, it can be a potential bottleneck if used for development and debugging purposes.

As most industrial practitioners are used to using MathWorks products but are not as familiar with CSP, the use of SDV will most likely be the fastest and easiest way to do a formal verification. Unfamiliarity with CSP and RoboTool, which required a different way of thought and modelling, resulted in some challenges during both the modelling and verification processes. However, RoboTool has the advantage of being designed specifically for robotic systems, which gives it more targeted modelling options. During this work, we often learned about new functionalities and new ways to solve problems in RoboTool, which indicates that it is the better choice for more advanced use cases and experienced users.

To tap into this, future work involves further improvement of the RoboTool model. Instead of the simplifications made to the RoboTool model in order to reduce computation time, as mentioned in Sect. 4.1, it would be preferable to utilize distributed computation and parallel refinement checking capabilities of FDR. In this way, it could be possible to explore the possibility to include timed assertions and formulate requirements capturing the dynamic convergence of the HV_Actual to $HV\_SetPoint$. By increasing the model's complexity, future work will also look into how the tools perform with increasingly computationally heavy models. Also, the potential of using RoboSim to generate (verified) simulations from RoboChart, is currently being further investigated.

As far as MathWorks is considered, the Polyspace software tools provide some complementary verification capabilities, such as deadlock detection, that should be examined and utilized in future work. In order to continue the comparative study, updates and improvements will be made to the Simulink model as well in future work, to ensure a fair comparison with RoboTool. This includes, for instance, formulating a specification property that captures the dynamics of the set-point following.

In this work, formal verification has been used on the already rectified code, in order to ensure that the errors have been corrected. However, to further demonstrate the abilities of formal verification as a supplement to testing, it would be interesting to repeat the process on the faulty code. This would increase the confidence that our modelling captures the behaviour properly, by showing that the errors would have been detected earlier if formal verification had been applied. Thus, future work will include repeating the verification steps on the faulty code as well.

Acknowledgements. The authors gratefully acknowledge the value of all the input and support provided by ABB Robotics research group at Bryne, Norway, most prominently by Dr. Morten Mossige and Cato Jensen.

The research presented in this paper has received funding from the Norwegian Research Council, SFI Offshore Mechatronics, project number 237896. Pedro Ribeiro is funded by the UK EPSRC under grant EP/M025756/1.

References

1. Seligman, E., Schubert, T., Kumar, M.V.A.K.: Formal Verification: An Essential Toolkit for Modern VLSI Design (2015)
2. Baier, C.: Principles of Model Checking. MIT Press, Cambridge (2008)
3. Chang, C., Lee, R.: Symbolic Logic and Mechanical Theorem Proving. Computer Science and Applied Mathematics. Academic Press, Cambridge (1973)
4. Weißmann, M., Bedenk, S., Buckl, C., Knoll, A.: Model checking industrial robot systems. In: Groce, A., Musuvathi, M. (eds.) SPIN 2011. LNCS, vol. 6823, pp. 161–176. Springer, Heidelberg (2011). https://doi.org/10.1007/978-3-642-22306-8_11
5. MathWorks: Simulink Design Verifier. https://www.mathworks.com/products/simulink-design-verifier.html. Accessed 5 Mar 2020
6. Miyazawa, A., Cavalcanti, A., Ribeiro, P., Li, W., Woodcock, J., Timmis, J.: RoboChart reference manual. Technical report, University of York, February 2016
7. Miyazawa, A., Ribeiro, P., Wei, L., Cavalcanti, A.L.C., Timmis, J., Woodcock, J.C.P.: RoboChart: modelling and verification of the functional behaviour of robotic applications. Softw. Syst. Model. **18**(5), 3097–3149 (2019)
8. Alur, R., Courcoubetis, C., Henzinger, T.A., Ho, P.-H.: Hybrid automata: an algorithmic approach to the specification and verification of hybrid systems. In: Grossman, R.L., Nerode, A., Ravn, A.P., Rischel, H. (eds.) HS 1991-1992. LNCS, vol. 736, pp. 209–229. Springer, Heidelberg (1993). https://doi.org/10.1007/3-540-57318-6_30
9. Alur, R.: Formal verification of hybrid systems. In: Proceedings of the Ninth ACM International Conference on Embedded Software, EMSOFT 2011, New York, NY, USA, pp. 273–278. Association for Computing Machinery (2011)
10. Henzinger, T.A., Rusu, V.: Reachability verification for hybrid automata. In: Henzinger, T.A., Sastry, S. (eds.) HSCC 1998. LNCS, vol. 1386, pp. 190–204. Springer, Heidelberg (1998). https://doi.org/10.1007/3-540-64358-3_40
11. Henzinger, T.A., Kopke, P.W., Puri, A., Varaiya, P.: What's decidable about hybrid automata? J. Comput. Syst. Sci. **57**(1), 94–124 (1998)
12. Bresolin, D., Di Guglielmo, L., Geretti, L., Muradore, R., Fiorini, P., Villa, T.: Open problems in verification and refinement of autonomous robotic systems. In: 2012 15th Euromicro Conference on Digital System Design, pp. 469–476 (2012)

13. Geretti, L., Muradore, R., Bresolin, D., Fiorini, P., Villa, T.: Parametric formal verification: the robotic paint spraying case study. IFAC-PapersOnLine **50**(1), 9248–9253 (2017). 20th IFAC World Congress
14. Roscoe, A.W.: Understanding Concurrent Systems. Springer, London (2010). https://doi.org/10.1007/978-1-84882-258-0
15. Gibson-Robinson, T., Armstrong, P., Boulgakov, A., Roscoe, A.W.: FDR3 — a modern refinement checker for CSP. In: Ábrahám, E., Havelund, K. (eds.) TACAS 2014. LNCS, vol. 8413, pp. 187–201. Springer, Heidelberg (2014). https://doi.org/10.1007/978-3-642-54862-8_13
16. University of Oxford: FDR4 — The CSP Refinement Checker. https://cocotec.io/fdr. Accessed 11 May 2020
17. Miyazawa, A.: RoboTool RoboChart Tool Manual. University of York, May 2019
18. MathWorks: Acknowledgments. https://se.mathworks.com/help/sldv/ug/acknowledgments.html. Accessed 10 Sept 2020
19. Sheeran, M., Stålmarck, G.: A tutorial on Stålmarck's proof procedure for propositional logic. Form. Methods Syst. Des. **16**, 23–58 (2000). https://doi.org/10.1023/A:1008725524946

Statistical Model Checking in Drug Repurposing for Alzheimer's Disease

Herbert Rausch Fernandes[1,3]([✉]) [iD], Giovanni Freitas Gomes[2],
Antonio Carlos Pinheiro de Oliveira[2][iD], and Sérgio Vale Aguiar Campos[3]

[1] Department of Computation and Civil Engineering, CEFET-MG, Varginha, Brazil
hrausch@cefetmg.br
[2] Department of Pharmacology, Universidade Federal de Minas Gerais,
Belo Horizonte, Brazil
acpoliveira@gmail.com
[3] Department of Computer Science, Universidade Federal de Minas Gerais,
Belo Horizonte, Brazil
scampos@dcc.ufmg.br

Abstract. Dementia is a disease that is characterized by the gradual loss of memory and cognition of patients due to the death of neurons. The future perspective is that the number of patients will increase, due to the aging of the population, reaching up to one third of the world population over 65 years. Alzheimer's disease is the most common form of dementia and there is no medication to prevent or cure the disease. In this sense, the discovery of an efficient treatment for the disease is a real need, and the repositioning of drugs and *in silico* techniques can contribute to this purpose. Computational methods, such as Statistical Model Checking, which is a formal verification technique, contribute to this field of research, aiding to analyze the evolution of the protein and drugs interactions at a lower cost than the laboratory experiments. In this work, we present a model of the PI3K/AKT/mTOR pathway and we connected it with Tau and Aβ, which are two important proteins that contribute to the evolution of Alzheimer's disease. We analyzed the effect of rapamycin, an immunosuppressive drug, on those proteins. Our results show that this medicine has the potential to slow down one of the biological processes that causes neuronal death. In addition, we could show the formal model verification technique can be an efficient tool to design pharmacological strategies reducing experimental cost.

Keywords: Statistical Model Checking · Alzheimer's disease · Systems biology

1 Introduction

Alzheimer's disease (AD) is the most common cause of dementia, representing about 50%–75% of all those cases [24]. AD is a progressive neurodegenerative disease associated with memory loss, and behavioral and cognitive impairment [43].

© Springer Nature Switzerland AG 2020
G. Carvalho and V. Stolz (Eds.): SBMF 2020, LNCS 12475, pp. 64–80, 2020.
https://doi.org/10.1007/978-3-030-63882-5_5

Patients also usually develop apathy, depression, eating and sleeping disorders, aggressiveness and other behavioral changes [4,41]. AD is a multifactorial condition and risk factors associated with the disease include age, gender, ethnic origin, lifestyle, genetic factors, cardiovascular and metabolic comorbidities, and others. The number of people affected by AD has risen over the years due to the increase of population life expectancy, once aging is the main risk factor for the disease [24].

There is no cure yet for the disease or drugs that reduce its progression [22]. In addition, a reliable biomarker for the early diagnosis of the disease is not already known [52]. If this situation remains, the World Health Organization estimates that, in 20 years, neurodegenerative diseases will become the second leading cause of mortality in the world, behind only cardiovascular diseases [17].

One of the strategies to find new treatments against AD is drug repurposing; that is an attempt for identifying new uses for a drug already known and tested, and that is currently used for the treatment of another disease. Some advantages of this approach are the reduction of investment and time required for testing the drug [17]. In this sense, anticancer and immunosuppressive drugs have proven to be an alternative for therapeutic application in AD. Studies indicate that there are shared signaling pathways for these diseases, such as mitochondrial dysfunction, oxidative stress and cellular metabolism [17].

System biology is a tool that can help biomedical researches for searching for disease treatment. This *in silico* approach consists of modelling biological interactions and checking how they evolve during the time [28]. This computational technique allows us to test different scenarios of protocols of treatment before doing *in vivo* or *in vitro* experiments, saving money and time. Besides that, it is possible to perform quantitative analysis of the system providing new insights [49].

Model Checking is a technique that can be applied to verify specifications, such as whether a medicine can inactivate a certain protein, of a systems biology model. The system is modeled in a finite state transition system and properties are specified in temporal language formulas. The model checker algorithms perform an exhaustive search in the state space of the system checking all configurations in order to verify if the property is satisfied. If the property is not satisfied, it returns a counter-example showing the decisions and values that make the specification false [12].

Although model checking is very efficient, it is limited by the exponential growth of the number of states in the model as the system complexity increases [55]. Frequently the representation of a model becomes so large that it cannot be represented in current computers. Statistical Model Checking (SMC) addresses this problem using controlled simulations in order to analyze the model [54]. Simulation is more efficient than a full model traversal, but it is not exhaustive. SMC, however, allows an error margin to be specified, and increases the number of simulations until the error margin is obtained. This way it executes faster than full model checking while maintaining control of the errors that might be incurred. Moreover, SMC can answer questions such as "What is the probability that a certain protein achieves a concentration after a drug being administered?", or "What is the probability that a protein activation implies in a knockout of another protein?". This is particularly useful given the nature of biological models. Often not all parameters of the model are known, making the models necessarily imprecise. It would be wasteful to use a precise technique on models that are approximate by construction [55].

In this work, we propose a formal model capable to provide insights and test hypotheses about the response of a medicine against AD. We modeled a survival and its related biological process to several diseases which have drugs in clinical trials or approved. In this case study, we tested whether a drug called rapamycin could be used for the treatment of AD and we could show that it leads Tau phosphorylation reductions.

Section 2 describes the main concepts related to formal methods, Alzheimer Disease and the biochemical pathway that the rapamycin targets. In Sect. 3 some mathematical models are shown and the proposed formal model is presented. The results of properties analyses are presented in Sect. 4, and the conclusion and the future work are found in Sect. 5.

2 Background

This section shows the concepts regarding Statistical Model Checking and its temporal logic, followed by the presentation of Alzheimer Disease and its behaviour. The PI3K/AKT/mTOR pathway and its interaction with AD is also described in this section.

2.1 Statistical Model Checking—SMC

SMC has emerged to handle the state-space explosion problem by allowing complex systems with stochastic behaviour to be analysed efficiently [3,55]. A stochastic system M is usually a Markov chain, that is, the next state of the system depends only on its current state and not on the whole system history [18].

Statistical model checking verifies the reachability of the transition system, but, in addition, it calculates the likelihoods to reach a defined state. It uses statistical inference methods in order verify whether the likelihood of a property θ being satisfied is greater than or equal to a threshold ϕ, that is, if $Pr \geq \theta(\phi) \in [0,1]$ [27].

UPPAAL [8] is one of the model checkers that implements the SMC algorithm. Figure 1 shows the overview of the method, in which the inputs are a stochastic model M, the statistical confidence parameters, and the specifications of the properties that will be verified. UPPAAL, then, generates simulation traces π and verifies if π satisfies the property ϕ. If the statistical significance given by the parameters has not been achieved, new simulation traces are generated. When the threshold defined is obtained, the tool returns the results obtained.

The systems in UPPAAL are represented by priced timed automatas (PTA) which are finite-state machines in which clocks evolve at different rates. The formal definition of a PTA is given by:

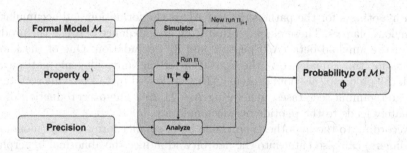

Fig. 1. From a model specification M, a property ϕ, and statistical parameters, UPPAAL generates traces of simulations which are verified if they satisfy the specification, and then, calculates the likelihood that the event happens.

Definition 1. *PTA is a tuple $A = (L, l_0, X, \Sigma, E, R, I)$ where (a) L is a finite set of states; (b) $l_0 \in L$ is the initial state; (c) X is a finite set of clocks; (d) $\Sigma = \Sigma_i \uplus \Sigma_o$ is a finite set of actions, divided into inputs (Σ_i) and outputs (Σ_o), (e) E is the set of edges; (f) R is a vector of rates for each clock; and (g) I assigns an invariant for each state [13].*

The properties of the system are written in weighted metric temporal logic formula ($WMTL_\leq$) which implements a subset of CTL properties [12] and a stochastic language capable of expressing temporal relationships between events and their probability. It is possible to verify whether $P_M(<>_{x \leq C} \phi) \geq p(p \in [0,1])$, where P_M is the probability of the model M satisfies the property, x is the clock, C is the time limit and ϕ is a state predicate. This temporal grammar also allows to define qualitative properties such as "the probability the concentration of active AKT is greater than the inactive AKT in 1000 units time is greater or equal than 0.7". This example is encoded in:

$$Pr[\leq 1000](<> aAKT > AKT) \geq 0.7$$

It is also possible to define quantitative properties in UPPAAL in order to estimate the probability the event occurrence, such as, "what is the probability that the concentration of active AKT is greater than the inative AKT in 1000 units time":

$$Pr[\leq 1000](<> aAKT > AKT)$$

2.2   Alzheimer's Disease Pathophysiology

AD is characterized as a neurodegenerative disease, which means that there is death and loss of neurons during the progress of this condition. Neuron loss is a consequence of a series of processes, including the accumulation of amyloid plaques in the brain, the destabilization of the neuron cytoskeleton, and metabolic changes and inflammation in the central nervous system [38]. The main hypothesis for the pathogenesis of AD is the formation and accumulation of amyloid plaques. These plaques result from an imbalance between the production of the amyloid-beta (Aβ) peptide and its degradation. One of the known reasons for this imbalance is the activation of the amyloidogenic pathway, in which the precursor amyloid protein (APP) is cleaved by two enzyme secretases, beta and gamma secretases, generating Aβ [11,15]. The overproduction of Aβ ultimately leads to the peptide overaccumulation.

According to the hypothesis amyloide beta, smaller forms of Aβ (monomers and dimers) can also enter into the neuron and induce the abnormal hyperphosphorylation of the Tau protein. Tau is a protein involved in the stabilization of the neuron cytoskeleton and hyperphosphorylated Tau results in the accumulation of neurofibrillary tangles (NFT) into the neuron and destabilization of neuron cytoskeleton, followed by the axon and dendrite degeneration, cell death, and loss of function [44].

The malfunction of degrading amyloid plaques and the NFT process can also contribute to maintain or increase the neuronal death and loss, resulting in cognitive decline [35]. One function that can assist to reduce those structures is the autophagy, which is an intracellular degradation process in which the cell self-digests its own components. Autophagy has an important role in the maintenance of homeostasis, energetic balance, and functional integrity, clearing dysfunctional species like toxic protein aggregates and damaged cell organelles, protecting neurons from death [30].

Autophagy is stimulated by different factors. The mammalian target of rapamycin (mTOR) is the main regulator that inhibits autophagic biogenesis [33,46]. Some studies have shown that the regulation of mTOR may improve cognitive impairments in transgenic animal models of Alzheimer's disease, what makes this pathway a target for a drug repurposing. In this sense, the mTOR pathway responsible for controlling the autophagic activity emerges as an important target for AD treatment [42].

2.3   PI3K/AKT/mTOR Pathway and Alzheimer Disease

The pathway starts with the phosphatidyl-inositol 3-kinase (PI3K) activation that leads to the protein kinase B (AKT) phosphorylation. Phosphorylated AKT is the activated form of this protein. After being activated, AKT phosphorylates various cellular substrates and acts in a series of functions, including the inhibition of glycogen synthase kinase 3β (GSK3β). GSK3β is one of the known kinases that phosphorylates Tau, and its inhibition can address a reduction in the NFT formation process and a reduction in neuronal loss. In addition, GSK3β cooperates with APP cleavage forming Aβ peptides and its inhibition can also slowdown the formation of Aβ plaques, reducing loss of function and symptoms of AD [29,34].

Another substrate activated by AKT is mTOR. One of the downstream of mTOR is the activation of p70S6 kinase (S6K1) that leads to a negative feedback inhibiting the PI3K activation [42]. mTOR inhibits the autophagy, and, in case of abnormal activities in this pathway, could promote a disrupted clearance of Aβ and NFT [19,23]. Impaired autophagic-mediated clearance of Aβ results in Aβ accumulation and in formation of plaques, ultimately leading to neuron injury and loss of function. Figure 2 shows this signaling cascade of the pathway and some of the biological functions it triggers.

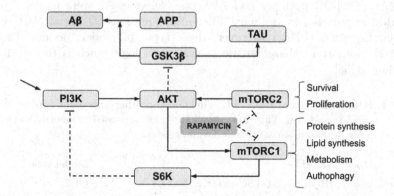

Fig. 2. The illustration of the pathway and its biological process related. The arrow means the protein activates the other protein. The dashed line means the protein inhibits the other protein.

There are several drugs that act regulating the mTOR pathway. The best known drug is rapamycin (Siromilus), which is an immunosuppressant used in human renal transplant, and other pathologies [31,35]. Although there are no clinical tests for Alzheimer's disease, studies in animal models show a protective effect of rapamycin on neurodegeneration, improving learning and cognitive parameters in mice [32,45].

Although these results suggest the drug is effective in cognitive parameters, mTOR signaling pathway is complex and requires a better understanding of its dynamic regulation. A Systems Biology approach can assist the understanding of this complex pathway beyond mere intuition by transforming experimental knowledge into a coherent formal model and testing hypotheses *in silico* [48].

3 Formal Model

3.1 Related Work

Model Checking has been used in different fields, such as hardware [7,36], real time systems [2,9,10], and robotics [25]. Furthermore, the technique can also be used to analyze biological systems. In the works [21] and [53] applied model checking to verify a pancreatic cancer model and the apoptosis, proliferation, cellular cycle, and the association with diabetes. A stochastic model and statistical model checking have been used to propose a new model for the interaction between the Na/Cl channels and the palitoxin, increasing the understanding of how the toxin affects ion channels [51].

In spite of that, Model Checking is not a common approach used in system biology. It is more common to use simulations and numerical techniques to analyze these types of systems. Table 1 shows some of works about the PI3K/AKT/mTOR pathway and Alzheimer Disease. All were modeled using numerical approaches by ordinary differential equations (ODE) or Partial Differential Equation (PDE). However, these types of models do not describe one of the important characteristic of system biology which is the stochastic behaviour [1,55].

Table 1. Related models of PI3K/AKT/mTOR and other important species for AD like $A\beta$, $GSK3\beta$, and Tau. This table shows the references used to identify the kinetic values in order to design our stochastic formal model.

Model	Variables	Model type
[39]	IR-IRS1-Akt-TSC-mTORC1-S6K1	ODE
[26]	IR-PI3K-Akt-mTOR-S6K-GSK3β	ODE
[20]	Rapamycin-mTOR	ODE
[50]	IR-IRS-Akt-mTORC1-mTORC2-DEPTOR	ODE
[16]	Rapamycin-mTORC1-mTORC2	ODE
[40]	APP-Aβ -GSK3β -Tau-NFT	ODE
[22]	APP-Aβ -GSK3β -Tau-NFT-Neuronal Death	PDE

In [39] a model with negative pathway feedback is presented, in which the activation of mTORC1 induces the inhibition of PI3K. In addition, this model includes the activation of mTORC2 by the action of PI3K. [26], in turn, describes a model in which the pathway is stimulated by insulin. This model also analyzes the effects on the phosphorylation of GSK3β , FOXO1 and mTORC1. In this model, the authors consider the negative feedback of mTORC1 on the insulin receptor complex through S6K. In [50] the model of inhibition of mTORC1 and mTORC2 is presented through the inhibitory activity of the Deptor subunit. This modeling also considers the negative feedback of the pathway in the inhibition of the insulin receptor complex by means of S6K phosphorylated by mTORC1. However, none of these works cover any variables related to AD like the proposed model.

The association, dissociation and IC50 values (50% of the maximum inhibitory concentration) of rapamycin, BEZ235 and LY294002 in the inhibition of mTORC1 and PI3K are presented in [20]. [16] describes a simplified model of the dynamics of inhibition of mTORC1 and mTORC2 using rapamycin at different times and concentrations. In this work, the authors did not consider other species involved, such as PI3K and AKT Besides that, both works only focus the behaviour of the drug and they do not present an analysis of the impact of the drug in other proteins.

A mathematical model of regulation of Tau phosphorylation and formation of amyloid plaques by GSK3β is presented in [40]. In this work, the authors consider the effects of AN-1792 (alzforum) on the route. [22] developed a Tau hyperphosphorylation model, formation of amyloid plaques, recruitment of astrocytes, microglia, release of pro and anti-inflammatory cytokines and, also, neuronal death. The model also considers the administration of an anti-amyloid drug, aducanumab, which acts on phagocytosis and the clearance of Aβ mediated by microglia. However, none of them describe the interaction of AD with the PI3K/AKT/mTOR which is an important aging signalling network.

3.2   The Proposed Model

In order to analyse the effect of rapamycin in Aβ and Tau protein, we designed a novel formal model which links the PI3K/AKT/mTOR pathway with Tau phosphorylation and the production of Aβ . For this, the initial values of variables and parameters of reactions were obtained from the works listed in Table 1 and adjusted as detailed in Sect. 4.

Some design decisions were made in this model: mTORC2 was not considered due to its drug resistance [23]; the full activation of AKT depends on PI3K, only; the hyper-phosphorylation of Tau by GSK3β in residues S404, S400 and S396 is also not addressed in our model, since this process occurs in a single step; and the degradation or synthesis of the proteins involved in the pathway is not covered. Although these simplifications could affect the system, like the time needed to the system stabilization, the biological behaviour is not changed and they are common in *in vivo* experiments as well.

The proposed formal model, illustrated in Fig. 3, considers two states for each protein. They are: the inactive state, represented by the name of the protein; and the active state, which has the letter "a" followed by the name of the protein. The transitions between the states constitute a biochemical reaction and they are listed in Table 2. For example, the reaction 3 represents the activation of one molecule of AKT in one molecule of aAKT. For this, a molecule of aPI3K is needed. The velocity, or rate, of this reaction can be defined by the law of mass action, that is, the rate would be obtained from the product of reactants concentration and the kinetic constant [14]. Considering the reaction's 3, its velocity is given by the Eq. (1).

$$0.005 \times AKT \times aPI3K \tag{1}$$

Each reaction was modeled as a PTA. The transition is triggered when the condition is satisfied and it depends on considering a rate given by the law of mass action. Hence, the number of molecules are updated. The automatas of the reactions are shown in Fig. 4.

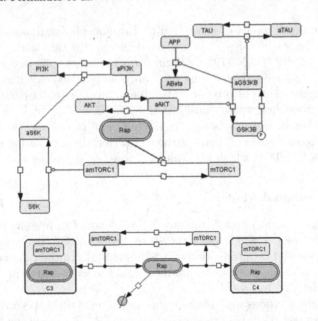

Fig. 3. Formal model representation of PI3K/AKT/mTOR and Aβ formation and Tau phosphorylation. Each state is assigned with the protein name, and the state that starts with "a" represents the active protein. For example: the state PI3K represents the protein PI3K inactive and the state "aPI3K" represents the protein active.

The administration of rapamycin is controlled by a specific automata, as shown in Fig. 5, and the degradation was modeled and we considered the drug binds to active and inactive mTORC1. In this example we add the drug at times 100, 200 and 300 h in a dose of 50ηM. These values can be adjusted, making *in silico* modeling an excellent tool for test and designing experiments *in vivo* or *in vitro*.

The UPPAAL model file is available at http://luar.dcc.ufmg.br/downloads/smc-alzheimer/.

4　Results

In this section the process used to adjust the parameters. The effects of the rapamycin in Tau and Aβ species and the discussion are also presented.

4.1　Simulations

The negative feedback of the signaling pathway is one of the pharmacological challenges [42] and it leads to the oscillatory behaviour shown in [50]. Several simulation executions were performed to adjust our parameters to reproduce this behaviour of mTOR as presented in Fig. 6. These simulations were also important to understand how the variable evolved overtime.

Table 2. List of reactions and rates modeled in Uppaal.

Id.	Reaction	Kinetic constant
1	$PI3K \longrightarrow aPI3K$	0.1
2	$aPI3K \longrightarrow PI3K$	1
3	$AKT + aPI3K \longrightarrow aAKT + aPI3K$	0.005
4	$aAKT \longrightarrow AKT$	2
5	$mTORC1 + aAKT \longrightarrow amTORC1 + aAKT$	0.1
6	$amTORC1 \longrightarrow mTORC1$	1
7	$S6K + amTORC1 \longrightarrow aS6K + amTORC1$	1
8	$aS6K \longrightarrow S6K$	0.01
9	$aPI3K + aS6K \longrightarrow PI3K + aS6K$	0.1
10	$aGSK3 + aAKT \longrightarrow GSK3 + aAKT$	0.003
11	$aGSK3 \longrightarrow ABeta$	0.002
12	$TAU + aGSK3 \longrightarrow aTAU + aGSK3$	0.02
13	$aTAU \longrightarrow TAU$	0.01
14	$GSK3 \longrightarrow aGSK3$	0.1
15	$aGSK3 \longrightarrow aGSK3 + Abeta$	0.02
16	$mTORC1 + RAP \longrightarrow mTORC1\_RAP$	$.92 \times 10^{-6}$
17	$mTORC1_R AP \longrightarrow mTORC1 + RAP$	2.2×10^{-6}
18	$amTORC1 + RAP \longrightarrow amTORC1\_RAP$	1.92×10^{-6}
19	$amTORC1\_RAP \longrightarrow amTORC1 + RAP$	2.2×10^{-6}
20	$RAP \longrightarrow Degradation$	0.016

4.2   Effect of Rapamycin in Tau

We analyzed the effect of rapamycin in Tau phosphorylation. For that, we simulated the system over the period of 300 h in four different scenarios: the first is the control scenario in which no drug was added; the other three different scenarios the rapamycin was inserted in doses 50 ηM , 500 ηM , and 5000 ηM at 100 h. Figure 7 shows how the Tau phosphorylation evolved and it is observed, in all scenarios, the phosphorylation achieves a peak at the initial moments, and stabilizes below this peak. A reduction in Tau phosphorylation was expected after the drug addition. However, this result could not be identified in this simulation process. Property 1 was defined, using WMTL, in order to better understand the effect of rapamycin in Tau phosphorylation.

$$Property1 : Pr[\leq 200](<> \phi_1 > \phi_2 \ \&\& \ \phi_3)$$

The ϕ_1 is aTAU; ϕ_2 is TAUactivation.maxATAU; and ϕ_3 is the variable *drugAdded*.

This verifies the likelihood of Tau being phosphorylated after rapamycin had been added to the system. The results are in Table 3 and reveals the best

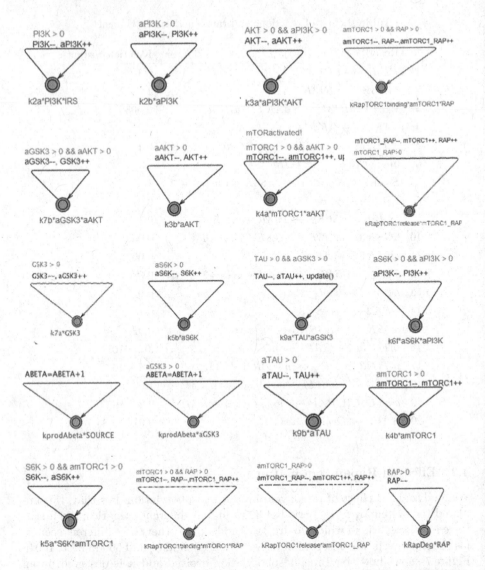

Fig. 4. Each reaction of the signaling network was modeled as a PTA in UPPAAL.

dose of rapamycin to reduce Tau phosphorylation is 500 ηM . In this dose, the probability range for Tau phosphorylation to exceed its maximum peak - that occurs before the system stabilization - is between 1.5% and 11.23%, whereas in a control scenario this probability is between from 8.56% to 18.53%. This means the rapamycin reduces the occurrence of Tau phosphorylation reaction. Moreover, the continuous use of rapamycin in 50 ηM shows good results reducing the phosphorylation of Tau. This behaviour of Tau in presence of rapamycin was observed in animal models [33, 37] supporting our abstraction of the pathway.

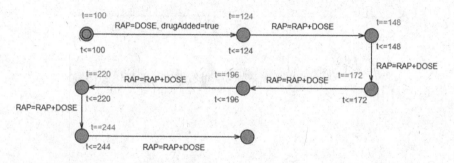

Fig. 5. This automata represents the addition of the rapamycin at the system at the dose 50 ηM daily during 7 days.

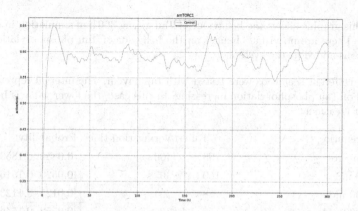

Fig. 6. The evolution of activation of mTORC1. The curve shows the species oscillates over the period after the initial peak. The oscillation occurs the negative feedback of the pathway which mTORC1 activates S6K which is an inhibitor of PI3K.

The Table 3 likewise shows the number of simulations needed to check the property with 95% degree of confidence. Each scenario required a different number of runs which is calculated by UPPAAL during the verification process. The number of runs is indicative of how easy, or how hard it was to check the property.

4.3   Effect of Rapamycin in Aβ

The formation of Aβ was checked through property 2 which evaluates the average quantity produced for this peptide. Rapamycin did not interfere with the production of the peptide in any of the tested scenarios as shown at Table 4. One reason for this is the rapamycin did not affect the activity of APP as shown *in vivo* experiments [47].

$$Property2 : E[\leq 300; 100](max : ABeta)$$

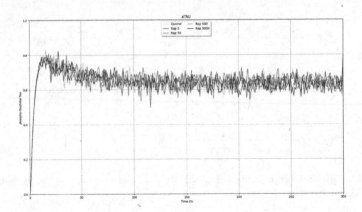

Fig. 7. This graphic shows the behaviour of Tau a long 300 h of simulation in different scenarios. There are no visual changes on the behavior of Tau phosphorylation when the drug was added at the system.

Table 3. Different scenarios were tested with rapamycin. The interval represents the likelihood of Tau phosphorylation increasing. In this case, the lower value is better for Alzheimer treatment.

Scenario	# Runs	Verification time	Probability
Control	193	466 s	[0.0856, 0.1853]
50 ηM	150	307 s	[0.0520, 0.1516]
500 ηM	88	204 s	[0.0125, 0.1123]
5000 ηM	155	329 s	[0.0552, 0.1546]
50 ηM daily during 7 days	124	454 s	[0.0337, 0.1331]

4.4   Discussion

One of the benefits of *in silico* techniques is the possibility of identifying a behavior of the biological system before carrying out an experiment. In our approach we could identify that it is not necessary to increase the drug dose to get the obtain minimum Tau phosphorylation. We could also show rapamycin develops a positive effect on reducing Tau phosphorylation even though it did not cause a reduction in the formation of Aβ. The biological works [33,37], and [47] corroborate our model. Therefore, this indicates that our model can be potentially used to design and test, *in silico*, other potential drugs which target the PI3K/AKT/mTOR pathway and analyze their consequence in AD.

Table 4. Average number of Aβ peptides produced during 300 h.

Scenario	Avg Aβ
Control	113.3 ± 0.7522
50 ηM	113.06 ± 0.7049
500 ηM	113.26 ± 0.6888
5000 ηM	113.38 ± 0.7905
50 ηM daily during 7 days	113.1 ± 0.6800

UPPAAL proved to be an efficient tool when analyzing and processing the properties of the model. A personal computer, with 8 GB of RAM, and an Intel Core i5-2450M 2.5 GHz processor was used for that and the response time of UPPAAL can be considered low for the number of simulations and the complexity of the system.

5 Conclusion

Alzheimer's disease is the most common case of dementia, and the disease is expected to increase with an aging population. Currently, there is no medicine capable of reducing the effects caused by the disease. Drug repositioning is a strategy that can reduce the time and investment required for drug and treatment development. *In silico* models can contribute to this research by enabling hypothesis tests before *in vitro* or *in silico* experiments saving money and time.

In this work, we presented an innovative stochastic formal model capable of analysing how the proteins evolve during the time and how they were affected when a medicine is added on the system. In this case study, the rapamycin, a drug used in the treatment for renal transplant, was used in different doses to investigate its impact on the Aβ formation and Tau phosphorylation. Our finding suggests it is a potential drug to be applied against AD since it does not stimulate Aβ formation and it can reduce the phosphorylation of Tau, consequently it can contribute reducing the neuronal'death. Our model can also be used to test other drugs that target the pathway modeled, like NVP-BEZ235 which has being studied for AD treatment [5,6].

Furthermore, this work showed the SMC technique can be applied in system biology studies since it is able to verify properties in stochastic systems efficiently. This type of work provides a better understanding of how species behave and the effects caused by a disturbance from a drug. It can be considered a powerful tool to outline pharmacological strategies reducing time and cost in experiments development.

Future Work includes incorporating the autophagy process in our model. Autophagy is directly impacted by the drug and can influence in degrading the Aβ plaques and NFT. We plan also to investigate other properties, scenarios, and test other drugs that target the pathway like NVP-BEZ235.

Acknowledgments. The authors would like to thank Fundação de Amparo à Pesquisa de Minas Gerais – FAPEMIG, Conselho Nacional de Desenvolvimento Científico e Tecnológico – CNPq, and Coordenação de Aperfeiçoamento de Pessoal de Nível Superios – CAPES for partially funding this research.

References

1. Agha, G., Palmskog, K.: A survey of statistical model checking. ACM Trans. Model. Comput. Simul. **28**(1), 1–39 (2018)
2. Alur, R., Dill, D.L.: A theory of timed automata. Theor. Comput. Sci. **126**(2), 183–235 (1994)
3. Bakir, M.E., Konur, S., Gheorghe, M., Krasnogor, N., Stannett, M.: Automatic selection of verification tools for efficient analysis of biochemical models. Bioinformatics **34**, 3187–3195 (2018)
4. Baumgartner, G., Renner, K.H.: Humor in the elderly with dementia: development and initial validation of a behavioral observation system. Curr. Psychol., 1–14 (2019)
5. Bellozi, P.M.Q., et al.: NVP-BEZ235 (dactolisib) has protective effects in a transgenic mouse model of Alzheimer's disease. Front. Pharmacol. **10**, 1–11 (2019)
6. Bellozi, P.M.Q., et al.: Neuroprotective effects of the anticancer drug NVP-BEZ235 (dactolisib) on amyloid-β 1-42 induced neurotoxicity and memory impairment. Sci. Rep. **6**, 25226 (2016)
7. örg Bormann, J., Lohse, J., Payer, M., Vezin, G.: Model checking in industrial hardware design. In: 32nd Design Automation Conference, pp. 298–303. IEEE (1995)
8. Bulychev, P., et al.: Monitor-based statistical model checking for weighted metric temporal logic. In: Bjørner, N., Voronkov, A. (eds.) LPAR 2012. LNCS, vol. 7180, pp. 168–182. Springer, Heidelberg (2012). https://doi.org/10.1007/978-3-642-28717-6_15
9. Campos, S., Clarke, E., Marrero, W., Minea, M., Hiraishi, H.: Computing quantitative characteristics of finite-state real-time systems. In: Proceedings Real-Time Systems Symposium REAL-94, pp. 266–270. IEEE Comput. Soc. Press (1994)
10. Campos, S., Clarke, E.M., Minea, M.: Symbolic techniques for formally verifying industrial systems. Sci. Comput. Program. **29**, 79–98 (1997)
11. Christensen, B.D.D.: Alzheimer's disease: progress in the development of anti-amyloid disease-modifying therapies. CNS Spectr. **12**(2), 113–123 (2007)
12. Clarke, E.M., Grumberg, O., Peled, D.A.: Model Checking. MIT Press, Cambridge (1999)
13. David, A., et al.: Statistical model checking for networks of priced timed automata. In: Fahrenberg, U., Tripakis, S. (eds.) FORMATS 2011. LNCS, vol. 6919, pp. 80–96. Springer, Heidelberg (2011). https://doi.org/10.1007/978-3-642-24310-3_7
14. David, A., Larsen, K.G., Legay, A., Mikučionis, M., Poulsen, D.B.: UPPAAL SMC tutorial. Int. J. Softw. Tools Technol. Transf. **17**(4), 397–415 (2015). https://doi.org/10.1007/s10009-014-0361-y
15. De Strooper, B., Vassar, R., Golde, T.: The secretases: enzymes with therapeutic potential in Alzheimer disease. Nat. Rev. Neurol. **6**(2), 99–107 (2010)
16. Dorvash, M., et al.: Dynamic modeling of signal transduction by mTOR complexes in cancer. J. Theor. Biol. **483**, 109992 (2019)
17. Durães, F., Pinto, M., Sousa, E.: Old drugs as new treatments for neurodegenerative diseases. Pharmaceuticals **11**(2), 1–21 (2018)

18. Ferreira, B., et al.: Intelligent service to perform overtaking in vehicular networks. In: Proceedings - IEEE Symposium on Computers and Communications 2016-Febru, pp. 669–676 (2016)
19. Gabbouj, S., et al.: Altered insulin signaling in Alzheimer's disease brain - special emphasis on PI3K-Akt pathway. Front. Neurosci. **13**, 1–8 (2019)
20. Goltsov, A., Tashkandi, G., Langdon, S.P., Harrison, D.J., Bown, J.L.: Kinetic modelling of in vitro data of PI3K, mTOR1, PTEN enzymes and on-target inhibitors Rapamycin, BEZ235, and LY294002. Eur. J. Pharm. Sci. **97**, 170–181 (2017)
21. Gong, H., Zuliani, P., Clarke, E.M.: Model checking of a diabetes-cancer model. AIP Conf. Proc. **1371**, 234–243 (2011)
22. Hao, W., Friedman, A.: Mathematical model on Alzheimer's disease. BMC Syst. Biol. **10**(1), 108 (2016)
23. Heras-Sandoval, D., Pérez-Rojas, J.M., Hernández-Damián, J., Pedraza-Chaverri, J.: The role of PI3K/AKT/mTOR pathway in the modulation of autophagy and the clearance of protein aggregates in neurodegeneration. Cell. Signal. **26**(12), 2694–2701 (2014)
24. Hurd, M.D., Martorell, P., Delavande, A., Mullen, K.J., Langa, K.M.: Monetary costs of dementia in the United States. N. Engl. J. Med. **368**(14), 1326–1334 (2013)
25. Konur, S., Dixon, C., Fisher, M.: Analysing robot swarm behaviour via probabilistic model checking. Robot. Auton. Syst. **60**(2), 199–213 (2012)
26. Kubota, H., et al.: Temporal coding of insulin action through multiplexing of the AKT pathway. Mol. Cell **46**(6), 820–832 (2012)
27. Kwiatkowska, M., Norman, G., Parker, D.: Stochastic model checking. In: Bernardo, M., Hillston, J. (eds.) SFM 2007. LNCS, vol. 4486, pp. 220–270. Springer, Heidelberg (2007). https://doi.org/10.1007/978-3-540-72522-0_6
28. Le Novère, N.: Quantitative and logic modelling of molecular and gene networks. Nat. Rev. Genet. **16**, 146–158 (2015)
29. Lee, Y.S., Chow, W.N.V., Lau, K.F.: Phosphorylation of FE65 at threonine 579 by GSK3β stimulates amyloid precursor protein processing. Sci. Rep. **7**(1), 1–10 (2017)
30. Levine, B., Kroemer, G.: Autophagy in the pathogenesis of disease. Cell **132**(1), 27–42 (2008)
31. Li, J., Kim, S.G., Blenis, J.: Rapamycin: one drug, many effects (2014)
32. Lin, A.L., et al.: Rapamycin rescues vascular, metabolic and learning deficits in apolipoprotein E4 transgenic mice with pre-symptomatic Alzheimer's disease. J. Cereb. Blood Flow Metab. **37**(1), 217–226 (2017)
33. Liu, Y., et al.: Rapamycin decreases Tau phosphorylation at Ser214 through regulation of cAMP-dependent kinase. Neurochem. Int. **62**(4), 458–467 (2013)
34. Llorens-Martín, M., Jurado, J., Hernández, F., Ávila, J.: GSK-3β, a pivotal kinase in Alzheimer disease. Front. Mol. Neurosci. **7**, 1–11 (2014)
35. Majd, S., Power, J., Majd, Z.: Alzheimer's disease and cancer: when two monsters cannot be together. Front. Neurosci. **13**, 1–11 (2019)
36. McMillan, K.L.: A methodology for hardware verification using compositional model checking. Sci. Comput. Program. **37**(1–3), 279–309 (2000)
37. Ozcelik, S., et al.: Rapamycin attenuates the progression of Tau pathology in P301S Tau transgenic mice. PLoS ONE **8**(5), 2–8 (2013)
38. Patel, A.N., Jhamandas, J.H.: Neuronal receptors as targets for the action of amyloid-beta protein (a [beta]) in the brain. Expert. Rev. Mol. Med. **14** (2012)
39. Pezze, P.D., et al.: A dynamic network model of mTOR signaling reveals TSC-independent mTORC2 regulation. Sci. Signal. **5**(217), 1–18 (2012)

40. Proctor, C.J., Gray, D.A.: GSK3 and p53 - is there a link in Alzheimer's disease? Mol. Neurodegener. **5**(1), 1–15 (2010)
41. Ryu, S.H., et al.: Incidence and course of depression in patients with Alzheimer's disease. Psychiatry Investig. **14**(3), 271 (2017)
42. Saxton, R.A., Sabatini, D.M.: mTOR signaling in growth, metabolism, and disease. Cell **168**(6), 960–976 (2017)
43. Selles, M.C., Oliveira, M.M., Ferreira, S.T.: Brain inflammation connects cognitive and non-cognitive symptoms in Alzheimer's disease. J. Alzheimer's Dis. **64**(s1), S313–S327 (2018)
44. Siegel, G.J.: Basic Neurochemistry: Molecular, Cellular, and Medical Aspects, 7th edn. Elsevier, Amsterdam (2006)
45. Siman, R., Cocca, R., Dong, Y.: The mTOR inhibitor rapamycin mitigates perforant pathway neurodegeneration and synapse loss in a mouse model of early-stage Alzheimer-type tauopathy. PLoS ONE **10**(11), 1–21 (2015)
46. Singh, A.K., Kashyap, M.P., Tripathi, V.K., Singh, S., Garg, G., Rizvi, S.I.: Neuroprotection through rapamycin-induced activation of autophagy and PI3K/Akt1/mTOR/CREB signaling against amyloid-β-induced oxidative stress, synaptic/neurotransmission dysfunction, and neurodegeneration in adult rats. Mol. Neurobiol. **54**(8), 5815–5828 (2017)
47. Spilman, P., et al.: Inhibition of mTOR by rapamycin abolishes cognitive deficits and reduces amyloid-β levels in a mouse model of Alzheimer's disease. PLoS ONE **5**(4), 1–8 (2010)
48. Sulaimanov, N., Klose, M., Busch, H., Boerries, M.: Understanding the mTOR signaling pathway via mathematical modeling. WIREs Syst. Biol. Med. **9** (2017)
49. Tenazinha, N., Vinga, S.: A survey on methods for modeling and analyzing integrated biological networks. IEEE/ACM Trans. Comput. Biol. Bioinform. **8**(4), 943–958 (2011)
50. Varusai, T.M., Nguyen, L.K.: Dynamic modelling of the mTOR signalling network reveals complex emergent behaviours conferred by DEPTOR. Sci. Rep. **8**(1), 1–14 (2018)
51. Vilallonga, G.D., De Almeida, A.C.G., Ribeiro, K.T., Campos, S.V., Rodrigues, A.M.: Hypothesized diprotomeric enzyme complex supported by stochastic modelling of palytoxin-induced Na/K pump channels. R. Soc. Open Sci. **5**(3) (2018)
52. Wang, J., Gu, B.J., Masters, C.L., Wang, Y.J.: A systemic view of Alzheimer disease - Insights from amyloid-β metabolism beyond the brain. Nat. Rev. Neurol. **13**(10), 612–623 (2017)
53. Wang, Q., Clarke, E.M.: Formal methods for biological systems : languages, algorithms, and applications. Ph.D. thesis, Carnegie Mellon University (2016)
54. Younes, H.L.S.: Verification and Planning for Stochastic Processes with Asynchronous Events (2005)
55. Zuliani, P.: Statistical model checking for biological applications. Int. J. Softw. Tools Technol. Transf. **17**(4), 527–536 (2014)

Models, Languages and Semantics

Calculational Proofs in Relational Graphical Linear Algebra

João Paixão[1]([✉]) and Paweł Sobociński[2]

[1] Universidade Federal do Rio de Janeiro, Rio de Janeiro, Brazil
jpaixao@dcc.ufrj.br
[2] Tallinn University of Technology, Tallinn, Estonia

Abstract. We showcase a modular, graphical language—graphical linear algebra—and use it as high-level language to reason calculationally about linear algebra. We propose a minimal framework of six axioms that highlight the dualities and symmetries of linear algebra, and use the resulting diagrammatic calculus as a convenient tool to prove a number of diverse theorems. Our work develops a relational approach to linear algebra, closely connected to classical relational algebra.

Keywords: Graphical linear algebra · Calculational proofs · Diagrammatic language · Galois connections · Relational mathematics

1 Introduction

This article is an introduction to Graphical Linear Algebra (GLA), a rigorous diagrammatic language for linear algebra. Its equational theory is known as the theory of Interacting Hopf Algebras [10,25], and it has been applied (and adapted) in a series of papers [3–5,7–9] to the modelling of signal flow graphs, Petri nets and even (non-passive) electrical circuits. In this paper, however, we focus on elucidating its status as an alternative language for linear algebra; that is, external to any specific applications. Some of this development was the focus of the second author's blog [24].

The diagrammatic syntax is extremely simple, yet powerful. Its simplicity is witnessed by the small number of concepts involved. Indeed, diagrams are built from just two structures, which we identify with black-white colouring. The black structure, roughly speaking, is *copying*; while the white structure is *adding*. Crucially, the interpretation of the diagrams is *relational*; instead of vector spaces and linear maps, the semantic universe is vector spaces and linear *relations* [1,12,13,18]. It is somewhat astonishing that *all* other concepts are derived from only the interaction between these two simple structures.

This research was supported by the ESF funded Estonian IT Academy research measure (project 2014-2020.4.05.19-0001). We thank Jason Erbele, Gabriel Ferreira, Lucas Rufino, and Iago Leal for fruitful conversations during various stages of this project.

G. Carvalho and V. Stolz (Eds.): SBMF 2020, LNCS 12475, pp. 83–100, 2020.
https://doi.org/10.1007/978-3-030-63882-5_6

One of our central contributions is the crystallisation of these interactions into six axioms. We show that they suffice to reconstruct the entire equational theory of Interacting Hopf Algebras. A divergence from that work is our focus on *inequations*. Indeed, our axioms are inspired by the notion of *abelian bicategory* of Carboni and Walters [11]. Inequational reasoning leads to shorter and more concise proofs, as known in the relational community; for examples see [15] and [6], the latter with results closely related to ours. Importantly, in spite of having roots in deep mathematical frameworks (functorial semantics [6,17], cartesian bicategories, abelian bicategories [11]) and its focus on universal properties and the use of high-level axioms, GLA is in fact a very simple system to work with: the rules of soundly manipulating diagrams can be easily taught to a student.

The semantics of diagrams is *compositional* – the meaning of a compound diagram is calculated from the meanings of its sub-diagrams. Here there is a connection with *relational algebra*, the two operations of diagram composition map to standard ways of composing relations: relational composition and cartesian product. In fact, the semantics of diagrams is captured as a monoidal *functor* from the category of diagrams GLA to the category of k-linear relations **LinRel**$_k$:

$$\mathsf{GLA} \to \mathbf{LinRel}_k$$

One of our favourite features of GLA is how it makes the underlying symmetries of linear algebra apparent. Two symmetries are immediately built into the syntax of diagrams: *(i) mirror-image*: any diagram can be "flipped around the y-axis", and *(ii) colour-swap*: any diagram can be replaced with its "photographic negative", swapping the black and white colouring. Thus one proof can sometimes result in four theorems. We feel like these important symmetries are sometimes hidden in traditional approaches; moreover, some classical "theorems" become trivial consequences of the diagrammatic syntax.

After introducing the language and the principles of diagrammatic reasoning, our goal is to demonstrate that GLA is naturally suitable for modular constructions. Indeed, we argue that GLA can be considered as **high-level specification language for linear algebra**. While traditional calculational techniques are built around matrix algebra, the diagrammatic language is a higher-level way of expressing concepts and constructions. Of course, the equational theory means that we can "compile" down to low-level matrix representations, when necessary.

The compositional nature of the syntax means that we can express many classical concepts in a straightforward and intuitive fashion. Traditional linear algebra, in spite of its underlying simplicity and elegance, has a tendency for conceptual and notational proliferation: Kernel, NullSpace, Image, sum of matrices, sum and intersection of vector spaces, etc. In GLA, all these concepts are expressible within the diagrammatic language. Moreover, the properties and relationships between the concepts can be derived via calculational proofs within the diagrammatic formalism. In many cases, these 2D proofs are shorter, more concise and more informative than their traditional 1D counterparts.

Finally, we compare the GLA approach with some recent work [20,22] on blocked linear algebra, which also focussed on calculational proofs.

To quip, we show that "Calculationally Blocked Linear Algebra!" can be done graphically! By doing so, and moving from block matrix algebra to block relational algebra, we extend the expressivity of the approach to deal with subspaces.

Structure of the Paper. In Sect. 2 we introduce the diagrammatic language, its semantics, and the six sound axioms for reasoning about linear relations. We then use those axioms in Sect. 3 to show that all of the equations of Interacting Hopf Algebras can be derived. In Sect. 4 we show how the diagrammatic language captures classical linear algebraic concepts, and relate it to recent work on block linear algebra. We conclude in Sect. 5 with some remarks about ongoing and future work.

2 Syntax and Semantics of Graphical Linear Algebra

In this section we introduce the diagrammatic language used throughout the paper. We explain how diagrams are constructed and outline basic principles of how to manipulate, and reason with them. Our diagrams are an instance of a particular class of *string diagrams*, which are well-known [23] to characterise the arrows of free strict monoidal categories. They are, therefore, rigorous mathematical objects.

We emphasise a syntactic approach: we generate string diagrams as terms and then quotient them w.r.t. the laws of strict symmetric monoidal categories. This quotienting process is particularly pleasant and corresponds to a topological understanding of diagrams where only the connectivity matters: intuitive deformations of diagrams do not change their meaning. Thus our work does not require extensive familiarity of (monoidal) category theory: the rules of constructing and manipulating the diagrams can be easily explained.

2.1 Syntax

Our starting point is the simple grammar for a language of diagrams, generated from the BNF below.

$$c, d \quad ::= \quad \text{—•} \mid \text{—<} \mid \text{>—} \mid \text{o—} \mid \text{•—} \mid \text{>—} \mid \text{—<} \mid \text{—o}$$

$$\mid \text{□} \mid \text{—} \mid \text{✕} \mid c; d \mid c \oplus d \tag{1}$$

The first line of (1) consists of eight constants that we refer to as *generators*. Although they are given in diagrammatic form, for now we can consider them as mere symbols. Already here we can see two fundamental symmetries that are present throughout this paper: for every generator there is a "mirror image" generator (inverted in the "y-axis"), and for every generator there is a "colour inverse" generator (swapping black with white). Thus, it suffices to note that

there are generators ─●, ─< and that the set of generators is closed w.r.t
the two symmetries. We shall discuss the formal semantics of the syntax in
Sect. 2.2, but it is useful to already provide some intuition at this point. It is
helpful to think of ─●, ─< as gates that, respectively, *discard* and *copy* the
value on the left, and of ○─, >─ as *zero* and *add* gates. The mirror-image
versions have the same intuitions, but from right-to-left.

The second line of (1) contains some structural terms and two binary operations for composing diagrams. The term ⌐⌐ is the empty diagram, ── is a wire
and $\times$ allows swapping the order of two wires. The two binary operations ; and
$\oplus$ allow us to construct diagrams from smaller diagrams. Indeed, the diagrammatic convention is to draw c; c' (or as $c' \cdot c$) as series composition, connecting
the "dangling" wires on the right of c with those on the left of c', and to draw
$c \oplus c'$ as c stacked on top of c', that is:

$$c; c' \text{ is drawn } \boxed{c}\ \boxed{c'} \quad \text{and } c \oplus c' \text{ is drawn } \begin{array}{c}\boxed{c}\\\boxed{c'}\end{array}.$$

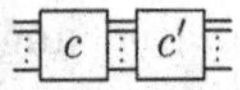

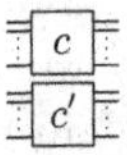

The simple sorting discipline of Fig. 1 counts the "dangling" wires and thus
ensures that the diagrammatic convention for ; makes sense. A *sort* is a pair of
natural numbers (m, n): m counts the dangling wires on the left and n those on
the right. We consider only those terms of (1) that have a sort. It is not difficult
to show that if a term has a sort, it is unique.

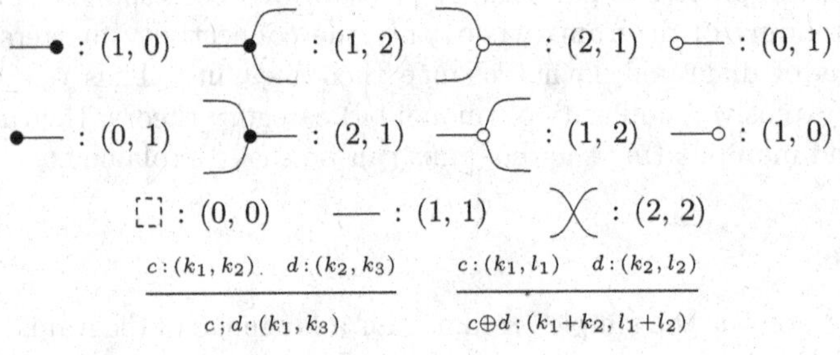

$$─● : (1, 0) \quad ─< : (1, 2) \quad >─ : (2, 1) \quad ○─ : (0, 1)$$

$$●─ : (0, 1) \quad >─ : (2, 1) \quad ─< : (1, 2) \quad ─○ : (1, 0)$$

$$⌐⌐ : (0, 0) \quad ── : (1, 1) \quad \times : (2, 2)$$

$$\frac{c:(k_1, k_2) \quad d:(k_2, k_3)}{c; d:(k_1, k_3)} \qquad \frac{c:(k_1, l_1) \quad d:(k_2, l_2)}{c \oplus d:(k_1+k_2, l_1+l_2)}$$

Fig. 1. The sorting discipline.

Example 1. Consider the term $\left(\left((── \oplus ─●) \oplus ─<\right) ; \left(>─ \oplus ──\right)\right)$;
$\times$. It has sort $(3, 2)$ and the diagrammatic representation is

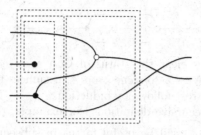

where the dashed-line boxes play the role of disambiguating associativity of operations.

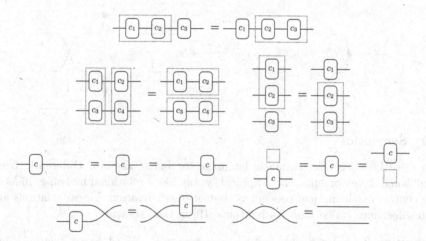

Fig. 2. Laws of symmetric monoidal categories. Sort labels are omitted for readability.

Raw terms are quotiented w.r.t. the laws of symmetric strict monoidal (SSM) categories, summarised in Fig. 2. We omit the (well-known) details [23] here and mention only that this amounts to eschewing the need for "dotted line boxes" and ensuring that diagrams which have the same topological connectivity are equated.

We refer to terms-modulo-SSM-equations as *string diagrams*. The resulting string diagrams are then the arrows of a SSM category known as a prop.

Definition 1. *A prop is a SSM category where the set of objects is the set of natural numbers, and, on objects $m \oplus n := m + n$. String diagrams generated from (1) are the arrows of a prop* GLA.

The idea is that the set of arrows from m to n is the set of string diagrams with m "dangling wires" on the left and n on the right.

In fact, GLA is the *free* prop on the set of generators

$$\left\{ \; \text{⟩─•─, ─•, ─⟨ , •─, •─⟨ , ─• , } \right\}. \tag{2}$$

This perspective makes clear the status of GLA as a *syntax*: for example to define a morphism GLA → $\mathbb{X}$ to some prop $\mathbb{X}$, it suffices to define its action on the generators (2): the rest follows by induction.

We can also give recursive definitions, for example, the following generalisation of copying ─• will be useful for us in subsequent sections. Similar constructions can be given for the other generators in (2).

Definition 2.

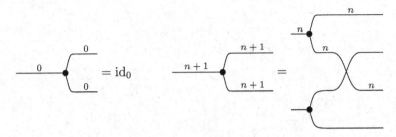

2.2 Semantics

We use GLA as a diagrammatic language for linear algebra. Differently from traditional developments, the graphical syntax has a relational meaning. Indeed, the central mathematical concept is that of *linear relation*. Linear relations are also sometimes called *additive* relations [19] in the literature.

Definition 3. *Fix a field* k *and* k-*vector spaces* V, W. *A linear relation from* V *to* W *is a set* $R \subseteq V \times W$ *that is a subspace of* $V \times W$, *considered as a* k-*vector space. Explicitly this means that* $(0,0) \in R$, *given* $k \in k$ *and* $(v,w) \in R$, $(kv, kw) \in R$, *and given* $(v,w), (v',w') \in R$, $(v + v', w + w') \in R$.

Given a field k, the prop **LinRel**$_k$ is of particular interest.

Definition 4. *The prop* **LinRel**$_k$ *has as arrows* $m \to n$ *linear relations* $R \subseteq k^m \times k^n$. *Composition is relational composition, and monoidal product is cartesian product of relations.*

We now give the interpretation of the string diagrams of our language GLA as linear relations.

$$\text{GLA} \to \textbf{LinRel}_k \tag{3}$$

Given that GLA is a free prop, it suffices to define the action on the generators.

$$\text{─⟨} \; \longmapsto \left\{ \left(x, \binom{x}{x} \right) \mid x \in k \right\} \subseteq k \times k^2 \qquad \text{─•} \longmapsto \{ (x, \star) \mid x \in k \} \subseteq k \times k^0$$

$$\mathrm{D}\!\!-\ \longmapsto\ \left\{\left(\begin{pmatrix}x\\y\end{pmatrix},\,x+y\right)\ \middle|\ x,y\in\mathsf{k}\right\}\subseteq\mathsf{k}^2\times\mathsf{k}\qquad \mathrm{o}\!\!-\ \longmapsto\ \{(\star,0)\}\subseteq\mathsf{k}^0\times\mathsf{k}$$

The generators $\mathrm{D}\!-$, $\bullet\!-$, $-\!\!\mathrm{C}$, $-\!\!\mathrm{o}$ map, respectively, to the opposite relations of the above, as hinted by the symmetric diagrammatic notation. As we shall see in the following, this semantic interpretation is canonical.

Intuitively, therefore, the *black structure* in diagrams refers to copying and discarding – indeed $-\!\!\blacktriangleleft$ is *copy*, and $-\!\!\bullet$ is *discard*. Instead, the *white structure* refers to addition in k – indeed $\mathrm{D}\!-$ is *add* and $\mathrm{o}\!-$ is *zero*.

Example 2. Consider the term of Example 1, reproduced below without the unnecessary dashed-line box annotations.

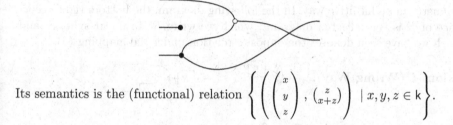

Its semantics is the (functional) relation $\left\{\left(\begin{pmatrix}x\\y\\z\end{pmatrix},\,\begin{pmatrix}z\\x+z\end{pmatrix}\right)\ \middle|\ x,y,z\in\mathsf{k}\right\}.$

2.3   Diagrammatic Reasoning

In this section we identify the (in)equational theory of GLA. It is common to define algebraic structure in a prop as a *monoidal theory* – roughly speaking, the prop version of an equational algebraic theory. Our goal, instead, is to arrive at a powerful calculus for linear algebra, with few high level axioms. These are inspired by the notion of *abelian bicategory* of Carboni and Walters [11].

Axiom 1 (Commutative comonoid). The copy structure satisfies the equations of commutative comonoids, that is, *associativity*, *commutativity* and *unitality*, as listed below:

Inequalities. Instead of a purely equational axiomatisation, we find the use of inequalities very convenient in proofs. From a technical point of view this means the extension of the semantic mapping (3) to a (2-)functor between poset-enriched monoidal categories. Indeed, **LinRel**$_\mathsf{k}$ has a natural poset-enrichment given by (set-theoretical) *inclusion* of relations.

We state three axioms below. Here R ranges over arbitrary string diagrams of GLA. Given that R can have arbitrary sort, the axioms make use of Definition 2.

Axiom 2 (Discard). $\le$

The axiom is sound; the left-hand-side denotes $LHS = \{(x, \star) \mid \exists y.\, xRy\}$, while right hand side denotes the relation $RHS = \{(x, \star) \mid \top\}$. Clearly $LHS \subseteq RHS$.

Axiom 3 (Copy). $\le$

Soundness is again easy: the left-hand-side is the relation $LHS = \{(x, \binom{y}{y}) \mid xRy\}$, while the right-hand-side is $RHS = \{(x, \binom{y}{y'}) \mid xRy \wedge xRy'\}$. Again $LHS \subseteq RHS$.

The diagrammatic notation for R allows us to represent the mirror image symmetry in an intuitive way. In the following diagram, the bottom right occurrence of R is the reflected diagram—which we write R^o in linear syntax—and which we have seen denotes the opposite relation under the mapping (3).

Axiom 4 (Wrong Way). $\le$

For example, let = , then Axiom 4 says that

For another example, let = = , then Axiom 4 says that

Soundness of Axiom 4 is very similar to the soundness of Axiom 3. It is worthwhile to explain the relationship between Axioms 3 and 4. In tandem, they capture a topological intuition: a relation that is adjacent to black node can "commute" with the node, resulting in a potentially larger relation. In Axiom 3 the relation approaches from the left. In Axiom 4 the relation comes from the "wrong side", it can still commute with the node to obtain a larger relation, but one must take care of the lower right wire that "curves around". It is this "curving around" that results in the R^o.

Symmetries. In Sect. 2.1, we saw that the generators of GLA are closed under two symmetries: the "mirror-image" $(-)^o$ and the "colour-swap". Henceforward we denote the colour swap symmetry by $(-)^\dagger$. Clearly, for any R, we have $R^{oo} = R$ and $R^{\dagger\dagger} = R$. We are now ready to state our final two axioms.

Axiom 5 (Converse). $R^o \leq S \iff R \leq S^o$, or in diagrams:

$$-\boxed{R}- \ \leq \ -\boxed{S}- \iff -\boxed{R}- \ \leq \ -\boxed{S}-$$

In particular, the mirror-image symmetry is *covariant*: if $R \leq S$ then $R^o \leq S^o$. Soundness is immediate.

Axiom 6 (Colour inverse). $R^\dagger \leq S \iff R \geq S^\dagger$, or in diagrams:

$$-\boxed{R}- \ \leq \ -\boxed{S}- \iff -\boxed{R}- \ \geq \ -\boxed{S}-$$

Thus the colour-swap symmetry is *contravariant*: if $R \leq S$ then $S^\dagger \leq R^\dagger$. Here soundness is not as obvious: one way is to show that the inequalities of Axioms 2, 3 and 4 reverse when it is the white structure that is under consideration. First it is easy to see that the two operations commute.

Theorem 1. $(R^o)^\dagger = (R^\dagger)^o$

By the above Theorem we can define the transpose operation.

Definition 5. $R^t := (R^o)^\dagger = (R^\dagger)^o$.

Prove One, Get Three Theorems for Free Principle. We will explore the symmetries of Axioms 5–6 throughout the paper. When we prove a result, we will usually assume we can use any of the other three theorems (its converse theorem, its colour inverse theorem, and its transpose theorem) afterwards just by referencing the original result. For example when we use, in a proof, the colour inverse of Axiom 3 we will simply denote Ax. 3.

3 Algebraic Structure

In this section we identify some of the algebraic structure that is a consequence of our six axioms. The two structures that play an important role are *bialgebras* and *special Frobenius algebras*. As Lack explains in [16], these are two canonical ways in which monoids and comonoids can interact. See *loc. cit.* for additional information on the provenance and importance of these two algebraic structures.

First note that it is an easy consequence of Axioms 5 and 6 that the group of generators $\{-\!\!\prec\ , -\!\!o\}$ is a commutative comonoid, and that $\{\ \succ\!\!-, o\!\!-\}$, $\{\ \succ\!\!-, \bullet\!\!-\}$ are both commutative monoids.

3.1 Bialgebra Structure

White and black structures act as bialgebras when they interact. This can be summarised by the following equations.

Theorem 2 (Bialgebra).

$$\succ\!\!-\!\!\prec \;=\; \bowtie \qquad \circ\!\!-\!\!\prec \;=\; \overset{\circ}{\underset{\circ}{-}}$$

$$\succ\!\!-\!\bullet \;=\; \overset{\bullet}{\underset{\bullet}{-}} \qquad \circ\!\!-\!\bullet \;=\; \square$$

Proof.

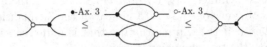

We use Axiom 3 in the first inequality and its color inverse in the second inequality. Note that while using Axiom 3 in the proof, we must use Definition 2. The other derivations are similar.

Hom Posets. Every hom-set, i.e. the set of $(m,\ n)$ string diagrams for $m, n \in \mathbb{N}$, has a top and bottom element. Indeed:

Theorem 3 (Top Element). $-\boxed{R}- \;\leq\; -\!\!\bullet\;\bullet\!\!-$

Proof. $-\boxed{R}- \overset{\text{Ax. 1}}{\leq} -\boxed{R}\!\!-\!\!\bullet\!\!\prec \overset{\text{Ax. 4}}{\leq} -\boxed{R}\!\!-\!\!\bullet\;\bullet\!\!- \overset{\text{Ax. 2}}{\leq} -\!\!\bullet\;\bullet\!\!-$

In the second step, we are using the second example of Axiom 4.

Using Axiom 6, we obtain, dually that $-\!\!\circ\;\circ\!\!-$ is the bottom element.

Frobenius Structure. We have seen that the white and black structure interact according to the rules of bialgebras. On the other hand, individually the white and black structures interact as (extraspecial) Frobenius algebras.

Theorem 4 (Frobenius). *The following equations hold.*

$$\overset{(1)}{=} \qquad \overset{(3)}{=}$$

$$\overset{(2)}{=} \qquad \overset{(4)}{=} \;\square$$

Proof. 1.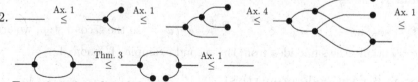

In the second step, we are using the first example of Axiom 4.

2.

Equations 3 and 4 of the theorem can be proven similarly.

With the previous theorem we can show now that the set of (m, n) string diagrams for $m, n \in \mathbb{N}$, has also a meet and join operation, expressible within the GLA structure, as we show below.

Theorem 5 (Universal property of meet).

Proof.

The other inequality follows similarly.

Corollary 1. *The partial order $\leq$ is a meet semi-lattice with top, where meet of R and S, written here as $R \cap S$, is* ——————— *and the top element is given by Theorem 3.*

By duality of Axiom 6, we obtain the join and the bottom element just switching the colours. Therefore we have:

Corollary 2. *The partial order $\leq$ is a lattice with top, bottom, meet and join.*

In the semantics, meet is intersection $R \cap S$, while join is the smallest subspace containing R and S: i.e. the subspace closure of the union $R \cup S$, usually denoted $R + S$.

Antipode. One of the most surprising facts about this presentation of linear algebra is the plethora of concepts derivable from the basic components of copying and adding (black and white) structures. This includes the notion of *antipode* a, i.e. -1. The following proofs were inspired by [14].

Definition 6 (Antipode). [figure] :=

Before proving properties of the antipode, we prove an useful lemma.

Lemma 1. [figure]

Proof. [figure] $\overset{\text{Ax. 4}}{\leq}$ [figure] $\overset{\text{Thm. 3}}{\leq}$ [figure] In the second step, we are using essentially the same idea from the second example of Axiom 4.

Theorem 6 (Antipode properties).

1. (Hopf) [figure] = [figure]

2. [figure] = [figure] = [figure] = [figure] $(a = a^o = a^\dagger = a^t)$

3. [figure] = [figure]

4. [figure] *is an isomorphism.*

Proof. 1.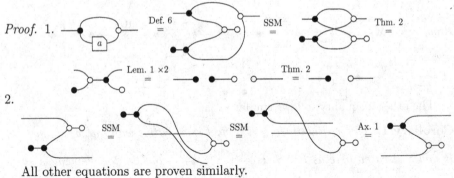

$\overset{\text{Def. 6}}{=}$ ... $\overset{\text{SSM}}{=}$ ... $\overset{\text{Thm. 2}}{=}$

$\overset{\text{Lem. 1} \times 2}{=}$ ... $\overset{\text{Thm. 2}}{=}$

2.

$\overset{\text{SSM}}{=}$ ... $\overset{\text{SSM}}{=}$ ... $\overset{\text{Ax. 1}}{=}$

All other equations are proven similarly.

3.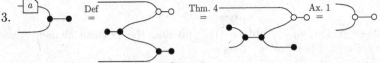

$\overset{\text{Def}}{=}$ ... $\overset{\text{Thm. 4}}{=}$ ... $\overset{\text{Ax. 1}}{=}$

4. We postpone this proof to Sect. 4.

The complete set of equations is known as the theory of Interacting Hopf (IH) Algebras [10]. In fact, given the results of this section (Theorems 2, 4, and 6) we have our main result.

Theorem 7. *Axioms 1–6 suffice to derive all of the algebraic structure of Interacting Hopf (IH) algebras. In fact, they are also sound in that theory. In particular, the prop obtained from* GLA, *quotiented by the axioms, is isomorphic to* LinRel$_\mathbb{Q}$, *the prop of linear relations over the rationals.*

The above result justifies our claims about the canonicity of the semantics (3). While the base language (of adding and copying) is powerful enough to express any rational number, for other fields (e.g. the set of real numbers) we can add additional generators to our base language in a principled way [10]. We omit the details here.

4 Applications

In this section, we will show how the graphical language, developed over the last few sections, can be used to reason about classical concepts and results in linear algebra.

4.1 Dictionary

The goal of this subsection is to provide a dictionary, showing how familiar linear algebraic concepts manifest in the graphical language. Given a diagram R, we first define some derived diagrams from R directly in GLA but which are inspired by classical relations and subspaces in linear algebra and relational algebra.

Definition 7 (Derived diagrams).

1. *the nullspace of R: $N(R) := \,$ —[R]—○ ,*
2. *the multivalued part of R: $Mul(R) := \,$ ○—[R]— ,*
3. *the range of R: $Ran(R) := \,$ ●—[R]— ,*
4. *and the domain of R: $Dom(R) := \,$ —[R]—● .*

Definition 8 (Dictionary). *Let R be a diagram. We call R*

injective (INJ) if   —○ ≥ —[R]—○ ;   total (TOT) if   —● ≤ —[R]—● ;
single-valued (SV) if   ○— ≥ ○—[R]— ; surjective (SUR) if   ●— ≤ ●—[R]— .

Moreover, since the converses of these inequalities hold in GLA, the four inequalities are actually equalities. We define a *map* to be a diagram that is both single-valued and total, $co-map$ is a diagram that is both surjective and injective, and finally an *Isomorphism* is a diagram that is map and a co-map. With the definition above we clearly obtain a nice symmetry.

Theorem 8 (Dictionary symmetry). *R is total $\iff R^{o}$ is surjective $\iff R^{\dagger}$ is injective $\iff (R^{\dagger})^{o}$ is single-valued.*

The next theorem shows that the notions in Definition 8 that were described through the converse inequalities of Axiom 2, can also be characterized by universal properties (item 1 from Theorem 9), the converse inequalities of Axioms 3 (item 3 from Theorem 9) and 4 (item 4 from Theorem 9), or by comparing their kernel and image relation with the identity (item 5 from Theorem 9).

Theorem 9 (Total). *All the following statements are equivalent.*

1. $\boxed{X}\ \boxed{R}\ \leq\ \boxed{Y}\ \Rightarrow\ \boxed{X}\ \leq\ \boxed{Y}\ \boxed{R}$

2. $\bullet\!\!-\!\!-\ \leq\ \bullet\!\!-\!\boxed{R}$

3. $\underset{X}{\rightarrow}\boxed{R}\!\!<\!\!\underset{Y}{\ }\ \geq\ X\!\!\circ\!\!\begin{array}{c}\boxed{R}\,Y\\ \boxed{R}\,Y\end{array}$

4. $\begin{array}{c}X\\ \end{array}\!\!>\!\!\boxed{R}\underset{Y}{\circ}\ \geq\ X\!\!-\!\!\boxed{R}\!\!\circ\!\!\begin{array}{c}Y\\ \boxed{R}\end{array}$

5. $-\!\!-\!\!-\ \leq\ \boxed{R}\,\boxed{R}$

Proof. $(1 \Rightarrow 2)$ TRUE $\overset{\text{Ax. 2}}{\Longleftrightarrow}\ \bullet\!\!-\!\boxed{R}\ \leq\ \bullet\!\!-\!\!-\ \overset{\text{Hyp}}{\Rightarrow}\ \bullet\!\!-\!\!-\ \leq\ \bullet\!\!-\!\boxed{R}$

$(2\qquad\qquad\qquad\qquad\qquad\qquad\qquad\qquad\qquad\qquad\Rightarrow\qquad\qquad\qquad\qquad\qquad\qquad\qquad\qquad\qquad 5)$

$-\!\!-\!\!-\ \overset{\text{Ax. 1}}{=}\ \rightarrow\!\!<\!\!\overset{\bullet}{\ }\ \overset{\text{Hyp}}{\leq}\ \rightarrow\!\!<\!\!\overset{\boxed{R}\,\bullet}{\ }\ \overset{\text{Ax. 4}}{\leq}\ \boxed{R}\!\!\circ\!\!<\!\!\begin{array}{c}\ \\ \boxed{R}\end{array}\ \overset{\text{Ax. 1}}{=}\ \boxed{R}\,\boxed{R}$

$(5 \Rightarrow 1)\ \boxed{X}\ \overset{\text{Hyp}}{\leq}\ \boxed{X}\,\boxed{R}\,\boxed{R}\ \overset{\text{Hyp}}{\leq}\ \boxed{Y}\,\boxed{R}$

The proofs that $1 \Rightarrow 3 \Rightarrow 5 \Rightarrow 1$ and $1 \Rightarrow 4 \Rightarrow 5 \Rightarrow 1$ are similar.

With the symmetries described in Theorem 8, we are able to obtain the same characterizations for injective, single-valued and surjective.

Observation. When using Theorem 9 and its 3 other symmetrical variants in proofs, we refer to the initials TOT (Theorem 9), SV, INJ, and SUR.

Theorem 10. *1. R is Total* $\iff XR \subseteq Y \implies X \subseteq YR^o$
2. R is Single Valued $\iff XR \subseteq Y \impliedby X \subseteq YR^o$
3. R is Surjective $\iff XR \supseteq Y \implies X \supseteq YR^o$
4. R is Injective $\iff XR \supseteq Y \impliedby X \supseteq YR^o$
5. R is function (total and single valued) $\iff XR \subseteq Y \iff X \subseteq YR^o$
6. R is Co-function (injective and surjective) $\iff RX \subseteq Y \iff X \subseteq R^oY$
7. R is Injective and total $\iff XR = Y \implies X = YR^o.$
8. R is Isomorphism $\iff XR = Y \iff X = YR^o.$

These properties are essentially "shunting rules" inspired from relational algebra and its Galois connections [2,21] which you can derive generic properties from them and allow you to reason effectively. We can use them in the proof of the following useful corollaries in GLA.

Corollary 3. *1. A function f is an isomorphism iff its converse f^o is a function.*
2. Smaller than injective (single valued) is injective (single valued).
3. Larger than total (surjective) is total (surjective).

To end this section, we present an antipode property that we postponed in an earlier section.

Theorem 11. *The antipode is an isomorphism.*

Proof. We show that the antipode is single valued:

$$\text{--}\boxed{a}\text{--} \overset{Def}{=} \quad \cdots \quad \overset{Ax.\ 1}{=} \quad \cdots \quad \overset{Lem.\ 1}{=} \quad \cdots \quad \overset{Thm.\ 2}{=} \quad \cdots$$

The other three properties *(surjective, injective and total)* have similar proofs.

4.2 Classical Existence Theorems

In this next subsection, we demonstrate how GLA can also prove classical *existence* theorems of linear algebra which connect subspaces, maps, and inverses. We begin with a common theorem in any undergraduate linear algebra class which gives sufficient conditions for the existence of a solution of a linear system $AX = B$. In linear algebra textbooks, this theorem is usually proven with Gaussian Elimination, LU decomposition, or RREF (Reduced Row Echelon Form). Here, we prove it completely in the graphical language.

Theorem 12. *If B is a map, A is an injective map, and* $\bullet\text{--}\boxed{B}\text{--} \leq \bullet\text{--}\boxed{A}\text{--}$, *then there exists a map X such that* $\text{--}\boxed{X}\,\boxed{A}\text{--} = \text{--}\boxed{B}\text{--}$.

Proof. First let $\text{--}\boxed{X}\text{--} := \text{--}\boxed{B}\text{--}\boxed{A}\text{--}$, we will first show, in the first two items, that X is a map (single-valued and total) and then prove the equality in the last two items using Theorem 9 and its variants.

1. (X is SV) $\circ\text{--}\boxed{X}\text{--} \overset{Def}{=} \circ\text{--}\boxed{B}\text{--}\boxed{A}\text{--} \overset{B\ SV}{\leq} \circ\text{--}\boxed{A}\text{--} \overset{A\ INJ}{\leq} \circ\text{--}$

2. (X is TOT) $\text{--}\boxed{X}\text{--}\bullet \overset{Def}{=} \text{--}\boxed{B}\text{--}\boxed{A}\text{--}\bullet \overset{Hyp}{\geq} \text{--}\boxed{B}\text{--}\boxed{B}\text{--}\bullet \overset{B\ TOT}{\geq} \text{--}\bullet$

3. $\text{--}\boxed{X}\text{--}\boxed{A}\text{--} \overset{Def}{=} \text{--}\boxed{B}\text{--}\boxed{A}\text{--}\boxed{A}\text{--} \overset{A\ SV}{\leq} \text{--}\boxed{B}\text{--}$

4. $\text{--}\boxed{X}\text{--}\boxed{A}\text{--} \overset{B\ SV}{\geq} \text{--}\boxed{X}\text{--}\boxed{A}\text{--}\boxed{B}\text{--}\boxed{B}\text{--} \overset{Item\ 3}{\geq} \text{--}\boxed{X}\text{--}\boxed{A}\text{--}\boxed{A}\text{--}\boxed{X}\text{--}\boxed{B}\text{--} \overset{A\ TOT}{\geq}$

   $\text{--}\boxed{X}\text{--}\boxed{X}\text{--}\boxed{B}\text{--} \overset{X\ TOT}{\geq} \text{--}\boxed{B}\text{--}$

The last proof demonstrate the usefulness of Theorem 9 and its variants. Also we are able to define the solution X even though A might not be invertible, which shows the "high level expressivity" of GLA. The next theorem shows the connection between existence of complementary subspaces and existence of left inverses.

Theorem 13. *Let T be an injective map, there exists a* $\boxed{N}\text{--}$ *such that*

$$\cdots \geq \text{--}\bullet \quad and \quad \cdots \leq \text{--}\circ \iff \text{there exists a map } \text{--}\boxed{X}\text{--} \text{ such}$$

that $\text{--}\boxed{T}\text{--}\boxed{X}\text{--} = \text{--------}$.

Proof. $\Rightarrow$ Let $\text{--}\boxed{X}\text{--} := \cdots$

1. Claim: $-\boxed{T}\!-\!\boxed{N}-$ $\overset{\text{Ax. 1}}{\leq}$ ... $\overset{\text{Ax. 4}}{\leq}$ $-\boxed{T}$ ... $\overset{\text{Hyp}}{\leq}$ $-\boxed{T}\!-\!\!\circ$ $\overset{\text{T INJ}}{\leq}$ $\longrightarrow\circ$

2. (X is TOT) $-\boxed{X}\!-\!\!\bullet$ $\overset{\text{Def}}{=}$ ... $\overset{\text{Hyp}}{\geq}$ $\longrightarrow\!\bullet$

3. (X is SV)

$\circ\!-\!\boxed{X}\!-$ $\overset{\text{Def}}{=}$ ... $\overset{\text{T SV}}{\leq}$ $\circ\!-\!\boxed{T}$ ... $\overset{\text{T TOT}}{\leq}$ $\circ\!-\!$ ... $\boxed{T}\!-\!\boxed{N}$ $\overset{\text{Above}}{\leq}$

$\circ\!-\!$ ... $\overset{\text{Ax. 1}}{\leq}$ $\circ\!-\!$

4. (X is the left inverse of T)

$-\boxed{T}\!-\!\boxed{X}\!-$ $\overset{\text{Def}}{=}$ $-\boxed{T}$ ... $\overset{\text{T TOT}}{=}$ ... $\boxed{T}\!-\!\boxed{N}$ $\overset{\text{Above}}{=}$ ... $\overset{\text{Ax. 1}}{=}$ —

4.3 Dotted Line Associativity in Block Linear Algebra

In this short section we present the power of the dotted line associativity mentioned in the beginning of the paper. To make one final connection with classical linear algebra we define:

$$\left[\frac{R}{S}\right] := \quad\quad\quad\quad [R\,|\,S] := $$

The notation is inspired by the semantics of the copy and add generators in the case that R and S are matrices (linear functions), which are horizontal or vertical block matrices R and S [24].

In GLA, we are able to immediately get the following properties by dotted line associativity, by looking and "grouping" the 2D syntax in two different ways such as, we did in example in Fig. 2.

Theorem 14 (Dotted line associativity).

1. $N(\left[\frac{R}{S}\right]) = N(R) \cap N(S)$

2. $Ran([\,R|S\,]) = Ran(R) + Ran(S)$.

3. *(Absorption)* $(T \oplus U) \cdot \left[\frac{R}{S}\right] = \left[\frac{T \cdot R}{U \cdot S}\right]$

4. $\left[\frac{R_1}{R_2}\right]^o \cdot \left[\frac{S_1}{S_2}\right] = R_1^o \cdot S_1 \cap R_2^o \cdot S_2$

5. *(Exchange Law)* $\left[\left[\frac{R}{S}\right]\left[\frac{T}{U}\right]\right] = \left[\left[\frac{R|T}{S|U}\right]\right]$

Proof. 1)$N(R) \cap N(S) = $ ... $=$ ... $= N(\left[\frac{R}{S}\right])$ All the

others items are also proven with dotted line associativity.

5   Conclusions and Future Work

We showcased *Graphical Linear Algebra*, a simple bichromatic diagrammatic language for linear algebra. We introduced a high level axiomatisation—which we argue is especially convenient for use in calculational proofs—and showed that it suffices to derive all of the algebraic structure of the theory of Interacting Hopf Algebras. We also focused on the modular nature of the language and how it captures many of the classical concepts of linear algebra.

A direction where future work will be especially fruitful is diagrammatic descriptions of various normal form theorems and matrix factorisations (Smith Normal Form, singular value decomposition, etc.); both in elucidating the classical theory, as well as obtaining useful relational generalisations.

References

1. Arens, R., et al.: Operational calculus of linear relations. Pac. J. Math. **11**(1), 9–23 (1961)
2. Backhouse, R.: Galois connections and fixed point calculus. In: Backhouse, R., Crole, R., Gibbons, J. (eds.) Algebraic and Coalgebraic Methods in the Mathematics of Program Construction. LNCS, vol. 2297, pp. 89–150. Springer, Heidelberg (2002). https://doi.org/10.1007/3-540-47797-7_4
3. Baez, J., Erbele, J.: Categories in control. Theory Appl. Categ. **30**, 836–881 (2015)
4. Bonchi, F., Holland, J., Pavlovic, D., Sobocinski, P.: Refinement for signal flow graphs. In: 28th International Conference on Concurrency Theory (CONCUR 2017). Schloss Dagstuhl-Leibniz-Zentrum fuer Informatik (2017)
5. Bonchi, F., Holland, J., Piedeleu, R., Sobociński, P., Zanasi, F.: Diagrammatic algebra: from linear to concurrent systems. Proc. ACM Program. Lang. **3(POPL)**, 1–28 (2019)
6. Bonchi, F., Pavlovic, D., Sobocinski, P.: Functorial semantics for relational theories. arXiv preprint arXiv:1711.08699 (2017)
7. Bonchi, F., Piedeleu, R., Fabio Zanasi, P.S.: Graphical affine algebra. In: ACM/IEEE Symposium on Logic and Computer Science (LiCS 2019) (2019)
8. Bonchi, F., Sobociński, P., Zanasi, F.: A categorical semantics of signal flow graphs. In: Baldan, P., Gorla, D. (eds.) CONCUR 2014. LNCS, vol. 8704, pp. 435–450. Springer, Heidelberg (2014). https://doi.org/10.1007/978-3-662-44584-6_30
9. Bonchi, F., Sobocinski, P., Zanasi, F.: Full abstraction for signal flow graphs. In: POPL 2015, pp. 515–526. ACM (2015)
10. Bonchi, F., Sobociński, P., Zanasi, F.: Interacting Hopf algebras. J. Pure Appl. Algebra **221**(1), 144–184 (2017)
11. Carboni, A., Walters, R.F.: Cartesian bicategories I. J. Pure Appl. Algebra **49**(1–2), 11–32 (1987)
12. Coddington, E.A.: Extension Theory of Formally Normal and Symmetric Subspaces, vol. 134. American Mathematical Soc. (1973)
13. Cross, R.: Multivalued Linear Operators, vol. 213. CRC Press, Boca Raton (1998)
14. Erbele, J.: Redundancy and zebra snakes. https://graphicallinearalgebra.net/2017/10/23/episode-r1-redundancy-and-zebra-snakes/
15. Freyd, P.J., Scedrov, A.: Categories, Allegories, vol. 39. Elsevier, Amsterdam (1990)
16. Lack, S.: Composing props. Theory Appl. Categ. **13**(9), 147–163 (2004)

17. Lawvere, F.W.: Functorial semantics of algebraic theories. Proc. Natl. Acad. Sci. **50**(5), 869–872 (1963)
18. Mac Lane, S.: An algebra of additive relations. Proc. Natl. Acad. Sci. U. S. A. **47**(7), 1043 (1961)
19. Mac Lane, S.: An algebra of additive relations. Proc. Natl. Acad. Sci. U. S. A. **47**(7), 1043–1051 (1961)
20. Macedo, H.D., Oliveira, J.N.: Typing linear algebra: a biproduct-oriented approach. Sci. Comput. Program. **78**(11), 2160–2191 (2013)
21. Mu, S.C., Oliveira, J.N.: Programming from Galois connections. J. Log. Algebraic Program. **81**(6), 680–704 (2012)
22. Santos, A., Oliveira, J.N.: Type your matrices for great good: a haskell library of typed matrices and applications (functional pearl). In: Proceedings of the 13th ACM SIGPLAN International Symposium on Haskell, p. 54–66. Haskell 2020, Association for Computing Machinery, New York (2020). https://doi.org/10.1145/3406088.3409019
23. Selinger, P.: A survey of graphical languages for monoidal categories. In: Coecke, B. (ed.) New Structures for Physics. LNP, vol. 813, pp. 289–355. Springer, Heidelberg (2010). https://doi.org/10.1007/978-3-642-12821-9_4
24. Sobociński, P.: Graphical linear algebra. Mathematical blog. https://graphicallinearalgebra.net
25. Zanasi, F.: Interacting Hopf Algebras: the theory of linear systems. Ph.D. thesis, Ecole Normale Supérieure de Lyon (2015)

Modeling Big Data Processing Programs

João Batista de Souza Neto[1]($^\boxtimes$) (iD), Anamaria Martins Moreira[2] (iD),
Genoveva Vargas-Solar[3] (iD), and Martin A. Musicante[1] (iD)

[1] Department of Informatics and Applied Mathematics (DIMAp),
Federal University of Rio Grande do Norte, Natal, Brazil
`jbsneto@ppgsc.ufrn.br, mam@dimap.ufrn.br`
[2] Computer Science Department (DCC),
Federal University of Rio de Janeiro, Rio de Janeiro, Brazil
`anamaria@dcc.ufrj.br`
[3] Univ. Grenoble Alpes, CNRS, Grenoble INP, LIG-LAFMIA, Grenoble, France
`genoveva.vargas@imag.fr`

Abstract. We propose a new model for data processing programs. Our
model generalizes the data flow programming style implemented by systems such as Apache Spark, DryadLINQ, Apache Beam and Apache
Flink. The model uses directed acyclic graphs (DAGs) to represent the
main aspects of data flow-based systems, namely, operations over data
(filtering, aggregation, join) and program execution, defined by data
dependence between operations. We use *Monoid Algebra* to model operations over distributed, partitioned datasets and *Petri Nets* to represent
the data flow. This approach allows the data processing program specification to be agnostic of the target Big Data processing system. As a
first application of the model, we used it to formalize mutation operators
for the application of mutation testing in Big Data processing programs.
The testing tool TRANSMUT-SPARK implement these operators.

Keywords: Big Data processing · Data flow programming models ·
Petri Nets · Monoid Algebra

1 Introduction

The access to datasets with important volume, variety and velocity scales,
namely Big Data, calls for alternative parallel programming models, adapted to
the implementation of data analytic tasks and capable of exploiting the potential
of those datasets. These programming models have been implemented by large
scale data processing systems that provide execution infrastructures for large
scale computing and memory resources.

Large scale data processing systems can be classified according to their purpose in general-purpose, SQL, graph processing, and stream processing [2]. These

This study was financed in part by the Coordenação de Aperfeiçoamento de Pessoal
de Nível Superior - Brasil (CAPES) - Finance Code 001.

© Springer Nature Switzerland AG 2020
G. Carvalho and V. Stolz (Eds.): SBMF 2020, LNCS 12475, pp. 101–118, 2020.
https://doi.org/10.1007/978-3-030-63882-5_7

systems adopt different approaches to represent and process data. Examples of general-purpose systems are *Apache Hadoop* [10], *DryadLINQ* [23], *Apache Flink* [5], *Apache Beam* [3] and *Apache Spark* [24]. According to the programming model adopted for processing data, general-purpose systems can be control flow-based (like Apache Hadoop) or data flow-based (like Apache Spark). In these systems, a program built to process distributed datasets composes individual processing blocks. These processing blocks implement operations that perform *transformations* on the data. The interaction between these blocks defines the *data flow* that specifies the order to perform operations. Datasets exchanged among the blocks are modeled by data structures such as key-value tuples or tables. The system infrastructure manages the parallel and distributed processing of datasets transparently. This allows developers to avoid having to deal with low-level details inherent to the distributed and parallel environments.

Yet, according to the dataset properties (velocity, volume), performance expectations and computing infrastructure characteristics (cluster, cloud, HPC nodes), it is often an important programmers' decision to choose a well-adapted target system to be used for running data processing programs. Indeed, each hardware/software facility has its particularities concerning the infrastructure and optimizations made to run the program in a parallel and distributed way. This means that the systems can have different performance scores depending on their context or available resources. The choice depends on non-functional requirements of the project, available infrastructure and even preferences of the team that develops and execute the program. In order to address these subjective criteria, we believe that data processing programs design must be agnostic of the target execution platform.

This paper proposes a **model for data processing programs** that provides an abstract representation of the main aspects of data flow-based data processing systems: *(i)* operations applied on data (e.g., filtering, aggregation, join); *(ii)* representation of programs execution through directed acyclic graphs (DAGs) where vertices represent operations and datasets, and edges represent data communication. According to the proposed model, a program is defined as a bipartite DAG composed of successive transformations (i.e., operations) over datasets being processed.

Our model represents the DAG of the data flow and transformations (i.e., operations) separately. We use *Petri Nets* [17] to represent the data flow, and *Monoid Algebra* [8,9], an algebra for processing distributed data, to model transformations. This allows the same program to be implemented independently of target Big Data processing systems, requiring adjustments about the programming language and API when deployed on a target system (*Apache Spark*, *DryadLINQ, Apache Beam* and *Apache Flink.*).

The proposed model provides a formal and infrastructure-independent specification of data processing programs implemented according to data flow-based programming models. For the time being, works addressing Big Data processing programs have merely concentrated efforts on technical and engineering challenging aspects. Yet, few works, such as [6,22], and [18] have worked on formal specifications that can reason about their execution abstractly. This can be important for comparing infrastructures, for pipelines for testing parallel data processing programs, and eventually verifying programs properties (like correctness, completeness, concurrent access to data). In this work, we use the model to define mutation operators which can be instantiated into the different reference systems and to represent programs in a tool for mutation testing of Spark programs.

The remainder of the paper is organized as follows. Section 2 presents the background concepts of the model, namely, Petri Nets and Monoid Algebra. Section 3 presents the model for formally expressing Big Data processing programs. Section 4 describes a case study where we applied the model. Section 5 introduces related work addressing approaches for generalizing control and data flow parallel programming models. Section 6 concludes the paper and discusses future work.

2   Background

This section briefly presents Petri Nets and Monoid Algebra, upon which our model is built. For a more detailed presentation, the reader can refer to [8,17].

Petri Nets. [19] is a formal tool that allows to model and analyze the behavior of distributed, concurrent, asynchronous, and/or non-deterministic systems [17]. A Petri Net is defined as a directed bipartite graph that contains two types of nodes: *places* and *transitions*. Places represent the system's state variables, while transitions represent the actions performed by the system. These two components are connected through directed edges that connect places to transitions and transitions to places. With these three components, it is possible to represent the different states of a system (places), the actions that take the system from one state to another (transitions) and how the change of state is made due to actions (edges). This is done by using *tokens* to decorate places of the net. The distribution of the tokens among places indicates that the system is in a given state. The execution of an action (transition) takes tokens from one state (place) to another.

Formally, a Petri net is a quintuple $PN = (P, T, F, W, M_0)$ where $P \cap T = \emptyset$, $P \cup T \neq \emptyset$ and:

$P = \{p_1, p_2, \ldots, p_m\}$ is a finite set of *places*,

$T = \{t_1, t_2, \ldots, t_n\}$ is a finite set of *transitions*,

$F \subseteq (P \times T) \cup (T \times P)$ is a finite set of *edges*,

$W : F \to \{1, 2, 3, \ldots\}$ is a set of weights associated to edges,

$M_0 : P \to \{0, 1, 2, 3, \ldots\}$ is a function defining the initial marking of a net,

The execution of a system is defined by *firing* transitions. Firing a transition t consumes $W(s, t)$ tokens from all its input places s, and produces $W(t, s')$ tokens to each of its output places s'.

Monoid Algebra was proposed in [8] as an algebraic formalism for data-centric distributed computing operations based on monoids and monoid homomorphisms. A monoid is a triad $(S, \oplus, e_\oplus)$ formed by a set S, an associative operation $\oplus$ in S and a neutral element $e_\oplus$ (consider that $\oplus$ identifies the monoid). A monoid homomorphism is a function H over two monoids, from $\otimes$ to $\oplus$, which respects:

$$H(X \otimes Y) = H(X) \oplus H(Y) \quad \text{for all } X \text{ and } Y \text{ of type } S$$
$$H(e_\otimes) = e_\oplus$$

Monoid algebra uses the concepts of monoid and monoid homomorphism to define operations on distributed datasets, which are represented as monoid collections. One type of monoid collection is the *bag*, an unordered data collection of type α (denoted as $Bag[\alpha]$) that has the unit injection function $\mathbb{U}_\uplus$, which generates the bag $\{\!\{x\}\!\}$ from the unitary element x ($\mathbb{U}_\uplus(x) = \{\!\{x\}\!\}$), the associative operation $\uplus$, which unites two bags ($\{\!\{x\}\!\} \uplus \{\!\{y\}\!\} = \{\!\{x, y\}\!\}$), and the neutral element $\{\!\{\}\!\}$, which is an empty bag. Another type of monoid collection is the list, which can be considered an ordered bag ($List[\alpha]$ denotes a list of type α), with $\mathbb{U}_{+\!\!+}$ as the unit injection function, $+\!\!+$ as the associative operation and $[\,]$ as the neutral element.

Monoid algebra defines distributed operations as monoid homomorphisms over monoid collections (which represent distributed datasets). These homomorphisms are defined to abstractly describe the basic blocks of distributed data processing systems such as map/reduce or data flow systems.

The **flatmap** operation receives a function f of type $\alpha \to Bag[\beta]$ and a collection X of type $Bag[\alpha]$ as input and returns a collection $Bag[\beta]$ resulting from the union of the results of applying f to the elements of X. This operation captures the essence of parallel processing since f can be executed in parallel on different data partitions in a distributed dataset. Notice that **flatmap** f is a monoid homomorphism since it is a function that preserves the structure of bags.

The operations **groupby** and **cogroup** capture the data shuffling process by representing the reorganization and grouping of data. The **groupby** operation groups the elements of $Bag[\kappa \times \alpha]$ through the first component (key) of type κ and results in a collection $Bag[\kappa \times Bag[\alpha]]$, where the second component is a collection containing all elements of type α to which were associated with the same key k in the initial collection. The **cogroup** operation works similarly to **groupby**, but it operates on two collections that have a key of the same type κ.

The **reduce** operation represents the aggregation of the elements of $Bag[\alpha]$ into a single element of type α from the application of an associative function f of type $\alpha \to \alpha \to \alpha$. The operation **orderby** represents the transformation of a bag $Bag[\kappa \times \alpha]$ into a list $List[\kappa \times \alpha]$ ordered by the key of type κ which supports the total order $\leq$.

In addition, monoid algebra also supports the use of lambda expressions ($\lambda x.e$), conditionals (**if-then-else**), and the union operation on bags ($\uplus$).

Our proposal combines the use of Petri Nets with Monoid Algebra to build abstract versions of the primitives present in Big Data processing applications. The main goal of our approach is to have a common, abstract representation of data-centric programs. This representation may be used to compare different frameworks, as well as an (intermediate) representation to translate, refine, or optimize programs.

3   Modeling Big Data Processing Programs

In this section, we present a formal model for Big Data processing programs. Our model is organized in two levels: *data flow*, and *transformations*. Data flow in our model is defined using Directed Acyclic Graphs (DAG), while the semantics of the transformations that are carried out on the data is modeled as monoid homomorphisms on datasets.

3.1   Data Flow

To define the DAG that represents the data flow of a data processing program, we rely on the data flow graph model presented in [14], which was formalized using Petri Nets [17].

A program P is defined as a bipartite directed graph where places stand for the distributed datasets (D) of the program, and transitions stand for its transformations (T). Datasets and transformations are connected by edges (E):

$$P = \langle D \cup T, E \rangle$$

To exemplify the model, let us consider the Spark program shown in Fig. 1. This program receives as input two datasets (RDDs) containing log messages (line 1), makes the union of these two datasets (line 2), removes duplicate logs (line 3), and ends by filtering headers, removing logs which match a specific pattern (line 4) and returning the filtered RDD (line 5).

```
1  def unionLogsProblem(firstLogs: RDD[String], secondLogs: RDD[String])
       : RDD[String] = {
2    val aggregatedLogLines = firstLogs.union(secondLogs)
3    val uniqueLogLines = aggregatedLogLines.distinct()
4    val cleanLogLines = uniqueLogLines.filter((line: String) => !(line.
         startsWith("host") && line.contains("bytes")))
5    return cleanLogLines
6  }
```

Fig. 1. Sample log union program in Spark.

In this program we can identify five RDDs, that will be referred to by using short names for conciseness. So, $D = \{d_1, d_2, d_3, d_4, d_5\}$, where $d_1 = $ firstLogs,

$d_2 = \texttt{secondLogs}$, $d_3 = \texttt{aggregatedLogLines}$, $d_4 = \texttt{uniqueLogLines}$, and $d_5 = \texttt{cleanLogLines}$. For simplicity, each RDD in the code was defined with a unique name. Still, the model considers references to the datasets, which are unique, independently of the identifier used in the code.

We can also identify the application of three transformations in P, thus the set T in our example is defined as $T = \{t_1, t_2, t_3\}$, where the transformations in T are $t_1 = \texttt{union}(d_1, d_2)$, $t_2 = \texttt{distinct}(d_3)$, and $t_3 = \texttt{filter((line: String) => !(line.startsWith(``host'') \&\& line.contains(``bytes'')), } d_4)$.

Each transformation in T receives one or two datasets belonging to D as input and produces a dataset al.so in D as output. Besides, the sets D and T are disjoint and finite.

Edges connect datasets with transformations. An edge may either be a pair in $D \times T$, representing the input dataset of a transformation; it can be a pair in $T \times D$, representing the output dataset of a transformation. In this way, the set of edges of P is defined as $E \subseteq (D \times T) \cup (T \times D)$.

The set E in our example program is, then:

$$E = \{(d_1, t_1), (d_2, t_1), (t_1, d_3), (d_3, t_2), (t_2, d_4), (d_4, t_3), (t_3, d_5)\}$$

Using these sets, the DAG representing the Spark program in Fig. 1 can be seen in Fig. 2. The distributed datasets in D are represented as circle nodes and the transformations in T are represented as thick bar nodes of the graph. The edges are represented by arrows that connect the datasets and transformations. The token marking in d_1 and d_2 indicate that the program is ready to be executed (initial marking).

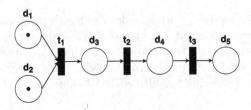

Fig. 2. Data flow representation of the program in Fig. 1.

3.2 Data Sets and Transformations

The data flow model presented above represents the datasets and transformations of a program P, as well as the order in which these transformations are processed when P is executed, but abstract from their actual contents or semantics.

To define the contents of datasets in D and the semantics of transformations in T, we make use of *Monoid Algebra* [8,9]. Datasets are represented as monoid collections and transformations are defined as operations supported by monoid algebra. These representations are detailed in the following.

Distributed Datasets. A distributed dataset in D can either be represented by a *bag* ($Bag[\alpha]$) or a *list* ($List[\alpha]$). Both structures represent collections of distributed data [9], capturing the essence of the concepts of *RDD* in Apache Spark, *PCollection* in Apache Beam, *DataSet* in Apache Flink and *DryadTable* in DryadLINQ. These structures provide an abstraction of the actual distributed data in a cluster in the form of a simple collection of items.

We define most of the transformations of our model in terms of bags. We consider lists only for transformations implementing sorts, which are the only ones in which the order of the elements in the dataset is relevant.

In monoid algebra, bags and lists can either represent distributed or local collections. These two kinds of collections are treated by monoid homomorphisms in a unified way [9]. In this way, we will not distinguish distributed and local collections when defining our transformations.

Transformations. In our model, transformations on datasets take one or two datasets as input and produce one dataset as an output. Transformations may also receive other types of parameters such as functions, which represent data processing operations defined by the developer, as well as literals such as boolean constants. A transformation t in the transformation set T of a program P is characterized by the operation it implements, the types of its input and output datasets, and its input parameters.

We define the transformations of our model in terms of the operations of monoid algebra defined in Sect. 2. We group transformations into categories, according to the types of operations that we identified in the data processing systems that we studied.

Mapping Transformations. Mapping transformations transform values of an input dataset into values of an output dataset through the application of a mapping function. Our model provides two mapping transformations: *flatMap* and *map*. Both transformations apply a given function f to every element of the input dataset to generate the output dataset, the only difference being the requirements on the type of f and its relation with the type of the generated dataset. Given an input dataset of type $Bag[\alpha]$, the *map* transformation accepts any $f : \alpha \rightarrow \beta$ and generates an output dataset of type $Bag[\beta]$, while the *flatMap* transformation requires $f : \alpha \rightarrow Bag[\beta]$ to produce a dataset of type $Bag[\beta]$ as output.

The definition of *flatMap* in our model is just the monoid algebra operation defined in Sect. 2:

$$flatMap :: (\alpha \rightarrow Bag[\beta]) \rightarrow Bag[\alpha] \rightarrow Bag[\beta]$$
$$flatMap(f, D) = \mathbf{flatmap}(f, D)$$

The *map* transformation derives data of type $Bag[\beta]$ when given a function $f : \alpha \rightarrow \beta$. For that to be modeled with the **flatmap** from monoid algebra, we create a lambda expression that receives an element x from the input dataset and results in a $Bag[\beta]$ collection containing only the result of applying f to x ($\lambda x.\{\!\{f(x)\}\!\}$). Thus, map is defined as:

$$map :: (\alpha \to \beta) \to Bag[\alpha] \to Bag[\beta]$$
$$map(f, D) = \textbf{flatmap}(\lambda x.\{\!\{f(x)\}\!\}, D)$$

Filter Transformation uses a boolean function to determine whether or not a data item should be mapped to the output dataset. As in the case of *map*, we use a lambda expression to build a singleton bag:

$$filter :: (\alpha \to boolean) \to Bag[\alpha] \to Bag[\alpha]$$
$$filter(p, D) = \textbf{flatmap}(\lambda x.\ \textbf{if}\ p(x)\ \textbf{then}\ \{\!\{x\}\!\}\ \textbf{else}\ \{\!\{\}\!\}, D)$$

For each element x of the input dataset D, the *filter* transformation checks the condition $p(x)$. It forms the singleton bag $\{\!\{x\}\!\}$ or the empty bag ($\{\!\{\}\!\}$), depending on the result of that test. This lambda expression is then applied to the input dataset using the **flatmap** operation.

For instance, consider the boolean function $p(x) = x \geq 3$ and a bag $D = \{\!\{1, 2, 3, 4, 5\}\!\}$. then, $filter(p, D) = \{\!\{3, 4, 5\}\!\}$.

Grouping Transformations group the elements of a dataset with respect to a key. We define two grouping transformations in our model: *groupByKey* and *groupBy*.

The *groupByKey* transformation is defined as the **groupBy** operation of Monoid Algebra. It maps a key-value dataset into a dataset associating each key to a bag. Our *groupBy* transformation uses a function k to map elements of the collection to a key *before* grouping the elements with respect to that key:

$$groupBy :: (\alpha \to \kappa) \to Bag[\alpha] \to Bag[\kappa \times Bag[\alpha]]$$
$$groupBy(k, D) = \textbf{groupby}(\textbf{flatmap}(\lambda x.\{\!\{(k(x), x)\}\!\}, D))$$

$$groupByKey :: Bag[\kappa \times \alpha] \to Bag[\kappa \times Bag[\alpha]]$$
$$groupByKey(D) = \textbf{groupby}(D)$$

For example, let us consider the identity function to define each key, and the datasets $D_1 = \{\!\{1, 2, 3, 2, 3, 3\}\!\}$, and $D_2 = \{\!\{(1, a), (2, b), (3, c), (1, e), (2, f)\}\!\}$. Applying *groupBy* and *groupByKey* to these sets results in:

$$groupBy(\lambda k.k, D_1) = \{\!\{(1, \{\!\{1\}\!\}), (2, \{\!\{2, 2\}\!\}), (3, \{\!\{3, 3, 3\}\!\})\}\!\}$$
$$groupByKey(D_2) = \{\!\{(1, \{\!\{a, e\}\!\}), (2, \{\!\{b, f\}\!\}), (3, \{\!\{c\}\!\})\}\!\}$$

Set (Bag) Transformations corresponds to binary mathematical collection operations on Bags. They operate on two collections of data of the same type and result in a new collection of the same type. The definition of these transformations is based on the definitions in [9].

The *union* transformation represents the union of elements from two datasets into a single dataset. This operation is represented in a simple way using the *bags* union operator ($\uplus$):

$$union :: Bag[\alpha] \rightarrow Bag[\alpha] \rightarrow Bag[\alpha]$$
$$union(D_x, D_y) = D_x \uplus D_y$$

We also define the *intersection* and *subtract* transformations:

$$intersection :: Bag[\alpha] \rightarrow Bag[\alpha] \rightarrow Bag[\alpha]$$
$$intersection(D_x, D_y) = \textbf{flatmap}(\lambda x. \text{ if } some(\lambda y.x = y, D_y)$$
$$\text{then } \{\!\{x\}\!\} \text{ else } \{\!\{\}\!\}), D_x)$$
$$subtract :: Bag[\alpha] \rightarrow Bag[\alpha] \rightarrow Bag[\alpha]$$
$$subtract(D_x, D_y) = \textbf{flatmap}(\lambda x. \text{ if } all(\lambda y.x \neq y, D_y)$$
$$\text{then } \{\!\{x\}\!\} \text{ else } \{\!\{\}\!\}), D_x)$$

where the auxiliary functions *some* and *all*, which represent the existential and universal quantifiers, respectively, are defined in [20].

The *intersection* of bags D_x and D_y selects all elements of D_x appearing at least once in D_y. Subtracting D_y from D_x selects all the elements of D_x that differ from every element of D_y.

Differently of the union operation in mathematical sets, the *union* transformation defined in our model maintains repeated elements from the two input datasets. To allow the removal of these repeated elements, we define the *distinct* transformation. To define *distinct*, we first map each element of the dataset to a key/value tuple containing the element itself as a key. After, we group this key/value dataset, which will result in a dataset in which the group is the repeated key itself. Last, we map the key/value elements only to the key, resulting in a dataset with no repetitions. The *distinct* transformation is defined as follows:

$$distinct :: Bag[\alpha] \rightarrow Bag[\alpha]$$
$$distinct(D) = \textbf{flatmap}(\lambda(k, g).\{\!\{k\}\!\}, t_2(D))$$
$$t_1(D) = \textbf{flatmap}(\lambda x.\{\!\{(x, x)\}\!\}, D)$$
$$t_2(D) = \textbf{groupby}(t_1(D))$$

Aggregation Transformations collapses elements of a dataset into a single element. The most common aggregations apply binary operations on the elements of a dataset to generate a single element, resulting in a single value, or on groups of values associated with a key. We represent these aggregations with the transformations *reduce*, which operates on the whole set, and *reduceByKey*, which operates on values grouped by key. The *reduce* transformation has the same behavior as the **reduce** operation of monoid algebra. The definition of *reduceByKey* is also defined in terms of **reduce**, but since its result is the aggregation of elements associated with each key rather than the aggregation of all elements of the set, we first need to group the elements of the dataset by their keys:

$$reduce :: (\alpha \to \alpha \to \alpha) \to Bag[\alpha] \to \alpha$$
$$reduce(f, D) = \mathbf{reduce}(f, D)$$

$$reduceByKey :: (\alpha \to \alpha \to \alpha) \to Bag[\kappa \times \alpha] \to Bag[\kappa \times \alpha]$$
$$reduceByKey(f, D) = \mathbf{flatmap}(\lambda(k, g).\{(k, \mathbf{reduce}(f, g))\}, \mathbf{groupby}(D))$$

Join Transformations implement relational join operations between two datasets. We define four join operations, which correspond to well-known operations in relational databases: *innerJoin*, *leftOuterJoin*, *rightOuterJoin*, and *fullOuterJoin*. The *innerJoin* operation combines the elements of two datasets based on a join-predicate expressed as a relationship, such as the same key. *LeftOuterJoin* and *rightOuterJoin* combine the elements of two sets like an *innerJoin* adding to the result all values in the left (right) set that do not match to the right (left) set. The *fullOuterJoin* of two sets forms a new relation containing all the information present in both sets.

See below the definition of the *innerJoin* transformation, which was based on the definition presented in [7]:

$$innerJoin :: Bag[\kappa \times \alpha] \to Bag[\kappa \times \beta] \to Bag[\kappa \times (\alpha \times \beta)]$$
$$innerJoin(D_x, D_y) = \mathbf{flatmap}(\lambda(k, (d_x, d_y)).t_2(k, d_x, d_y), t_1(D_x, D_y))$$
$$t_1(D_x, D_y) = \mathbf{cogroup}(D_x, D_y)$$
$$t_2(k, d_x, d_y) = \mathbf{flatmap}(\lambda x.t_3(k, x, d_y), d_x)$$
$$t_3(k, x, d_y) = \mathbf{flatmap}(\lambda y.\{(k, (x, y))\}, d_y)$$

The definition of the other joins follows a similar logic, but conditionals are included to verify the different relationships.

The types for our other join transformations are:

$$leftOuterJoin :: Bag[\kappa \times \alpha] \to Bag[\kappa \times \beta] \to Bag[\kappa \times (\alpha \times Bag[\beta])]$$
$$rightOuterJoin :: Bag[\kappa \times \alpha] \to Bag[\kappa \times \beta] \to Bag[\kappa \times (Bag[\alpha] \times \beta)]$$
$$fullOuterJoin :: Bag[\kappa \times \alpha] \to Bag[\kappa \times \beta] \to Bag[\kappa \times (Bag[\alpha] \times Bag[\beta])]$$

The full definition of our join operations is not included here due to lack of space. It can be found in [20].

Sorting Transformations add the notion of *order* to a bag. In practical terms, these operations receive a bag and form a list, ordered in accordance of some criteria. Sort transformations are defined in terms of the **orderby** operation of monoid algebra, which transforms a $Bag[\kappa \times \alpha]$ into a $List[\kappa \times \alpha]$ ordered by the key of type κ that supports the total order $\leq$ (we will also use the *inv* function, which reverses the total order of a list, thus using $\geq$ instead of $\leq$). We define two transformations, the *orderBy* transformation that sorts a dataset of type α, and the *orderByKey* transformation that sorts a key/value dataset by the key. The definitions of our sorting transformations are as follows:

$$orderBy :: boolean \rightarrow Bag[\alpha] \rightarrow List[\alpha]$$
$$orderBy(desc, D) = \textbf{flatmap}(\lambda(k,v).[k], \textbf{orderby}(t_1(desc, D)))$$
$$t_1(desc, D) = \textbf{if } desc \textbf{ then } t_2(D) \textbf{ else } t_3(D)$$
$$t_2(D) = \textbf{flatmap}(\lambda x.\{\!\{(inv(x), x)\}\!\}, D)$$
$$t_3(D) = \textbf{flatmap}(\lambda x.\{\!\{(x, x)\}\!\}, D)$$

$$orderByKey :: boolean \rightarrow Bag[\kappa \times \alpha] \rightarrow List[\kappa \times \alpha]$$
$$orderByKey(desc, D) = \textbf{orderby}(t_1(desc, D))$$
$$t_1(desc, D) = \textbf{if} desc \textbf{ then } t_2(D) \textbf{ else } D$$
$$t_2(D) = \textbf{flatmap}(\lambda(k,x).\{\!\{(inv(k), x)\}\!\}, D)$$

The boolean value used as first parameter defines if the direct order $\leq$ or its inverse is used.

To exemplify the use of sorting transformations let us consider $D_1 = \{\!\{1, 3, 2, 5, 4\}\!\}$ and $D_2 = \{\!\{(1, a), (3, c), (2, a), (5, e), (4, d)\}\!\}$. Then:

$$orderBy(false, D_1) = [1, 2, 3, 4, 5]$$
$$orderBy(true, D_1) = [5, 4, 3, 2, 1]$$
$$orderByKey(false, D_2) = [(1, a), (2, b), (3, c), (4, d), (5, e)]$$
$$orderByKey(true, D_2) = [(5, e), (4, d), (3, c), (2, b), (1, a)]$$

3.3   Abstracting Features from Big Data Processing Systems

The model presented in this paper was based on the main characteristics of the programming models of the systems *Apache Spark* [24], *DryadLINQ* [23], *Apache Flink* [5] and *Apache Beam* [3]. Even having differences in the way they deal with program execution, different ways of optimization and data treatment, all these systems use a similar DAG-based model to represent the workflow of data processing programs. These DAGs are composed of data processing operations that are connected through communication channels. These channels, in turn, are places for intermediate data storage between operations.

Our model captures these features in its Petri Net data flow component. The nodes for datasets symbolize the channels of communication between operations, working as a high level representation of the abstractions for distributed data sets present in these systems, such as the *RDD* in *Apache Spark*, as shown in the example of Figs. 1 and 2, but also *PCollection* in *Apache Beam*, *DataSet* in *Apache Flink* and *DryadTable* in *DryadLINQ*. Transformation nodes represent the processing operations that receive data from datasets and transmit the processing results to another dataset. The representations of the datasets and transformations in the data flow graph encompass the main abstractions of the

DAGs in these systems and allow us to represent and analyze a program independently of the system in which it will be executed. In this way, the particularities of each system, such as the way they deal with parallel and distributed execution, can be abstracted so that we can concentrate on the functionalities and behavior of the program.

The semantics of transformations and data sets is represented in the model using Monoid Algebra. Table 1 presents a comparison between the transformations that were defined in the model and the operations present in the Big Data processing systems considered. The operations defined in our model correspond to the main operations that can be found in these systems.

Table 1. Comparison between the operations in the model and the operations in the Big Data processing systems studied.

	Model	Apache Spark	Apache Flink	Apache Beam	DryadLINQ
Mapping	map, flatMap	map, flatMap	map, flatMap	ParDo, FlatMapElements, MapElements	Select, SelectMany
Filtering	filter	filter	filter	Filter	Where
Grouping	groupBy, groupByKey	groupBy, groupByKey	groupBy	GroupByKey	GroupBy
Sets	union, intersection, subtract, distinct	union, intersection, subtract, distinct	union, distinct	Flatten, Distinct	Union, Intersect, Except, Distinct
Aggregation	reduce, redubeByKey	reduce, reduceByKey, aggregateByKey	reduce, reduceGroup, aggregate	Combine	Aggregate
Joins	innerJoin, leftOuterJoin, rightOuterJoin, fullOuterJoin	join, leftOuterJoin, rightOuterJoin, fullOuterJoin	join, leftOuterJoin, rightOuterJoin, fullOuterJoin	CoGroupByKey	Join
Ordering	orderBy, orderByKey	sortBy, sortByKey	sortPartition, sortGroup		OrderBy

Some systems offer more specific operations that we do not define directly in our model. It is work on progress to guarantee complete coverage of all the operations of the considered systems. However, most of the operations that are not directly represented in the model can easily be represented using the transformations provided by the model. For example, classic aggregation operations, like maximum, minimum or the sum of the elements in a dataset. We can easily represent these operations using the *reduce* operation of the model:

$$max(D) = reduce(\lambda(x,y).\ \textbf{if}\ x > y\ \textbf{then}\ x\ \textbf{else}\ y, D)$$
$$min(D) = reduce(\lambda(x,y).\ \textbf{if}\ x < y\ \textbf{then}\ x\ \textbf{else}\ y, D)$$
$$sum(D) = reduce(\lambda(x,y).x + y, D)$$

This model is used as a representation tool for defining mutation operators for the application of mutation testing in Big Data processing program. In the next section, we briefly present how this is done in a testing tool we developed.

4   Applications of the Model

The model proposed in the previous section can be as an abstraction of existing data flow programming models used by processing systems. It provides abstractions of the data flow programming models that can be applied to specify parallel data processing programs independently of target systems. Finally, the abstract and formal concepts provided by the model, make it quite suitable for the automation of software development processes, such as those done by IDE tools.

We first applied the model to formalize the mutation operators presented in [21], where we explored the application of mutation testing in Spark programs, and in the tool TRANSMUT-SPARK[1] [20] that we developed to automate this process. Mutation testing is a fault-based testing technique that relies on simulating faults to design and evaluate test sets [1]. Faults are simulated by applying mutation operators, which are rules with modification patterns for programs (a modified program is called a mutant). In [21], we presented a set of mutation operators designed for Spark programs that are divided into two groups: *mutation operators for the data flow* and *mutation operators for transformations*. These mutation operators were based on faults that can be found in Spark programs with the idea of mimicking them.

Mutation operators for the data flow model changes in the DAG that defines the program. In general, we define three types of modifications in the data flow: replacement of one transformation with another (both existing in the program); swap the calling order of two transformations, and delete the call of a transformation in the data flow. These modifications involve changes to the edges of the program. Besides, the type consistency in the program must be maintained, i.e., when a transformation is replaced by another the I/O datasets of both transformations must be of the same type. In Fig. 3 we exemplify these mutations in the data flow that was presented in Fig. 2.

Mutation operators associated with transformations model the changes done on specific types of transformations, such as operators for aggregation transformations or set transformations. In general, we model two types of modifications: replacement of the function passed as a parameter of the transformation, and replacement of a transformation by another of the same group. In the first type, we defined specific substitution functions for each group of transformations. For example, for an aggregation transformation, we define five substitution functions (f_m) to replace an original function. Considering the aggregation transformation $t_1 = reduce(max(x,y),d)$, which receives as input a function that returns the

---

[1] TRANSMUT-SPARK is publicly available at https://github.com/jbsneto-ppgsc-ufrn/transmut-spark.

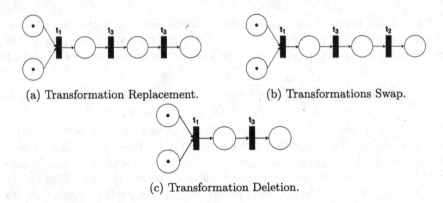

(a) Transformation Replacement.   (b) Transformations Swap.

(c) Transformation Deletion.

Fig. 3. Examples of mutants created with mutation operators for data flow.

greater of the two input parameters and an integer dataset, the mutation operator for aggregation transformation replacement will generate the following five mutants:

$$t_1 = reduce(f_m(x, y) = x, d)$$
$$t_1 = reduce(f_m(x, y) = y, d)$$
$$t_1 = reduce(f_m(x, y) = max(x, x), d)$$
$$t_1 = reduce(f_m(x, y) = max(y, y), d)$$
$$t_1 = reduce(f_m(x, y) = max(y, x), d)$$

In the other type of modification, we replace a transformation with others from the same group. For example, for set transformations (union, intersection and subtract), we replace one transformation with the remaining two, besides, we replace the transformation for the identity of each of the two input datasets and we also invert the order of the input datasets. Considering the set transformation $t_1 = subtract(d_1, d_2)$, which receives two integer datasets a input, the set transformation replacement operator will generate the following mutants:

$$t_1 = union(d_1, d_2)$$
$$t_1 = intersection(d_1, d_2)$$
$$t_1 = identity(d_1)$$
$$t_1 = identity(d_2)$$
$$t_1 = subtract(d_2, d_1)$$

The mutation operators for the other groups of transformations follow these two types of modifications, respecting the type consistency and the particularities of each group. The tool TRANSMUT-SPARK [20] uses the model as an intermediate representation. The tool reads a Spark program and translates it into an implementation of the model, so the mutation operators are applied to the model. We use the model as an intermediate representation in the tool to expand it in the future to apply the mutation test to programs in *Apache Flink*, *Apache Beam* and *DryadLINQ*.

5   Related Work

Data flow processing that defines a pipeline of operations or tasks applied on datasets, where tasks exchange data, has been traditionally formalised using (coloured) Petri Nets [15]. They seem well adapted for modeling the organization (flow) of the processing tasks that receive and produce data. In the case of data processing programs based on data flow models, in general, proposals use Petri Nets to model the flow and they use other formal tools for modeling the operations applied on data. For example, [11,12] uses nested relational calculus for formalizing operations applied to non first normal form compliant data. Next, we describe works that have addressed the formalization of data processing parallel programming models. The analysis focuses on the kind of tools and strategies used for formalizing either control/data flows and data processing operations.

The authors in [22] formalize MapReduce using *CSP* [4]. The objective is to formalize the behaviour of a parallel system that implements the MapReduce programming model. The system is formalized with respect to four components: *Master*, *Mapper*, *Reducer* and *FS* (file system). The Master manages the execution process and the interaction between the other components. The Mapper and Reducer components represent, respectively, the processes for executing the map and reduce operations. Finally, the FS represents the file system that stores the data processed in the program. These components implement the data processing pipeline implemented by these systems which loading data from an FS, executing a map function (by a number of mappers), shuffling and sorting, and then executing a reduce function by reducers. The model allows the analysis of properties and interaction between these processes implemented by MapReduce systems.

In [18] MapReduce applications are formalized with *Coq*, an interactive theorem proving systems. As in [22], the authors also formalized the components and execution process of MapReduce systems. The user-defined functions of the map and reduce operations are also formalized with Coq. Then these formal definitions are used to prove the correctness of MapReduce programs. This is different from the work presented in [22] (described above) that formalizes only the MapReduce system.

More recent work has proposed formal models for data flow programming models, particularly associated with Spark. The work in [6] introduces *PureSpark*, a functional and executable specification for Apache Spark written in Haskell. The purpose of PureSpark is to specify parallel aggregation operations of Spark. Based on this specification, necessary and sufficient conditions are extracted to verify whether the outputs of aggregations in a Spark program are deterministic.

The work [16] presents a formal model for Spark applications based on temporal logic. The model takes into account the DAG that forms the program, information about the execution environment, such as the number of CPU cores available, the number of tasks of the program and the average execution time of the tasks. Then, the model is used to check time constraints and make predictions about the program's execution time.

6 Conclusions and Future Work

This paper introduced a model of data flow processing programs that formally specifies the data flow using Petri Nets and operations performed on data using Monoid Algebra. The paper gave the specification of data processing operations (i.e., transformations) provided as built-in operations in Apache Spark, DryadLINQ, Apache Beam and Apache Flink.

Our model combines two existing proposals: Monoid Algebra and Petri Nets. Monoid Algebra is an abstract way to specify operations over partitioned datasets. Petri nets are widely used to specify parallel computation. Our proposal simply combines these to models to have an intermediate representation of data flow-based programs so that we can manipulate them.

Beyond the interest of providing a formal model for data flow-based programs, the model can be a comparison tool of target systems, and be used to define program testing pipelines. We also showed how operations can be combined into data flows for implementing data mutation operations in mutation testing approaches. The model was used for specifying mutation operators that were then implemented in TRANSMUT-SPARK, a software engineering tool for mutation testing of Spark programs. A natural extension to this work would be to instantiate the tool for other systems of the data flow family (*DryadLINQ, Apache Beam, Apache Flink*). This can be done by adapting TRANSMUT-SPARK's front and back ends so that a program originally written in any of them can be tested using the mutation testing approach proposed in [21].

This line of work, where the model is only used as the internal format, is suited for the more practical users, not willing to see the formality behind their tools. However, when exploring the similarities of these systems, the model may be used as a platform-agnostic form of formally specifying and analyzing properties of a program before its implementation. Coloured Petri Nets and tools such as CPN Tools [13], can be powerful allies in the rigorous development process of such programs. As future work, we intend to study the mapping of our model into the input notation of CPN Tools for model simulation and analysis. Also, we plan to work on the use of this specification for code generation in data flow systems similar to Apache Spark.

References

1. Ammann, P., Offutt, J.: Introduction to Software Testing, 2nd edn. Cambridge University Press, New York (2017)
2. Bajaber, F., Elshawi, R., Batarfi, O., Altalhi, A., Barnawi, A., Sakr, S.: Big Data 2.0 processing systems: taxonomy and open challenges. J. Grid Comput. **14**(3), 379–405 (2016). https://doi.org/10.1007/s10723-016-9371-1

3. Beam, A.: Apache Beam: an advanced unified programming model (2016). https://beam.apache.org/

4. Brookes, S.D., Hoare, C.A.R., Roscoe, A.W.: A theory of communicating sequential processes. J. ACM **31**(3), 560–599 (1984). https://doi.org/10.1145/828.833

5. Carbone, P., Ewen, S., Haridi, S., Katsifodimos, A., Markl, V., Tzoumas, K.: Apache flink: stream and batch processing in a single engine. IEEE Data Eng. Bull. **38**(4), 28–38 (2015)

6. Chen, Y.-F., Hong, C.-D., Lengál, O., Mu, S.-C., Sinha, N., Wang, B.-Y.: An executable sequential specification for Spark aggregation. In: El Abbadi, A., Garbinato, B. (eds.) NETYS 2017. LNCS, vol. 10299, pp. 421–438. Springer, Cham (2017). https://doi.org/10.1007/978-3-319-59647-1_31

7. Chlyah, S., Gesbert, N., Genevès, P., Layaïda, N.: An Algebra with a Fixpoint Operator for Distributed Data Collections, March 2019. https://hal.inria.fr/hal-02066649

8. Fegaras, L.: An algebra for distributed Big Data analytics. J. Funct. Program. **27**, e27 (2017). https://doi.org/10.1017/S0956796817000193

9. Fegaras, L.: Compile-time query optimization for Big Data analytics. Open J. Big Data (OJBD) **5**(1), 35–61 (2019). https://www.ronpub.com/ojbd/OJBD2019v5i1n02Fegaras.html

10. Hadoop: Apache Hadoop Documentation (2019). https://hadoop.apache.org/docs/r2.7.3/

11. Hidders, J., Kwasnikowska, N., Sroka, J., Tyszkiewicz, J., Van den Bussche, J.: Petri Net + nested relational calculus = dataflow. In: Meersman, R., Tari, Z. (eds.) OTM 2005. LNCS, vol. 3760, pp. 220–237. Springer, Heidelberg (2005). https://doi.org/10.1007/11575771_16

12. Hidders, J., Kwasnikowska, N., Sroka, J., Tyszkiewicz, J., Van den Bussche, J.: DFL: a dataflow language based on Petri Nets and nested relational calculus. Inf. Syst. **33**(3), 261–284 (2008)

13. Jensen, K., Kristensen, L.M., Wells, L.: Coloured Petri Nets and CPN tools for modelling and validation of concurrent systems. Int. J. Softw. Tools Technol. Transf. **9**(3), 213–254 (2007). https://doi.org/10.1007/s10009-007-0038-x

14. Kavi, K.M., Buckles, B.P., Bhat, N.: A formal definition of data flow graph models. IEEE Trans. Comput. **C-35**(11), 940–948 (1986). https://doi.org/10.1109/TC.1986.1676696

15. Lee, E., Messerschmitt, D.: Pipeline interleaved programmable DSP's: synchronous data flow programming. IEEE Trans. Acoust. Speech Signal Process. **35**(9), 1334–1345 (1987)

16. Marconi, F., Quattrocchi, G., Baresi, L., Bersani, M.M., Rossi, M.: On the timed analysis of Big-Data applications. In: Dutle, A., Muñoz, C., Narkawicz, A. (eds.) NFM 2018. LNCS, vol. 10811, pp. 315–332. Springer, Cham (2018). https://doi.org/10.1007/978-3-319-77935-5_22

17. Murata, T.: Petri Nets: properties, analysis and applications. Proc. IEEE **77**(4), 541–580 (1989). https://doi.org/10.1109/5.24143

18. Ono, K., Hirai, Y., Tanabe, Y., Noda, N., Hagiya, M.: Using Coq in specification and program extraction of Hadoop MapReduce applications. In: Barthe, G., Pardo, A., Schneider, G. (eds.) SEFM 2011. LNCS, vol. 7041, pp. 350–365. Springer, Heidelberg (2011). https://doi.org/10.1007/978-3-642-24690-6_24

19. Petri, C.A.: Kommunikation mit Automaten. Ph.D. thesis, Universität Hamburg (1962). (in German)

20. Souza Neto, J.B.: Transformation mutation for Spark programs testing. Ph.D. thesis, Federal University of Rio Grande do Norte (UFRN), Natal/RN, Brazil (2020). (in Portuguese)

21. Souza Neto, J.B., Martins Moreira, A., Vargas-Solar, G., Musicante, M.A.: Mutation operators for large scale data processing programs in Spark. In: Dustdar, S., Yu, E., Salinesi, C., Rieu, D., Pant, V. (eds.) CAiSE 2020. LNCS, vol. 12127, pp. 482–497. Springer, Cham (2020). https://doi.org/10.1007/978-3-030-49435-3_30

22. Yang, F., Su, W., Zhu, H., Li, Q.: Formalizing MapReduce with CSP. In: 2010 17th IEEE International Conference and Workshops on Engineering of Computer Based Systems, pp. 358–367 (2010)

23. Yu, Y., et al.: DryadLINQ: a system for general-purpose distributed data-parallel computing using a high-level language. In: Proceedings of the 8th USENIX Conference on Operating Systems Design and Implementation, OSDI 2008, pp. 1–14. USENIX Association, Berkeley, CA, USA (2008). http://dl.acm.org/citation.cfm?id=1855741.1855742

24. Zaharia, M., Chowdhury, M., Franklin, M.J., Shenker, S., Stoica, I.: Spark: cluster computing with working sets. In: Proceedings of the 2nd USENIX Conference on Hot Topics in Cloud Computing, HotCloud 2010, p. 10. USENIX Association, Berkeley, CA, USA (2010). http://dl.acm.org/citation.cfm?id=1863103.1863113

Optimization of Timed Scenarios

Neda Saeedloei[1(✉)] and Feliks Kluźniak[2]

[1] Towson University, Towson, USA
nsaeedloei@towson.edu
[2] LogicBlox, Atlanta, Georgia
feliks.kluzniak@logicblox.com

Abstract. Given a consistent timed scenario, we use its stable distance table, which is a canonical representation for the entire class of equivalent scenarios, to optimise a scenario. We present a general algorithm that can be combined with different heuristics in order to achieve different optimisation goals. In the limited setting of scenarios this algorithm is stronger than the DBM reduction technique.

1   Introduction

Using scenarios for specification and implementation of complex systems, including real time systems, has been an active area of research for several decades [1,5,6,8,15,16]. Synthesis of formal models of systems from scenarios (including scenarios with time) has also been studied in the past [5,8,15,16], and recently there has been renewed interest in this area [4,9,12].

Our own foray into the field [13] was guided by very specific goals. We wanted to develop, from first principles, a notation for scenarios that would be quite formal, but as simple as possible: simple enough to be used by, say, domain experts with little or no training in formal models. We wanted to use such scenarios to automatically synthesize formal models in the form of timed automata with reasonably few resources [3].

One result was a canonical representation (a "stable distance table") for the entire class of scenarios that are equivalent to the given one. This allowed us to *optimise*[1] a scenario by replacing it with an equivalent one, whose properties are more desirable (especially for synthesizing a timed automaton).

In particular, given a distance table corresponding to a scenario we were able to minimize the maximum constant in the scenario. Our optimization algorithm was simple and effective, but we did not have much control over—or insight into—how it works. Moreover, its results were not entirely satisfactory, as it often generated some redundant constraints.

In this paper we examine the question of optimisation in greater depth. We develop a general algorithm that—together with some specific strategies—minimises the maximum constant, but also tends to decrease the other constants,

---

[1] We use "optimisation" as it is used in the field of compiler theory, i.e., "improvement" that does not necessarily lead to a result that is strictly optimal in some sense.

© Springer Nature Switzerland AG 2020
G. Carvalho and V. Stolz (Eds.): SBMF 2020, LNCS 12475, pp. 119–136, 2020.
https://doi.org/10.1007/978-3-030-63882-5_8

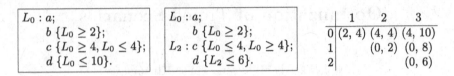

Fig. 1. Two equivalent scenarios and their stable distance table

as well as the number of clocks that would be needed after converting a scenario to a timed automaton.

As noted in the cited work [13], our stable distance table, though derived in a very different fashion, turned out to be in some ways essentially equivalent to Dill's Difference Bounds Matrices (DBMs) [7]. However, when applied to the particular case of scenarios, the constraint reduction technique developed for DBMs [10] is weaker than the new optimisation algorithm presented here, which is developed directly from our method of stabilising a distance table.

2   A General, Flexible Optimisation Algorithm

2.1   Preliminaries

(This subsection briefly recounts our earlier work [13].)

Let Σ be a finite set of symbols called *events*. A *behaviour*[2] over Σ is a sequence $(e_0, t_0)(e_1, t_1)(e_2, t_2) \ldots$, such that $e_i \in \Sigma$, $t_i \in \mathbb{R}^{\geq 0}$ and $t_{i-1} \leq t_i$ for $i \in \{1, 2 \ldots\}$. In this paper we will consider mostly finite behaviours.

For a behaviour $\mathcal{B} = (e_0, t_0)(e_1, t_1) \ldots (e_{n-1}, t_{n-1})$ of length n, and for any $0 \leq i < j < n$, we use $t_{ij}^{\mathcal{B}}$ to denote the *distance*, in time units, of event j from event i in $\mathcal{B}$. That is, $t_{ij}^{\mathcal{B}} = t_j - t_i$.

Given a natural number n, we use $\Phi(n)$ to denote the set of *constraints* of the form $d \sim c$, where $\sim \in \{\leq, \geq\}$[3] and c is a constant in the set of rational numbers, $\mathbb{Q}$. d is the symbol $\tau_{i,j}$, for some integers $0 \leq i < j < n$.

A *timed scenario* of length $n \in \mathbb{N}$ over Σ is a pair $(\mathcal{E}, \mathcal{C})$, where $\mathcal{E} = e_0 e_1 \ldots e_{n-1}$ is a sequence of events, and $\mathcal{C} \subset \Phi(n)$ is a finite set of constraints. We will use $events(\xi)$ to denote $\mathcal{E}$ and $constraints(\xi)$ to denote $\mathcal{C}$.

In the remainder of the paper we will use the term "scenarios" instead of "timed scenarios". A scenario will be written as a sequence of events, separated by semicolons and terminated by a period. If the scenario contains a constraint such as $\tau_{i,j} \leq c$, then event i in the sequence will be labelled by a unique symbol L_i, and event j will be annotated with a set of constraints that contains $L_i \leq c$.

The second scenario in Fig. 1 is $(abcd, \{\tau_{0,1} \geq 2, \tau_{0,2} \leq 4, \tau_{0,2} \geq 4, \tau_{2,3} \leq 6\})$.

A behaviour $\mathcal{B} = (e_0, t_0)(e_1, t_1) \ldots (e_{n-1}, t_{n-1})$ over Σ is *allowed* by scenario ξ iff $events(\xi) = e_0 \ldots e_{n-1}$ and every $\tau_{i,j} \sim c$ in $constraints(\xi)$ evaluates to true after $\tau_{i,j}$ is replaced by $t_{ij}^{\mathcal{B}}$.

---

[2] The notion of "behaviour" is equivalent to that of Alur's "timed word".

[3] To keep the presentation compact, we do not allow sharp inequalities [13]. Equality is expressed in terms of $\leq$ and $\geq$.

L_0 : a;
L_1 : b $\{L_0 \leq 1\}$;
L_2 : c $\{L_1 \leq 5\}$;
L_3 : d $\{L_1 \leq 4, L_2 \geq 2\}$;
    e $\{L_1 \leq 11, L_2 \geq 4,$
        $L_3 \leq 4\}.$

	1	2	3	4		1	2	3	4
0	(0, 1)	(0, ∞)	(0, ∞)	(0, ∞)	0	(0, 1)	(0, 3)	(2, 5)	(4, 9)
1		(0, 5)	(0, 4)	(0, 11)	1		(0, 2)	(2, 4)	(4, 8)
2			(2, ∞)	(4, ∞)	2			(2, 4)	(4, 8)
3				(0, 4)	3				(0, 4)

Fig. 2. A scenario, its distance table and the stable version of the table

The constraints $\tau_{i,j} \geq 0$ and $\tau_{i,j} \leq \infty$, which always evaluate to true after we replace them with some t_{ij}, will be called *default constraints*.

The *semantics* of scenario ξ, denoted by $[\![\xi]\!]$, is the set of behaviours that are allowed by ξ. Let η be the second scenario in Fig. 1, then $[\![\eta]\!] = \{(a, t_0)(b, t_1)(c, t_2)(d, t_3) \mid t_3 \geq t_2 \geq t_1 \geq t_0 \wedge t_1 - t_0 \geq 2 \wedge t_2 - t_0 \leq 4 \wedge t_2 - t_0 \geq 4 \wedge t_3 - t_2 \leq 6\}$.

A scenario ξ is *consistent* iff $[\![\xi]\!] \neq \emptyset$. It is *inconsistent* iff $[\![\xi]\!] = \emptyset$.

For a consistent scenario ξ of length n, and for $0 \leq i < j < n$, we define $m_{ij}^\xi = min\{t_{ij}^\mathcal{B} \mid \mathcal{B} \in [\![\xi]\!]\}$ and $M_{ij}^\xi = max\{t_{ij}^\mathcal{B} \mid \mathcal{B} \in [\![\xi]\!]\}$. The absence of an upper bound for some i and j will be denoted by $M_{ij}^\xi = \infty$. We will often write just m_{ij} and M_{ij} when ξ is understood.

Obviously, for any behaviour in $[\![\xi]\!]$, $0 \leq m_{ij} \leq t_{ij} \leq M_{ij} \leq \infty$.

For a consistent scenario ξ of length n, and for any $0 \leq i < j < k < n$ the following inequations hold:

$$m_{ij} + m_{jk} \leq m_{ik} \leq \left\{ \begin{array}{l} m_{ij} + M_{jk} \\ M_{ij} + m_{jk} \end{array} \right\} \leq M_{ik} \leq M_{ij} + M_{jk} \qquad (1)$$

Let $\xi = (\mathcal{E}, \mathcal{C})$ be a scenario of length n, such that, for any $0 \leq i < j < n$, $\mathcal{C}$ contains at most one constraint of the form $\tau_{i,j} \geq c$ and at most one of the form $\tau_{i,j} \leq c$. A *distance table* for ξ is a representation of $\mathcal{C}$ in the form of a triangular matrix $\mathcal{D}^\xi$. For $0 \leq i < j < n$, $\mathcal{D}_{ij}^\xi = (l_{ij}, h_{ij})$, where l_{ij} and h_{ij} are rational numbers. If $\tau_{i,j} \geq c \in \mathcal{C}$ then $l_{ij} = c$, otherwise $l_{ij} = 0$; if $\tau_{i,j} \leq c \in \mathcal{C}$ then $h_{ij} = c$, otherwise $h_{ij} = \infty$. (See the example in Fig. 2.)

A distance table of size n is *valid* iff $l_{ij} \leq h_{ij}$, for all $0 \leq i < j < n$. A table that is not valid is *invalid*. If $\mathcal{D}^\xi$ is invalid, then ξ is obviously inconsistent.

A distance table of size n is *stable* iff, for all $0 \leq i < j < k < n$,

$$l_{ij} + l_{jk} \leq l_{ik} \leq \left\{ \begin{array}{l} l_{ij} + h_{jk} \\ h_{ij} + l_{jk} \end{array} \right\} \leq h_{ik} \leq h_{ij} + h_{jk} \qquad (1')$$

If $\mathcal{D}^\xi$ is stable then ξ is consistent.

To determine whether a scenario ξ is consistent, we attempt to *stabilise* $\mathcal{D}^\xi$ by repeatedly applying the following six rules until the table becomes either invalid or stable. We assume that $0 \leq i < j < k < n$.

$$l_{ij} + l_{jk} > l_{ik} \longrightarrow l_{ik} := l_{ij} + l_{jk} \tag{R1}$$

$$l_{ik} > l_{ij} + h_{jk} \longrightarrow l_{ij} := l_{ik} - h_{jk} \tag{R2}$$

$$l_{ik} > h_{ij} + l_{jk} \longrightarrow l_{jk} := l_{ik} - h_{ij} \tag{R3}$$

$$l_{ij} + h_{jk} > h_{ik} \longrightarrow h_{jk} := h_{ik} - l_{ij} \tag{R4}$$

$$h_{ij} + l_{jk} > h_{ik} \longrightarrow h_{ij} := h_{ik} - l_{jk} \tag{R5}$$

$$h_{ik} > h_{ij} + h_{jk} \longrightarrow h_{ik} := h_{ij} + h_{jk} \tag{R6}$$

If the scenario is consistent, then (1) holds, so application of these rules modifies the set of constraints without changing the semantics.

The right-hand side of Fig. 2 shows the result of stabilising the original distance table (shown in the middle). The right hand side of Fig. 1 shows the stable distance table obtained from the constraints of either of the two scenarios in the figure (which shows that they are equivalent).

2.2   Implied Constraints

Given a scenario $\xi = (\mathcal{E}, \mathcal{C})$, our general objective is to replace $\mathcal{C}$ with an equivalent set of constraints $\mathcal{C}'$, in the sense that if $\xi' = (\mathcal{E}, \mathcal{C}')$, then $[\![\xi]\!] = [\![\xi']\!]$. We normally want $\mathcal{C}'$ to be *minimal*, i.e., such that removing any constraint from $\mathcal{C}'$ would change the semantics of the associated scenario. In general, a minimal set will not be unique, so we might have to apply various strategies in order to obtain the one that is most satisfactory in some respect.

We obtain $\mathcal{C}'$ by identifying those constraints that are "implied" by other constraints (see Definition 2), and either removing them entirely, or replacing them with different ones.

The lynchpin of our approach is the notion of a stable distance table (Sect. 2.1). If $\mathcal{D}_s^\xi$ is stable, $l_{ij} = m_{ij}^\xi$ and $h_{ij} = M_{ij}^\xi$.

Given a scenario ξ with its stable distance table $\mathcal{D}_s^\xi$, we use $\mathcal{C}(\mathcal{D}_s^\xi)$ to denote the set of constraints represented by $\mathcal{D}_s^\xi$. Some of the constraints are generated during the stabilisation: they are, in effect, implied by other constraints, so they can be safely removed without changing the semantics of the scenario.

As an example consider the scenario on the left-hand side of Fig. 1. The max value at row 1, column 3 of the stable distance table, i.e., M_{13}, is 8. Since it was initially ∞, the value 8 must have been obtained during stabilisation of the table. We see that the value can be calculated by applying rule R6:

$8 = h_{13} = h_{12} + h_{23} = 2 + 6$

The constraint $\tau_{1,3} \le 8$ is, in effect, implied by $\tau_{1,2} \le 2$ and $\tau_{2,3} \le 6$. These two are also not present in the original scenario and were derived by R4:

$2 = h_{12} = h_{02} - l_{01} = 4 - 2$ and $6 = h_{23} = h_{03} - l_{02} = 10 - 4$

The constraint in the table, $\tau_{1,3} \le 8$, is thus implied by a conjunction of four of the original constraints: $\tau_{0,2} \le 4$, $\tau_{0,1} \ge 2$, $\tau_{0,3} \le 10$ and $\tau_{0,2} \ge 4$.

We now notice that rule R6 can be used to derive M_{03} as follows:

$10 = h_{03} = h_{02} + h_{23} = 4 + 6$

So, if we replace the original constraint $\tau_{0,3} \le 10$ with $\tau_{2,3} \le 6$, we will obtain an equivalent scenario (shown in the middle of Fig. 1).

Since we are using the word "implied", we should have some kind of transitivity: if c is implied by d and e, and if e is implied by f and g, then c is implied by d and f and g. We have already noticed this phenomenon in the example above.

Definition 1. *Let ξ be a scenario of length n, $\mathcal{D}_s^\xi$ be its stable table, $c \in \mathcal{C}(\mathcal{D}_s^\xi)$, $S \subset \mathcal{C}(\mathcal{D}_s^\xi)$, and $0 \le i < j < k < n$. We say that c is directly implied by S, denoted by $S \rightsquigarrow c$, iff c and S satisfy one of the following six conditions:*

1. $c = \tau_{i,k} \ge u$, $S = \{\tau_{i,j} \ge v, \tau_{j,k} \ge w\}$, *and* $u = v + w$.
2. $c = \tau_{i,j} \ge u$, $S = \{\tau_{i,k} \ge v, \tau_{j,k} \le w\}$, *and* $u = v - w$.
3. $c = \tau_{j,k} \ge u$, $S = \{\tau_{i,k} \ge v, \tau_{i,j} \le w\}$, *and* $u = v - w$.
4. $c = \tau_{j,k} \le u$, $S = \{\tau_{i,k} \le v, \tau_{i,j} \ge w\}$, *and* $u = v - w$.
5. $c = \tau_{i,j} \le u$, $S = \{\tau_{i,k} \le v, \tau_{j,k} \ge w\}$, *and* $u = v - w$.
6. $c = \tau_{i,k} \le u$, $S = \{\tau_{i,j} \le v, \tau_{j,k} \le w\}$, *and* $u = v + w$.

Intuitively, S represents the conjunction of its elements.

Observe the close similarity of these six cases to rules (R1)–(R6).

Definition 2. *Let $\mathcal{D}_s^\xi$ be a stable distance table. $\rightsquigarrow^+ \subset 2^{\mathcal{C}(\mathcal{D}_s^\xi)} \times \mathcal{C}(\mathcal{D}_s^\xi)$ is the smallest relation that satisfies the following two conditions:*

- *If $S \rightsquigarrow c$ then $S \rightsquigarrow^+ c$;*
- *If $S \rightsquigarrow^+ c$ and there is a constraint $d \in S$ such that, for some S', $S' \rightsquigarrow d$ and $c \notin S'$, then $(S \setminus \{d\}) \cup S' \rightsquigarrow^+ c$.*

When $S \rightsquigarrow^+ c$, we say that c is implied *by S.*

It must be stressed that the notions used in Definitions 1 and 2 are relative to a given distance table. Strictly speaking, the symbols $\rightsquigarrow$ and $\rightsquigarrow^+$ ought to be annotated with $\mathcal{D}_s^\xi$, but that would make the notation too heavy.

Observation 1. *If $S \rightsquigarrow^+ c$, then $c \notin S$.*

Proof. A direct consequence of Definition 2. □

2.3   The Notion of Support

Note: In what follows, every set of constraints is assumed to be a subset of the set of constraints described by some given distance table. Implication is understood to be relative to that distance table.

Definition 3. *Let $\mathcal{C}$ be a set of constraints, $c \in \mathcal{C}$ be a non-default constraint, and $S \subset \mathcal{C}$. We say that c is* supported *by S iff $S \rightsquigarrow^+ c$. S is then called a* support *of c. We sometimes say simply that c has a support, when there is no need to specify S.*

From the definition we can see that a support contains at least two elements.

Intuitively, when a constraint c in a set C is supported by some $S \subset C$, then c can be removed from C as long as *all* the members of its support are present in C: the resulting set of constraints will be equivalent to C.

A constraint might have more than one support. For instance, in the set of constraints described by the table generated from the first scenario of Fig. 1, both $\{\tau_{1,2} \leq 2, \tau_{2,3} \leq 6\}$) and $\{\tau_{0,3} \leq 10, \tau_{0,1} \geq 2\}$ are supports for $\tau_{1,3} \leq 8$.

Definition 4. *Given a set C of constraints, we define the direct support relation on C by $DSupp = \{(c, S) \in C \times 2^C \mid S \rightsquigarrow c$ and c is not a default constraint$\}$.*

Definition 5. *Given a set C of constraints, we define the support relation on C by $Supp = \{(c, S) \in C \times 2^C \mid S \rightsquigarrow^+ c$ and c is not a default constraint$\}$.*

Intuitively, *Supp* shows how the various members of C support each other: if $(c, S) \in Supp$, then c is supported by S.

Observation 2. *Let Supp be a support relation on a set C of constraints and (c, S) be a member of Supp. Then $C' = C \setminus \{c\}$ is equivalent to C.*

Proof. If we compute the stable distance table from the constraints in C', c will appear in the table, since it is implied by the members of S, and $S \subset C'$ ($c \notin S$: see Observation 1).   □

We are now ready to present our new optimisation algorithm.

2.4   The General Algorithm

2.4.1   A Bird's Eye View

We are given a stable distance table, $\mathcal{D}_s^\xi$, generated from some scenario ξ. $\mathcal{C}(\mathcal{D}_s^\xi)$ is the set of all the constraints described by the table. Our goal is to find a minimal subset of constraints that is still equivalent to $\mathcal{C}(\mathcal{D}_s^\xi)$. Since there are, in general, many such minimal subsets, we will allow our search to be guided by some strategy that is not a part of the general algorithm.

The algorithm uses two data structures, C and WS. C represents the current set of constraints, and WS ("working support") contains information about whether the constraints are supported.

The three important invariants are:

1. C is equivalent to $\mathcal{C}(\mathcal{D}_s^\xi)$;
2. WS represents a subset of *Supp*, the support relation associated with $\mathcal{D}_s^\xi$;
3. WS represents only those tuples in *Supp* that do not contain constraints from outside C.

Thanks to the second and third invariant, a constraint c that has support in WS can be removed from C without violating the first invariant (Observation 2). The resulting new version of C will not contain c, therefore WS must be updated to restore the third invariant, in a way that does not violate the second invariant.

We remove supported constraints, one by one, until none of the members of C has support in WS: the algorithm then terminates. All the remaining default constraints are then removed from C, so the resulting set is minimal. (We ensure that WS does not "lose" any relevant information from $Supp$: see Sect. 2.4.2.)

Termination is assured, because at each step we remove a constraint from a finite set of constraints. Correctness is ensured by the invariants.

At every step we may have a number of supported constraints. The choice of the one to remove depends on the strategy, which will be designed to achieve some particular objective.

2.4.2   Details

To establish the invariants, we initialise C to $\mathcal{C}(\mathcal{D}_s^\xi)$, and WS to a representation of $DSupp$, the direct support relation associated with $\mathcal{C}(\mathcal{D}_s^\xi)$.

Default constraints of the form $\tau_{i,j} \leq \infty$ never appear in supports, so we immediately remove them from C.

We then proceed with the iteration outlined above.

Whenever we modify C by removing a supported constraint c, we must update WS to restore the third invariant. This is done as follows:

1. For each $(c', S') \in WS$, such that $c \in S'$:
   - remove (c', S') from WS;
   - for each $(c, S) \in WS$, if $c' \notin S$, add $(c', S' \setminus \{c\} \cup S)$ to WS.
2. Remove from WS every tuple whose first element is c.

Notice that the first step above is a partial computation of the transitive closure of implication (see Definition 2).

It should be clear that this method of updating ensures that WS remains within $Supp$ and that we do not lose information about indirect supports in C.

2.4.3   An Example

Consider a set of constraints $C = \{a, b, c, d, e\}$ and let $WS = \{(a, \{b, c\}), (b, \{d, e\}), (b, \{a, d\}), (c, \{e, a\})\}$. Constraint b has a support, so it can be removed from C. After the removal, the support for a must be updated. The new support for a is obtained by replacing b with d and e or with a and d in a's original support, which would seem to yield $(a, \{d, e, c\})$ and $(a, \{a, d, c\})$. However, Definition 5 does not allow $(a, \{a, d, c\})$ to be in the relation, and quite rightly so: a constraint cannot support its own removal. So a will have only one support, namely $\{d, e, c\}$: after the update we have $WS = \{(a, \{d, e, c\}), (c, \{e, a\})\}$. Note that b has disappeared from the set of constraints, i.e., C, and also from WS.

At this point, either a or c can be removed, as both have supports.

If we remove a, then we must update the support for c, since it contains a. This will yield $\{e, d, c\}$. But this is not a valid support for c, as it includes c. So c has now lost its support, and therefore cannot be removed. At this point $C = \{c, d, e\}$ and $WS = \emptyset$.

L_0 : a ;		1	2	3		L_0 : a ;
$b\,\{L_0 \geq 2\}$;	0	(2, 5)	(2, 5)	(2, ∞)		L_1 : $b\,\{L_0 \geq 2, L_0 \leq 5\}$;
$c\,\{L_0 \leq 5\}$;	1		(0, 3)	(0, ∞)		$c\,\{L_0 \leq 5, L_1 \leq 3\}$;
d.	2			(0, ∞)		d.
ξ						η

Fig. 3. A scenario, its stable distance table, and an equivalent scenario

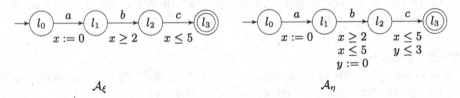

$$\mathcal{A}_\xi \qquad\qquad\qquad \mathcal{A}_\eta$$

Fig. 4. Two equivalent timed automata corresponding to the scenarios of Fig. 3

If we remove c instead of a, we will obtain $C = \{a, d, e\}$ and $WS = \emptyset$. So both $\{c, d, e\}$ and $\{a, d, e\}$ are equivalent to the original set of constraints, i.e., $\{a, b, c, d, e\}$.

2.5 An Application of the Algorithm

Given a collection of scenarios, our ultimate goal is to synthesize a timed automaton [2] whose language would be the set of behaviours allowed by appropriate combinations of the scenarios [14].

For a timed automaton with $|K|$ clocks, the number of clock regions is at most $R = |K|!4^{|K|}\Pi_{x \in K}(\mu_x + 1)$, where μ_x is the maximum constant with which clock x is compared [3]. Verification of a timed automaton can be computationally expensive, and the cost crucially depends on the number of regions of the automaton. Every attempt must be made to keep R as low as possible.

In this section we propose a heuristic that would allow the general algorithm of Sect. 2.4 to keep the value of R as low as possible. (We do not, however, claim that it achieves any strict optimality.)

Definition 6. *Let* $\xi = (\mathcal{E}, \mathcal{C})$ *be a scenario of length n. If* $\mathcal{C}$ *contains a constraint* $\tau_{i,j} \sim a$ *for some* $0 \leq i < j < n$, *then the index i is an* anchor.

An anchor i in ξ corresponds to a referenced label in the external representation of ξ. For example, in scenario η of Fig. 3, i.e., $(abcd, \{\tau_{0,1} \geq 2, \tau_{0,1} \leq 5, \tau_{0,2} \leq 5, \tau_{1,2} \leq 3\})$, the anchors 0 and 1 correspond to labels L_0 and L_1, respectively.

Definition 7. *Let* $\xi = (\mathcal{E}, \mathcal{C})$ *be a scenario of length n and* $0 \leq i < n - 1$ *be an anchor in* ξ. *Let* $0 < j < n$ *be the largest number such that* $\tau_{i,j} \sim a$ *is a constraint in* $\mathcal{C}$. *Then* $[i, j)$ *is the* range *of anchor i.*

Definition 8. *Let ξ be a scenario, and i_1 and i_2 be two anchors with ranges $[i_1, j_1)$ and $[i_2, j_2)$ in ξ. The two ranges overlap iff $i_1 < i_2 < j_1$ or $i_2 < i_1 < j_2$.*

In scenario η of Fig. 3, the range of 0 is $[0, 2)$ and the range of 1 is $[1, 2)$: these are overlapping ranges.

Let ξ be a scenario. By $Anch_\xi$ we denote the set of anchors of ξ. We assume the existence of a set X of clock variables.

Next, we formally define clock allocations for scenarios.[4]

Definition 9. *A clock allocation for ξ is a relation alloc $\subset Anch_\xi \times X$.*

If $(a, x) \in alloc$, then we say *alloc uses* clock x.

Definition 10. *The clock allocation alloc for ξ is complete iff for every anchor $i \in Anch_\xi$ there is a clock $x \in X$ such that $(i, x) \in alloc$.*

For instance, $\{(0, x), (1, y)\}$ is a complete clock allocation for scenario η of Fig. 3.

Definition 11. *A clock allocation alloc for ξ is incorrect iff there exist two different anchors i and j in $Anch_\xi$ whose ranges overlap, such that $(i, x) \in alloc$ and $(j, x) \in alloc$ for some $x \in X$. alloc is correct iff it is not incorrect.*

Intuitively, two overlapping ranges cannot be associated with the same clock. In scenario η of Fig. 3, associating the same clock x with two anchors 0 and 1 would create an incorrect clock allocation. It would, however, be correct to associate the same clock with two anchors 0 and 2 in the scenario in the middle of Fig. 1, since the ranges of the two anchors, $[0, 2)$ and $[2, 3)$, do not overlap.

Definition 12. *A correct and complete clock allocation is optimal if there is no other correct and complete allocation that uses fewer clocks.*

Definition 13. *Let $\xi = (\mathcal{E}, \mathcal{C})$ be a scenario, where $\mathcal{E} = e_0 e_1 \ldots e_{n-1}$. Let alloc be an optimal clock allocation for ξ. The timed automaton corresponding to ξ, $\mathcal{A}_\xi$, is defined as follows:[5]*

- *$\{l_0, l_1, \ldots l_n\}$ is the set of locations of $\mathcal{A}_\xi$. l_0 is the initial location and l_n is the final location;*
- *there is a transition r_i from l_i to l_{i+1}, labeled with e_i, for each $0 \le i < n$;*
- *$K = \{x \mid \exists_{i \in Anch_\xi} (i, x) \in alloc\}$ is the set of clocks of $\mathcal{A}_\xi$;*
- *if $(i, x) \in alloc$, then there is a clock reset $x := 0$ on transition r_i;*
- *if $\tau_{i,j} \sim a$ is a constraint in $\mathcal{C}$ and $(i, x) \in alloc$, then there is a clock constraint $x \sim a$ on transition r_j.*

(Strictly speaking, we should write $\mathcal{A}_\xi^{alloc}$, not $\mathcal{A}_\xi$, but we will be interested only in the number of clocks, not the details arising out of a particular allocation.)

The two automata $\mathcal{A}_\xi$ and $\mathcal{A}_\eta$ of Fig. 4 correspond to scenarios ξ and η of Fig. 3. Notice that $\mathcal{A}_\eta$ has more clocks, because η has redundant constraints.

---

[4] Some of the definitions in the remainder of this subsection are taken from our earlier work [11], and customized for the case of scenarios.

[5] This limited definition suffices for the purposes of this paper. Synthesis of timed automata from more than one scenario is addressed elsewhere [14].

2.5.1   The Specialised Strategy

Given a scenario $\xi = (\mathcal{E}, \mathcal{C})$, our strategy aims at replacing $\mathcal{C}$ with an equivalent set of constraints $\mathcal{C}'$ such that, if $\xi' = (\mathcal{E}, \mathcal{C}')$, then (i) the number of clocks in $\mathcal{A}_{\xi'}$ may be smaller, but is not larger than that in $\mathcal{A}_{\xi}$, (ii) the maximum constants corresponding to the clocks in $\mathcal{A}_{\xi'}$ may be smaller, but are not larger than those in $\mathcal{A}_{\xi}$.

To achieve these goals, we use a particular order for removing supported constraints from the original set of constraints, $\mathcal{C}(\mathcal{D}_s^{\xi})$. Specifically, we divide the processing into two phases. In phase 1 we proceed as follows:

1. We copy the supported constraints to a list L, and sort L so that constraints with larger constants precede those with lower constants.
2. At each step of the general algorithm we find the first constraint c on L such that $(c, \{\tau_{i,j} \leq M_{ij}, \tau_{j,k} \leq M_{jk}\}) \in WS$ or $(c, \{\tau_{i,j} \geq m_{ij}, \tau_{j,k} \geq m_{jk}\}) \in WS$. The constraint c is chosen for removal.

Once L no longer contains constraints that satisfy the condition in pt. 2, we move to phase 2, where we just remove the remaining supported constraints in an arbitrary order.

Phase 1 will remove the largest constants whenever possible. This tends to be beneficial for the number of clocks, as shorter ranges are less likely to overlap. Phase 2 may have a similar effect, as decreasing the number of constraints can decrease the length and/or the number of ranges.

It is easy to see that neither phase 1 nor phase 2 will increase the number of anchors. The number of overlapping ranges is also not increased, and therefore neither is the number of clocks.

As an example, consider the scenario of Fig. 5 along with its stable distance table. Table 1 summarizes the first phase of the algorithm that is run for this scenario. The first two columns show the non-default constraints of the scenario extracted from the distance table and their direct supports, respectively (a blank space signifies lack of support). During phase 1 the algorithm will remove two constraints: $\tau_{0,3} \geq 13$ and $\tau_{1,3} \geq 11$.

When the first constraint is removed, the supports for $\tau_{2,3} \geq 4$ and $\tau_{1,3} \geq 11$ are updated. The updated support for $\tau_{2,3} \geq 4$ is not valid, as it contains the constraint itself. So $\tau_{2,3} \geq 4$ loses its support. As for $\tau_{1,3} \geq 11$, one of its supports is updated: see the third column.

The constraint $\tau_{1,3} \geq 11$ does not appear in any support, so its removal will only delete the associated row from the table.

At the beginning of the second phase, there are only three constraints in WS that have support. Table 2 shows one particular order in which the supported constraints can be considered for removal. Only the removal of $\tau_{1,2} \geq 7$ results in an update in the supports. In particular, $\tau_{0,1} \leq 2$ loses its support and cannot be removed. The minimal set of constraints obtained after the second phase is $\{\tau_{0,2} \geq 9, \tau_{0,2} \leq 9, \tau_{2,3} \geq 4, \tau_{0,1} \leq 2\}$.

The final scenario is shown in Fig. 6. Observe that the automaton corresponding to this scenario requires only one clock whose maximum constant is

$L_0 : a;$
$L_1 : b \{L_0 \leq 2\};$
$L_2 : c \{L_0 \leq 9, L_0 \geq 9,$
$\qquad L_1 \geq 7\};$
$\quad d \{L_1 \geq 11, L_2 \geq 4\}.$

	1	2	3
0	(0, 2)	(9, 9)	(13, ∞)
1		(7, 9)	(11, ∞)
2			(4, ∞)

$L_0 : a;$
$\quad b \{L_0 \leq 2\};$
$L_2 : c \{L_0 \leq 9, L_0 \geq 9\};$
$\quad d \{L_2 \geq 4\}.$

Fig. 5. A scenario and its stable table   **Fig. 6.** An equivalent scenario

Table 1. The first phase of the algorithm for the scenario of Fig. 5

C	$DSupp$	WS after $\tau_{0,3} \geq 13$ is removed	WS after $\tau_{1,3} \geq 11$ is removed
$\tau_{0,3} \geq 13$	$\{\tau_{0,2} \geq 9, \tau_{2,3} \geq 4\}$		
$\tau_{1,3} \geq 11$	$\{\tau_{1,2} \geq 7, \tau_{2,3} \geq 4\},$ $\{\tau_{0,3} \geq 13, \tau_{0,1} \leq 2\}$	$\{\tau_{1,2} \geq 7, \tau_{2,3} \geq 4\},$ $\{\tau_{0,2} \geq 9, \tau_{2,3} \geq 4, \tau_{0,1} \leq 2\}$	
$\tau_{0,2} \geq 9$			
$\tau_{0,2} \leq 9$			
$\tau_{1,2} \leq 9$	$\{\tau_{0,2} \leq 9, \tau_{0,1} \geq 0\}$	$\{\tau_{0,2} \leq 9, \tau_{0,1} \geq 0\}$	$\{\tau_{0,2} \leq 9, \tau_{0,1} \geq 0\}$
$\tau_{1,2} \geq 7$	$\{\tau_{0,2} \geq 9, \tau_{0,1} \leq 2\}$	$\{\tau_{0,2} \geq 9, \tau_{0,1} \leq 2\}$	$\{\tau_{0,2} \geq 9, \tau_{0,1} \leq 2\}$
$\tau_{2,3} \geq 4$	$\{\tau_{0,3} \geq 13, \tau_{0,2} \leq 9\}$	~~$\{\tau_{0,2} \geq 9, \tau_{2,3} \geq 4, \tau_{0,2} \leq 9\}$~~	
$\tau_{0,1} \leq 2$	$\{\tau_{0,2} \leq 9, \tau_{1,2} \geq 7\}$	~~$\{\tau_{0,2} \leq 9, \tau_{1,2} \geq 7\}$~~	$\{\tau_{0,2} \leq 9, \tau_{1,2} \geq 7\}$

Table 2. The second phase of the algorithm for the scenario of Fig. 5

part of C	initial WS at phase 2	WS after $\tau_{1,2} \leq 9$ is removed	WS after $\tau_{1,2} \geq 7$ is removed
$\tau_{1,2} \leq 9$	$\{\tau_{0,2} \leq 9, \tau_{0,1} \geq 0\}$		
$\tau_{1,2} \geq 7$	$\{\tau_{0,2} \geq 9, \tau_{0,1} \leq 2\}$	$\{\tau_{0,2} \geq 9, \tau_{0,1} \leq 2\}$	
$\tau_{0,1} \leq 2$	$\{\tau_{0,2} \leq 9, \tau_{1,2} \geq 7\}$	$\{\tau_{0,2} \leq 9, \tau_{1,2} \geq 7\}$	~~$\{\tau_{0,2} \leq 9, \tau_{0,2} \geq 9, \tau_{0,1} \leq 2\}$~~

9, whereas the original scenario requires two clocks with maximum constants 9 and 11.

2.5.2 Another Refinement

Consider the scenario of Fig. 7 along with its distance table. Observe that $m_{02} = M_{02} = 11$, $m_{01} = 8$ and $M_{12} = 3$. Equations $m_{01} = m_{02} - M_{12}$ and $M_{12} = M_{02} - m_{01}$ both hold. That is, $\{\tau_{0,2} \geq 11, \tau_{1,2} \leq 3\} \rightsquigarrow \tau_{0,1} \geq 8$, and $\{\tau_{0,2} \leq 11, \tau_{0,1} \geq 8\} \rightsquigarrow \tau_{1,2} \leq 3$ (cases 2. and 4. of Definition 1). Figure 8 shows the initial constraints, while the two other diagrams illustrate the two alternatives for removing the implied constraints.

In the middle diagram, which corresponds to the removal of the "left leg", i.e., $\tau_{0,1} \geq 8$, there are two anchors whose ranges overlap. However, in the rightmost

	1	2	3
0	(8, 11)	(11, 11)	(11, 15)
1		(0, 3)	(0, 7)
2			(0, 4)

$L_0 : a;$
$L_1 : b \{L_0 \geq 8\};$
$L_2 : c \{L_0 \leq 11, L_0 \geq 11, L_1 \leq 3\};$
$\quad d \{L_1 \leq 7, L_2 \leq 4\}.$

Fig. 7. A scenario and its stable table

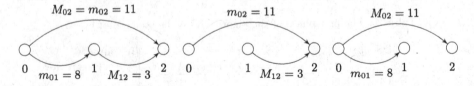

$M_{02} = m_{02} = 11 \qquad\qquad m_{02} = 11 \qquad\qquad M_{02} = 11$

$0 \quad m_{01} = 8 \quad^1 \; M_{12} = 3 \quad^2 \quad 0 \qquad^1 \; M_{12} = 3 \quad^2 \quad 0 \quad m_{01} = 8 \;^1 \qquad 2$

Fig. 8. An illustration of having a choice for removing a constraint

$L_0 : a;$
$L_1 : b;$
$L_2 : c \{L_0 \leq 11, L_0 \geq 11, L_1 \leq 3\};$
$\quad d \{L_2 \leq 4\}.$

$L_0 : a;$
$\quad b \{L_0 \geq 8\};$
$L_2 : c \{L_0 \leq 11, L_0 \geq 11\};$
$\quad d \{L_2 \leq 4\}.$

Fig. 9. Two scenarios equivalent to that of Fig. 7

diagram, which corresponds to the removal of the "right leg", i.e., $\tau_{1,2} \leq 3$, there is only one anchor with range $[0, 2)$. (See also Fig. 9.)

We amend the strategy of Sect. 2.5.1 to always remove the "right leg" of a distance, if possible. This is done by introducing an extra phase between phase 1 and phase 2. During this extra phase we traverse the stabilised distance table. For every $0 \leq i < j < k < n$ such that $m_{ik} = M_{ik}$ we check whether $\tau_{i,k} \geq m_{ik} \in C$ and $\tau_{i,k} \leq M_{ik} \in C$. If this is so, then:

- if $m_{ij} + M_{jk} = M_{ik}$, remove $\tau_{j,k} \leq M_{jk}$ if it is in C and has support in WS;
- if $M_{ij} + m_{jk} = m_{ik}$, remove $\tau_{j,k} \geq m_{jk}$ if it is in C and has support in WS.

It is not too difficult to think of other possible improvements to the heuristics presented here. One can easily experiment with various strategies, as they can affect only the effectiveness, but not the soundness of the general algorithm. This flexibility is an important strength of our method.

2.5.3   A Final Tweak

We judge a scenario by the size of R, i.e., the number of clock regions in the corresponding straight line timed automaton (recall the formula for R at the beginning of Sect. 2.5). If two scenarios are equivalent, the one that is associated with a lower R is "better".

We can now say that a scenario is *optimal* if the associated value of R is minimal for the class of equivalent scenarios.

Our algorithm starts from the complete set of constraints in the stable distance table. While it can be quite effective in improving a scenario (as shown by the examples in this paper), we do not claim that it can achieve strict optimality.

This means that in the class of equivalent scenarios represented by a given stable distance table there may, in principle, exist scenarios that are better than the one found by our algorithm.

If we start with such a scenario, then the result of optimisation may turn out not to be an improvement. In that case we simply retain the original scenario.

3   Comparison with Difference Bounds Matrices

Difference Bounds Matrices (DBMs) have been developed by Dill [7] as an efficient technique for representing clock zones in the context of verification of timed automata. A clock zone is a set of constraints that put bounds either on the values of a set of clocks, or on the differences between such values. Each constraint is of the form $c_i - c_j \sim C$, where $\sim \in \{<, \leq\}$ and C is a constant.[6] The constraint is represented by the pair $(C, \sim)$ in the (i, j)-th entry of a square matrix (the DBM). If there is no constraint, $C = \infty$.

A pair with a smaller constant represents a tighter constraint, so tightening up all the constraints (explicit or implied) can be carried out by treating the DBM as an adjacency matrix of a graph, and applying the Floyd-Warshall algorithm to compute the shortest path between any two nodes. If the result is such that, for some i and j, $c_i - c_j \leq a$, $c_j - c_i \leq -b$ and $a < b$, then the DBM is inconsistent. Otherwise the result is a *canonicalised* DBM, which is a canonical representation of all equivalent sets of constraints.

As mentioned in Sect. 2.5, given a scenario ξ, one can construct a timed automaton A_ξ whose language is equivalent to $[\![\xi]\!]$. If we make sure that every transition of A_ξ (including the last transition) is annotated with a new clock reset, then the DBM that corresponds to the final zone of the augmented A_ξ will contain information that is equivalent to the stable distance table for ξ.

For instance, consider ξ of Fig. 10. Assume A'_ξ is the automaton obtained by annotating transitions labeled with c and e in A_ξ with two new clock resets $c_2 := 0$ and $c_4 := 0$, respectively (A_ξ and A'_ξ are not shown here). Figure 10 shows the stable distance table of ξ and the DBM that represents the final zone of A'_ξ (we omit information about the operators, because we do not consider sharp inequalities).

It is tempting to take advantage of various techniques for DBMs and apply them to scenarios. The technique that is most relevant to our work is the method of removing redundant constraints from a DBM [10]. However, this method is quite different from ours and may result in different outcomes.

If the graph that corresponds to a canonical DBM contains zero cycles (i.e., cycles in which the sum of the weights of edges is zero), then it is converted to a

---

[6] A constraint such as $m \leq c_i - c_j < M$ is equivalent to two such simple constraints: $c_i - c_j < M$ and $c_j - c_i \leq -m$. A constraint of the form $c_i \sim C$ is represented as $c_i - c_{zero} \sim C$, where c_{zero} is a hypothetical clock whose value is always zero.

$L_0 : a;$
$L_1 : b;$
$\quad c\ \{L_0 \le 1\};$
$L_3 : d;$
$\quad e\ \{L_1 \ge 4, L_3 \le 2\}.$

	1	2	3	4
0	$(0,1)$	$(0,1)$	$(2,\infty)$	$(4,\infty)$
1		$(0,1)$	$(2,\infty)$	$(4,\infty)$
2			$(1,\infty)$	$(3,\infty)$
3				$(0,2)$

	c_0	c_1	c_2	c_3	c_4
c_0	0	1	1	∞	∞
c_1	0	0	1	∞	∞
c_2	0	0	0	∞	∞
c_3	-2	-2	-1	0	2
c_4	-4	-4	-3	0	0

Fig. 10. Scenario ξ, its stable distance table and the final DBM of A_ξ (with c_2 and c_4)

supergraph that contains no such cycles. The nodes are divided into equivalence classes: if two nodes appear in the same zero cycle, then they belong to the same equivalence class. The equivalence classes are the nodes of the supergraph.

In the supergraph there is an edge of weight w between two equivalence classes if in the original graph there is an edge of weight w between nodes that are chosen to be representatives of these equivalence classes.

Once the supergraph is obtained, it is subjected to a reduction procedure: if $w_{ij} + w_{jk} \le w_{ik}$, then the edge between nodes i and k can be removed (since an edge of weight at most $w_{ij} + w_{jk}$ would be restored between i and k during subsequent canonicalisation of the main graph). The edges that remain in the reduced supergraph represent a minimal set of constraints equivalent to the original constraints in the supergraph. The reduced version of the original graph is obtained by deleting all the original edges, adding those edges between representatives that remain in the reduced supergraph, and then, for each equivalence class, adding the edges of a zero cycle that connects the constituent nodes.

The representative of an equivalence class is selected arbitrarily (e.g., by choosing the node with the lowest number), so the supergraph that corresponds to a given DBM is not uniquely determined by the original set of constraints represented by the DBM. If there is more than one zero cycle between the nodes in an equivalence class, then the choice of edge upon restoration is also arbitrary. Therefore the final (reduced) set of constraints is not uniquely determined.

As an example consider the scenario and the table of Fig. 7 once more. The DBM, its graph representation and one possible supergraph are shown in Fig. 11. Observe that c_0 and c_2 belong to the same equivalence class and that c_2 is chosen as the representative of this class. Reduction of the supergraph results in removing the edges between c_1 and c_3 (because $3 + 4 \le 7$ and $0 + 0 \le 0$). The final reduced graph is shown in Fig. 12. The set of constraints represented by this graph is equivalent to the set obtained by our method, shown on the left-hand side of Fig. 9 (our best solution is on the right-hand side).

However, if we choose c_0 as the representative of $\{c_0, c_2\}$, then we obtain another supergraph, shown on the left-hand side of Fig. 13. Here, too, reduction eliminates the edges between c_1 and c_3 (because $-8 + 15 \le 7$ and $-11 + 11 \le 0$): the final reduced graph is shown on the right-hand side. The set of constraints represented by this graph is shown in the scenario of Fig. 14. Observe that the number of constraints is the same as in the original scenario (shown in Fig. 7); moreover, the maximum constant has increased from 11 to 15.

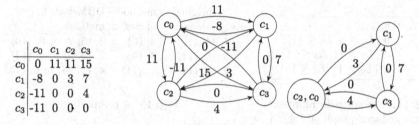

	c_0	c_1	c_2	c_3
c_0	0	11	11	15
c_1	-8	0	3	7
c_2	-11	0	0	4
c_3	-11	0	0	0

Fig. 11. The DBM equivalent to the table of Fig. 7, its graph and one of its supergraphs

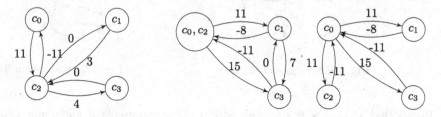

Fig. 12. The reduced graph for the supergraph of Fig. 11   **Fig. 13.** Another supergraph for the graph of Fig. 11 and its corresponding reduced graph

Figure 15 compares the results obtained by our optimisation method of Sect. 2 with the graph-based minimization method [10] for DBMs on some of the scenarios presented in this paper. For instance, the comparison for the scenario of Fig. 7, shown in the third row of the table, is interpreted as follows: the original scenario has 6 constraints and the required number of clocks for replacing the labels is two, with maximum constants 11 and 7. The scenario obtained by our method, shown on the right-hand side of Fig. 9, has 4 constraints, and requires one clock, say x, where $\mu_x = 11$. The graph-based approach can generate a scenario with 4 constraints which requires two clocks, say x and y, where $\mu_x = 11$ and $\mu_y = 3$. It can also generate another equivalent scenario with 6 constraints where only one clock with maximum 15 would be required.

For all the other examples in this paper the results obtained by the two methods were the same. Notice that our technique is not worse also in the reduction of the number of constraints, even though that was not our goal.

Observation 3. *If a canonicalised DBM represents the constraints of a scenario, and the corresponding graph does not contain zero cycles, then the reduction procedure [10] is equivalent to the optimisation algorithm of Sect. 2.*

Proof. Let G be the graph corresponding to the canonicalized DBM. Let a, b and c be three nodes, and $a \to b$, $b \to c$ and $a \to c$ three edges in G, such that $a \to c$ is removed during the reduction procedure (see Fig. 17). Since G is in closed form (it corresponds to a canonicalized DBM), we must have

$$w_{ab} + w_{bc} = w_{ac} \qquad (2)$$

$L_0:\ a;$
$\quad b\ \{L_0 \geq 8, L_0 \leq 11\};$
$\quad c\ \{L_0 \geq 11, L_0 \leq 11\};$
$\quad d\ \{L_0 \geq 11, L_0 \leq 15\}.$

Fig.	original scenario	method of Sec. 2	DBM-based method
1	4, (10)	4, (6)	4, (6, 2) or 6, (10)
5	6, (11, 9)	4, (9)	5, (9, 9) or 4, (13)
7	6, (11, 7)	4, (11)	4, (11, 3) or 6, (15)

Fig. 14. The scenario represented by the reduced graph of Fig. 13

Fig. 15. A comparison

	w_{ab}	w_{bc}	w_{ac}			w_{ab}	w_{bc}	w_{ac}
1.	−	−	−		4.	−	+	+
2.	−	+	−		5.	+	−	+
3.	+	−	−		6.	+	+	+

Fig. 16. Six cases of Eq. 2

$a \qquad b \qquad c$

Fig. 17. Observation 3

Recall that if $w_{xy} > 0$ then the edge $x \to y$ represents a maximum in the corresponding distance table, i.e., M_{xy}, and if $w_{xy} < 0$ the edge represents $-m_{yx}$.

Since the weights of edges can be positive or negative, there are six possible cases for Eq. 2, which are summarized in Fig. 16.

We consider one case, where w_{ab} and w_{ac} are negative and w_{bc} is positive (case 2 in Fig. 16). Then Eq. 2 becomes $-m_{ba} + M_{bc} = -m_{ca}$.

This implies that the events are ordered as follows: b, c, a.

Let $i = b$, $j = c$ and $k = a$. Then $-m_{ik} + M_{ij} = -m_{jk}$. That is, $m_{jk} = m_{ik} - M_{ij}$. This corresponds to pt. 3. of Definition 1. So the constraint corresponding to m_{jk}, represented by edge $a \to c$ in G, is removed by our optimization method.

The other five cases of Fig. 16 correspond to the remaining five cases of Definition 1. We omit the details, which are very similar. □

Observation 4. *If a DBM represents the constraints of a scenario, then the optimisation algorithm of Sect. 2 is stronger than the reduction procedure.*

Proof. If there are no zero cycles, the reduction procedure removes the same constraints as our algorithm (Observation 3).

In the presence of zero cycles the reduction procedure is applied to a supergraph. The set of edges in the supergraph is a subset of the set of edges of the original graph, and the set of removed edges is a subset of those that would have been removed from the original graph if it were modified by breaking the zero cycles. So reduction cannot remove constraints that would not have been removed by our method (Observation 3).

The examples above (Fig. 15) show that our algorithm sometimes removes more constraints than the DBM reduction technique. □

Intuitively, the strength of our approach arises from the fact that, thanks to our explicit maintenance of supports, we can make good use of equality constraints (i.e., such that $m_{ij} = M_{ij}$). Equality constraints correspond to zero cycles, and the reduction technique sidesteps those by creating the supergraph.

It must be stressed that the above observations apply only to the limited setting of scenarios. The DBM reduction technique [10] is, of course, applicable to more general settings, in which our techniques would not be useful.

4 Conclusions

We have previously developed a notion of timed scenarios and their semantics [13]. The semantics of a scenario is defined in terms of the set of behaviours that are allowed by the scenario. We also developed a method for checking the consistency of scenarios. Our consistency check was a simple byproduct of the construction of a "stable distance table". The particular value of our method of stabilising a distance table lies in the fact that it provides a natural stepping-stone towards interesting optimisations.

In the current paper we present a general algorithm that can reliably optimise scenarios according to different strategies, intended to achieve different goals: we illustrate this by specifying strategies that minimise the maximum constant, but also tend to decrease the other constants, as well as the number of clocks that would be needed after converting a scenario to a timed automaton. It turns out that in the case of scenarios these optimisations perform better than the DBM reduction technique [10] even at the task of reducing the number of constraints.

References

1. Akshay, S., Mukund, M., Kumar, K.N.: Checking Coverage for Infinite Collections of Timed Scenarios. In: Caires, L., Vasconcelos, V.T. (eds.) CONCUR 2007. LNCS, vol. 4703, pp. 181–196. Springer, Heidelberg (2007). https://doi.org/10.1007/978-3-540-74407-8_13
2. Alur, R., Henzinger, T.A.: A really temporal logic. J. ACM 41(1), 181–203 (1994)
3. Alur, R., Madhusudan, P.: Decision problems for timed automata: a survey. In: Bernardo, M., Corradini, F. (eds.) SFM-RT 2004. LNCS, vol. 3185, pp. 1–24. Springer, Heidelberg (2004). https://doi.org/10.1007/978-3-540-30080-9_1
4. Alur, R., Martin, M., Raghothaman, M., Stergiou, C., Tripakis, S., Udupa, A.: Synthesizing finite-state protocols from scenarios and requirements. In: Yahav, E. (ed.) HVC 2014. LNCS, vol. 8855, pp. 75–91. Springer, Cham (2014). https://doi.org/10.1007/978-3-319-13338-6_7
5. Bollig, B., Katoen, J.-P., Kern, C., Leucker, M.: Replaying play in and play out: synthesis of design models from scenarios by learning. In: Grumberg, O., Huth, M. (eds.) TACAS 2007. LNCS, vol. 4424, pp. 435–450. Springer, Heidelberg (2007). https://doi.org/10.1007/978-3-540-71209-1_33
6. Chandrasekaran, P., Mukund, M.: Matching scenarios with timing constraints. In: Asarin, E., Bouyer, P. (eds.) FORMATS 2006. LNCS, vol. 4202, pp. 98–112. Springer, Heidelberg (2006). https://doi.org/10.1007/11867340_8
7. Dill, D.L.: Timing assumptions and verification of finite-state concurrent systems. In: Sifakis, J. (ed.) CAV 1989. LNCS, vol. 407, pp. 197–212. Springer, Heidelberg (1990). https://doi.org/10.1007/3-540-52148-8_17

8. Harel, D., Kugler, H., Pnueli, A.: Synthesis revisited: generating statechart models from scenario-based requirements. In: Kreowski, H.-J., Montanari, U., Orejas, F., Rozenberg, G., Taentzer, G. (eds.) Formal Methods in Software and Systems Modeling. LNCS, vol. 3393, pp. 309–324. Springer, Heidelberg (2005). https://doi.org/10.1007/978-3-540-31847-7_18

9. Heitmeyer, C.L., et al.: Building high assurance human-centric decision systems. Autom. Softw. Eng. **22**(2), 159–197 (2014). https://doi.org/10.1007/s10515-014-0157-z

10. Larsen, K.G., Larsson, F., Pettersson, P., Yi, W.: Efficient verification of real-time systems: compact data structure and state-space reduction. In: 18th IEEE Real-Time Systems Symposium, pp. 14–24, December 1997

11. Saeedloei, N., Kluźniak, F.: Clock allocation in timed automata and graph colouring. In: Proceedings of the 21st International Conference on Hybrid Systems: computation and Control (part of CPS Week), HSCC, pp. 71–80 (2018)

12. Saeedloei, N., Kluźniak, F.: From scenarios to timed automata. In: Formal Methods: Foundations and Applications - 20th Brazilian Symposium, SBMF, Proceedings. pp. 33–51 (2017)

13. Saeedloei, N., Kluźniak, F.: Timed scenarios: consistency, equivalence and optimization. In: Formal Methods: Foundations and Applications - 21st Brazilian Symposium, SBMF, Proceedings, pp. 215–233 (2018)

14. Saeedloei, N., Kluźniak, F.: Synthesizing clock-efficient timed automata. In: Integrated Formal Methods - 16th International Conference, iFM 2020, Proceedings (2020), (To appear)

15. Somé, S., Dssouli, R., Vaucher, J.: From scenarios to timed automata: building specifications from users requirements. In: Proceedings of the Second Asia Pacific Software Engineering Conference, APSEC 1995, pp. 48–57. IEEE Computer Society (1995)

16. Uchitel, S., Kramer, J., Magee, J.: Synthesis of behavioral models from scenarios. IEEE Trans. Softw. Eng. **29**(2), 99–115 (2003)

Reversal Fuzzy Switch Graphs

Suene Campos[1,2], Regivan Santiago[2(✉)] [iD], Manuel A. Martins[3] [iD],
and Daniel Figueiredo[3]

[1] Centro de Ciências Exatas e Naturais, Universidade Federal Rural do Semi-Árido,
Mossoró, Brazil
suenecampos@ufersa.edu.br
[2] Departamento de Informática e Matemática Aplicada, Universidade Federal do Rio
Grande do Norte, Natal, Brazil
regivan@dimap.ufrn.br
[3] CIDMA & Departamento de Matemática, Universidade de Aveiro, Aveiro, Portugal
{martins,daniel.figueiredo}@ua.pt

Abstract. Fuzzy Switch Graphs (FSG) generalize the notion of Fuzzy
Graphs by adding high-order arrows and aggregation functions which
update the fuzzy values of arrows whenever a zero-order arrow is crossed.
In this paper, we propose a more general structure called Reversal Fuzzy
Switch Graph ($RFSG$), which promotes other actions in addition to
updating the fuzzy values of the arrows, namely: activation and deactivation of the arrows. $RFSG$s are able to model dynamical aspects of
some systems which generally appear in engineering, computer science
and some other fields. The paper also provides a logic to verify properties
of the modelled system and closes with an application.

Keywords: Reversal Fuzzy Switch Graphs · Reversal Fuzzy Reactive
Graphs · Fuzzy Switch Graphs · Fuzzy systems · Reactive systems

1 Introduction

Reactive graphs are structures whose the relations change when we move along
the graph. This concept has been introduced by Dov Gabbay in 2004 (see [7,8])
and generalizes the static notion of a graph by incorporating high-order edges
(called high-order arrows or switches). Graphs with these characteristics are
called *Switch Graphs*.

In [13], Santiago et al. introduce the notion of *Fuzzy Switchs Graphs* (FSGs).
These graphs are able to model reactive systems endowed with fuzziness and
extend the notion of fuzzy graphs, in the sense that crossing an edge (zero-order
arrow) induces an update of the system using high-order arrows and aggregation
functions. For systems which require different aggregations for updating different
arrows, Santiago et al. [13] introduced the *Fuzzy Reactive Graphs* (FRGs).

FSGs and FRGs, however, are not sufficient to model systems in which
other edges of the system are activated or deactivated when one edge is crossing. To incorporate this, we propose the notion of *Reversal Fuzzy Switch Graphs*

G. Carvalho and V. Stolz (Eds.): SBMF 2020, LNCS 12475, pp. 137–154, 2020.
https://doi.org/10.1007/978-3-030-63882-5_9

(*RFSGs*). We also introduce the cartesian product of *RFSGs* and a logic to verify properties of such structures. We close this paper by showing an application of *RFSGs*.

The paper is organized as follows: Sect. 2 presents some basic concepts. Section 3 introduces the notion of *RFSGs*, how they can be used to model the reactivity of some fuzzy systems and presents some algebraic operations. Section 4 provides a logic for *RFSGs*. Section 5 shows how *RFSGs* can be used to model a dynamic control system. Finally, Sect. 6 provides some final remarks.

2   Preliminaries

In this section we recall some concepts and results found in the literature in order to make this paper self-contained. We assume that the reader has some basic knowledge in fuzzy set theory.

Definition 1 ([10]). *A **fuzzy set** A, defined on a non-empty set X, is characterized by a **membership function** $\varphi_A : X \to [0,1]$. The value $\varphi_A(x) \in [0,1]$ measures the degree of membership of x in the set A.*

Definition 2 (Fuzzy Graphs [10]). *A **fuzzy graph** is a structure $\langle V, R \rangle$, such that V is a non-empty set called **set of vertices** and R is a fuzzy set $R : V \times V \to [0,1]$.*

For simplicity, we assume the set of vertices is a crisp set, in contrast to what is defined as a fuzzy graph in [10]. The Fig. 1(a) shows a fuzzy graph.

Dov Gabbay [2] provided graphs with high-order arrows in order to model reactive behaviors. This kind of graphs is defined as follows.

Definition 3 (Switch Graphs [2,6]). *A **switch graph** is a pair $\langle W, R \rangle$ s.t. W is a non-empty set (set of **worlds**) and $R \subseteq A(W)$ is a set of arrows, called **switches** or **high-order arrows**, where $A(W) = \bigcup_{i \in \mathbb{N}} A_i(W)$ with*

$$\begin{cases} A_0(W) = W \times W \\ A_{i+1}(W) = A_0(W) \times A_i(W) \end{cases} \tag{1}$$

Fuzzy Switch Graphs were introduced by Santiago et al. in [13].

Definition 4 (Fuzzy Switch Graphs [13]). *Let W be a non-empty finite set (set of **states** or **worlds**) and the set $S = \bigcup_{n \in \mathbb{N}} S^n$ where,*

$$\begin{cases} S^0 \subseteq W \times W \\ S^{n+1} \subseteq S^0 \times S^n \end{cases} \tag{2}$$

*A **fuzzy switch graph (FSG)** is a pair $M = \langle W, \varphi : S \to [0,1] \rangle$, where φ is a fuzzy subset of S. The elements $a_i^0 \in S^0 (i \in \mathbb{N})$ are called **zero-order arrows**. The elements of S^{n+1} are called **high-order arrows**.*

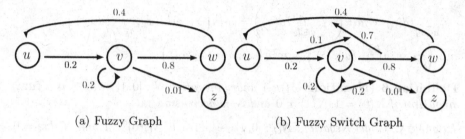

(a) Fuzzy Graph   (b) Fuzzy Switch Graph

Fig. 1. Santiago et al. (2020) [13].

Example 1. The Fig. 1 shows a fuzzy graph and a fuzzy switch graph.

Fuzzy Logic provides many proposals for logical connectives. In what follows we review the notions of fuzzy conjunctions, disjunctions, implications and negations. The first two are generalized by t-norms and t-conorms, respectively [9].

Definition 5 (t-norms and t-conorms). *A **uninorm** function is a bivariate function* $U : [0,1] \times [0,1] \to [0,1]$*, that is isotonic, commutative, associative with a neutral element* $e \in [0,1]$*. If* $e = 1$*, then* U *is called **t-norm** and if* $e = 0$*, then* U *is called **t-conorm**.*

Example 2. The functions $T_G(x,y) = min(x,y)$ and $T_L(x,y) = max(x + y - 1, 0)$ (*Łukasiewicz*) are t-norms. The functions $S_G(x,y) = max(x,y)$ and $S_L(x,y) = min(x+y,1)$ (*Łukasiewicz*) are t-conorms.

Notation: Let T be a t-norm, $f : [0,1] \to [0,1]$ and J_n a finite subset of $[0,1]$ with n elements ($J_0 = \emptyset$). We define $\underset{a \in J_n}{T}$ in this way,

$$\underset{a \in J_n}{T} f(a) = \begin{cases} 1, & \text{case } n = 0; \\ f(a), & \text{case } n = 1; \\ T\big(f(x), \underset{a \in J_m}{T} f(a)\big), & \text{case } n > 1, x \in J_n \text{ and } J_m = J_n \backslash \{x\}. \end{cases} \tag{3}$$

Similarly, for S t-conorm, we define $\underset{a \in J_n}{S}$ s.t.

$$\underset{a \in J_n}{S} f(a) = \begin{cases} 0, & \text{case } n = 0; \\ f(a), & \text{case } n = 1; \\ S\big(f(x), \underset{a \in J_m}{S} f(a)\big), & \text{case } n > 1, x \in J_n \text{ and } J_m = J_n \backslash \{x\}. \end{cases} \tag{4}$$

Note that, since T and S are commutative and associative, $\underset{a \in J_m}{T}$ and $\underset{a \in J_m}{S}$ are well defined. That is, it does not depend on the way we choice $x \in J_n$ to make $J_n = \{x\} \cup J_m$.

Example 3. Given the t-norm $T(x,y) = min(x,y)$, the identity function $Id : [0,1] \to [0,1]$ and the set $J_3 = \{x_1, x_2, x_3\} \subset [0,1]$, we have:

$$\underset{a \in J_3}{T} Id(a) = min\Big(x_1, \underset{a \in J_2}{T} Id(a)\Big) = min\Big(x_1, min\big(x_2, \underset{a \in J_1}{T} Id(a)\big)\Big) =$$
$$min\Big(x_1, min\big(x_2, Id(x_3)\big)\Big) = min\Big(x_1, min\big(x_2, x_3\big)\Big).$$

Definition 6 (Negations [1]). *A unary operation* $N : [0,1] \to [0,1]$ *is a* **fuzzy negation** *if* $N(0) = 1, N(1) = 0$ *and* N *is decreasing.*

Example 4. *Gödel Negation:* $N_G : [0,1] \to [0,1]$ *s.t.* $N_G(0) = 1$ *and* $N_G(x) = 0$, *whenever* $x > 0$.

Definition 7 (Implications [1]). *A bivariate function* $I : [0,1]^2 \to [0,1]$ *is a* **fuzzy implication** *if it is decreasing with respect to the first variable, increasing with respect to the second variable,* $I(0,0) = I(0,1) = I(1,1) = 1$ *and* $I(1,0) = 0$ *(boundary conditions).*

Example 5. *Gödel Implication:* $I_G : [0,1]^2 \to [0,1]$ *s.t.* $I_G(x,y) = 1$, *whenever* $x \le y$, *and* $I_G(x,y) = y$ *otherwise.*

Definition 8 (Bi-implications [11]). *A bivariate function* $B : [0,1]^2 \to [0,1]$ *is a* **fuzzy bi-implication** *if it is commutative,* $B(x,x) = 1$, $B(0,1) = 0$ *and* $B(w,z) \le B(x,y)$, *whenever* $w \le x \le y \le z$.

Example 6. *Gödel Bi-implication:* $B_G(x,y) = T_G(I_G(x,y), I_G(y,x))$.

Definition 9 (Fuzzy Semantics [4]). *A structure* $\mathcal{F} = \{[0,1], T, S, N, I, B, 0, 1\}$, *s.t.* T *is a t-norm,* S *is a t-conorm,* N *a fuzzy negation,* I *is a fuzzy implication, and* B *a fuzzy bi-implication is a called* **fuzzy semantics**.

Example 7. *Gödel Semantic:* $\mathcal{G} = \{[0,1], T_M, S_M, N_G, I_G, B_G, 0, 1\}$.

Aggregation functions are functions with special properties which generalize the means, like *arithmetic mean, weighted mean* and *geometric mean*.

Definition 10 (Aggregation Function [3]). *An* **aggregation function** *is a* n-*ary function* $A : [0,1]^n \to [0,1]$ *with* $A(0,0,...,0) = 0$, $A(1,1,...,1) = 1$ *and, for all* $\bar{x}, \bar{y} \in [0,1]^n$, $\bar{x} \le \bar{y}$ *implies* $A(\bar{x}) \le A(\bar{y})$.

Example 8. $A_n(\bar{x}) = \dfrac{1}{n}(x_1 + ... + x_n)$ *(Arithmetic mean),* $A_n(\bar{x}) = \sqrt[n]{x_1 \times ... \times x_n}$ *(Geometric mean),* t-norms, t-conorms and projection functions $\pi_j : A_1 \times ... \times A_j \times ... \times A_n \longrightarrow A_j$, *s.t.* $\pi_j(x_1, ..., x_j, ..., x_n) = x_j$, are aggregation functions.

Definition 11 ([3]). *For every* $\bar{x} \in [0,1]^n$, *an aggregation function* A *is* **averaging** *if* $min(\bar{x}) \le A(x) \le max(\bar{x})$, **conjunctive** *if* $A(x) \le min(\bar{x})$ *and* **disjunctive** *if* $A(x) \ge max(\bar{x})$.

Example 9. t-norms are conjunctive aggregations, t-conorms are disjunctive and means *(arithmetic, geometric, weighted)* are average aggregations. For example, given $x, y \in [0,1]$ we have:

$$xy \le min\{x,y\} \le \frac{x+y}{2} \le max\{x,y\}.$$

Definition 12. *An aggregation* $A : [0,1]^n \to [0,1]$ *is* **shift-invariant** *if, for all* $\lambda \in [-1,1]$ *and for all* $\bar{x} \in [0,1]^n$,

$$A(x_1 + \lambda, ..., x_n + \lambda) = A(x_1, ..., x_n) + \lambda$$

whenever $(x_1 + \lambda, ..., x_n + \lambda) \in [0,1]^n$ *and* $A(x_1, ..., x_n) + \lambda \in [0,1]$.

Definition 13. *An element* $a \in \,]0,1[$ *is a* **zero divisor** *of an aggregation* A *if, for all* $i \in \{1, ..., n\}$, *there is some* $\bar{x} \in \,]0,1]^n$ *such that its i-th component is* $x_i = a$ *and* $A(\bar{x}) = 0$, *i.e. the equality* $A(x_1, ..., x_{i-1}, a, x_{i+1}, ..., x_n) = 0$ *holds.*

Example 10. The function $A(x_1, x_2) = max(0, x_1 + x_2 - 1)$ is an aggregation with zero divisor $a = 0.999$.

In this paper, we avoid aggregations with zero divisors, since it will induce the disconnection of edges.

In [13], Santiago et al. extend the notion of $FSGs$ for *Fuzzy Reactive Graphs*.

Definition 14 (Fuzzy Reactive Graphs). *Let* $\mathcal{M} = \langle W, \varphi : S \to [0,1] \rangle$ *be a FSG, the set of zero-order arrows* $\Gamma_{\mathcal{M}} = \{a_i^0 \in S^0 : \varphi(a_i^0) > 0\}$, $A_{\mathcal{M}} = \{A_1, ..., A_k : [0,1]^3 \to [0,1]\}$ *a set of aggregation functions and a function* $Ag_{\mathcal{M}} : \Gamma_{\mathcal{M}} \to A_{\mathcal{M}}$. *The pair* $\mathcal{M}_R = \langle \mathcal{M}, Ag_{\mathcal{M}} \rangle$ *is called a* **fuzzy reactive graph (FRG).**

Example 11. Let $\mathcal{M}$ be the FSG in Fig. 1(b). Consider $\Gamma_{\mathcal{M}} = \{a_1^0 = (u,v), a_2^0 = (v,v), a_3^0 = (v,w), a_4^0 = (v,z), a_5^0 = (w,u)\}$ and $A_{\mathcal{M}} = \{arith, max\}$. Defining the application $Ag_{\mathcal{M}} : \Gamma_{\mathcal{M}} \to A_{\mathcal{M}}$ s.t. $Ag(a_1^0) = Ag(a_2^0) = arith$ and $Ag(a_3^0) = Ag(a_4^0) = Ag(a_5^0) = max$, we have the FRG $\mathcal{M}_R = \langle \mathcal{M}, Ag \rangle$. The Fig. 2(a) contains the reconfiguration of $\mathcal{M}_R$ after crossing $a_1^0 = (u,v)$ and having applied $Ag(a_1^0) = arith$ to the fuzzy values: 0.2, 0.1, 0.7. The Fig. 2(b) contains the reconfiguration of $\mathcal{M}_R$ after crossing $a_3^0 = (v,w)$ and having applied $Ag(a_3^0) = max$ to the fuzzy values: 0.8, 0.7, 0.4.

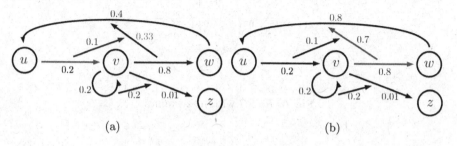

Fig. 2. Santiago et al. (2020) [13].

3   Reversal Fuzzy Switch Graphs

In this section we introduce the notion of Reversal Fuzzy Switch Graph, a structure which generalizes the notion of Fuzzy Switch Graph introduced by Santiago et al. [13]. This new kind of graph has in its structure two new types of high order-arrows, called connecting arrows and disconnecting arrows. These arrows allow to model reactive systems in which the accessibility to the worlds may be activated or deactivated by the transitions.

In what follows W and V are non-empty finite sets.

Definition 15 (Reversal Fuzzy Switch Graphs). *Let W be a set whose elements are called* **states** *or* **worlds**. *Consider the following family of sets defined recursively,*

$$\begin{cases} S^0 \subseteq W \times W \\ S^{n+1} \subseteq S^0 \times S^n \times \{\bullet, \circ\} \end{cases} \tag{5}$$

and $S = \bigcup_{n \in \mathbb{N}} S^n$. A **reversal fuzzy switch graph (RFSG)** *is a pair $M = \langle W, \mu : S \rightarrow [0,1] \times \{\text{ON}, \text{OFF}\}\rangle$. Arrows with $\bullet$ in their third component are called* **connecting arrows** *and arrows with $\circ$ in their third component are called* **disconnecting arrows**. *When the context is clear we denote a RFSG simply by $\langle W, \mu \rangle$.*

Active arrows are drawn with a normal line whereas inactive arrows are drawn with a dashed line. Moreover, connecting (disconnecting) arrows change the targeted arrow state for active (inactive) and are drawn with a black (white) arrowhead.

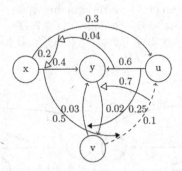

Fig. 3. *RFSG* with fuzzy values

For readability, we introduce some notation and nomenclatures:

- Arrows in S^n will be denoted by a_i^n, for $n \geq 0$ and $i \in \mathbb{N}$. Connecting (disconnecting) arrows receive an $\bullet(\circ)$ marker above. In this context, for $i \in \mathbb{N}$, a_i^0 are used to represent **zero-order arrows**, $\mathring{a}_i^1$ are used to represent **disconnecting one-order arrows**, $\mathring{a}_i^1$ are used to represent **connecting one-order arrows**, $\mathring{a}_i^2$ are used to represent **disconnecting two-order arrows**, $\mathring{a}_i^2$ are used to represent **connecting two-order arrows**, and so on.

- In the following, we make an abuse of notation. When necessary and if the context is clear, we will denote in more detail the arrows in S^n in a more expanded way. For example, a_i^0 from x to y will be denoted by $[xy]$, the disconnecting and connecting one-order arrows $\mathring{a}_i^1$ and $\mathring{a}_i^1$, from $[xy]$ to $[uv]$ will be denoted by $[[xy], [uv], \circ]$ and $[[xy], [uv], \bullet]$, respectively. When referring to any high-order arrow, we write $\sigma \in \{\circ, \bullet\}$ instead of $\circ$ or $\bullet$. For example, any one-order arrow from $[uv]$ to $[xy]$ will be written $[[uv], [xy], \sigma]$. Any two-order arrows from $[zw]$ to $[[xy], [uv], \sigma]$ will be denoted by $[[zw], [[xy], [uv], \sigma], \sigma]$.
- When there is no need to specify the order of the arrow belonging to set S, we will denote $a \in S$.
- Given the projection functions $\pi_1 : [0,1] \times \{\text{ON}, \text{OFF}\} \rightarrow [0,1]$ and $\pi_2 : [0,1] \times \{\text{ON}, \text{OFF}\} \rightarrow \{\text{ON}, \text{OFF}\}$, if $a \in S$ we write $\mu_1(a) = \pi_1(\mu(a))$ and $\mu_2(a) = \pi_2(\mu(a))$ to indicate the first and second components of $\mu(a)$.

In the following, we will consider the $RFSG$s $M = \langle W, \mu \rangle$ and $M' = \langle W, \mu' \rangle$.

Definition 16. *M is a **subgraph** of M' if $\mu_1(a) \leq \mu_1'(a)$ and $\mu_2(a) = \mu_2'(a)$, for all $a \in S$. M is a **supergraph** of M' if $\mu_1(a) \geq \mu_1'(a)$ and $\mu_2(a) = \mu_2'(a)$, for all $a \in S$.*

Definition 17. *M' is a **translation** of M by $\lambda \in [-1,1]$ if, for all $a \in S$ s.t. $\mu_1(a) > 0$, $\mu_1'(a) = \mu_1(a) + \lambda \in [0,1]$ and $\mu_2'(a) = \mu_2(a)$.*

3.1 Reactivity of $RFSG$s

Intuitively, a reactive graph is a graph that may change its configuration when a zero-order arrow is crossed. In order to model this global dependence in a $RFSG$, we consider the reactivity idea presented in [13] with the necessary adaptations: *Whenever a zero-order arrow is crossed, the fuzzy value and the arrow state (active or inactive) of its target arrows are updated.*

Definition 18. *Given M and an aggregation function $A : [0,1]^3 \rightarrow [0,1]$, a RFSG **based on** A after crossing a zero-order arrow a_i^0, is the RFSG $M_{a_i^0}^A = \langle W, \mu_{a_i^0}^A : S \rightarrow [0,1] \times \{\text{ON}, \text{OFF}\} \rangle$ s.t.*

$$
\mu_{a_i^0}^A(a) = \begin{cases} \left(A\big(\mu_1(a_i^0), \mu_1([a_i^0, a, \bullet]), \mu_1(a)\big), \text{ON} \right), & \text{if } [a_i^0, a, \bullet] \in S; \\ \left(A\big(\mu_1(a_i^0), \mu_1([a_i^0, a, \circ]), \mu_1(a)\big), \text{OFF} \right), & \text{if } [a_i^0, a, \circ] \in S; \\ \mu(a), \text{ otherwise.} \end{cases}
$$
(6)

*The RFSG $M_{a_i^0}^A$ is called **reconfiguration of** M, based on A, after crossing a_i^0.*

Let us see how this definition works in Fig. 4 using the *arithmetic mean* as aggregation function after crossing a sequence of zero-order arrows in Fig. 3. After the arrow $a_1^0 = [xu]$ has been crossed, Fig. 4(a), the arrow $a_2^0 = [xy]$ is *updated* due to $a_1^1 = [[xu], [xy], \circ]$ by the *arithmetic mean* between the fuzzy values $\mu_1(a_1^0), \mu_1(a_2^0)$ and $\mu_1(a_1^1)$, and by replacing the marker ON to OFF (the arrow a_2^0 becames inactive). In a second step and in the same manner, after the arrow $a_3^0 = [uy]$ be crossed, the arrow $a_1^1 = [[xu], [xy], \circ]$ has its fuzzy value updated and becomes inactive, however, the arrow $a_5^0 = [vy]$ has only its fuzzy value updated since it is an active arrow targeted by a connecting arrow (Fig. 4(b)).

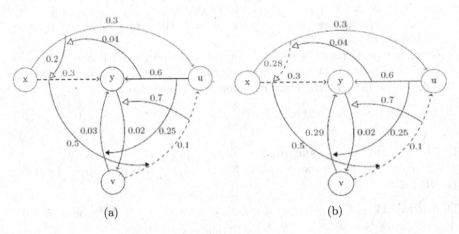

Fig. 4. Reactivity of $RFSG$ after crossing zero-order arrows $[xu]$ and $[xu][uy]$.

Proposition 1. *If A is a conjunctive (disjunctive) aggregation and $\left(\mu_{a_i^0}^A\right)_2 (b) = \mu_2(b)$ for all $b \in S$, then $M_{a_i^0}^A$ is a subgraph (supergraph) of M.*

Proof. Given $b \in S$ and denoting $(\mu_1(a_i^0), \mu_1([a_i^0, b, \sigma]), \mu_1(b)) = \overline{[a_i^0, b, \sigma]}$:

- Case $[a_i^0, b, \sigma] \in S$:

$$\left(\mu_{a_i^0}^A\right)_1 (b) = A(\overline{[a_i^0, b, \sigma]}) \le \min(\overline{[a_i^0, b, \sigma]}) \le \mu_1(b).$$

- Case $[a_i^0, b, \sigma] \notin S$:

$$\left(\mu_{a_i^0}^A\right)_1 (b) = \mu_1(b)$$

Then $M_{a_i^0}^A$ is subgraph of M. The dual statement follows straightforwardly.

Proposition 2. *Let M' be a translation of M by $\lambda \in [-1, 1]$. If A is shift-invariant, then $M'^A_{a^0_i}$ is a translation of $M^A_{a^0_i}$ by λ.*

Proof. Let $b \in S$. Denoting $\left(\mu'_1(a^0_i), \mu'_1([\![a^0_i, b, \sigma]\!]), \mu'_1(b)\right) = \overline{[\![a^0_i, b, \sigma]\!]}$ and supposing that $A\left(\mu_1(a^0_i), \mu_1([\![a^0_i, b, \sigma]\!]), \mu_1(b)\right) + \lambda \in [0, 1]$:

– Case $[\![a^0_i, b, \sigma]\!] \in S$:

$$\left(\mu'^A_{a^0_i}\right)_1 (b) = A(\overline{[\![a^0_i, b, \sigma]\!]})$$
$$= A\left(\mu_1(a^0_i) + \lambda, \mu_1([\![a^0_i, b, \sigma]\!]) + \lambda, \mu_1(b) + \lambda\right)$$
$$= A\left(\mu_1(a^0_i), \mu_1([\![a^0_i, b, \sigma]\!]), \mu_1(b)\right) + \lambda$$
$$= \left(\mu^A_{a^0_i}\right)_1 (b) + \lambda$$

– Case $[\![a^0_i, b, \sigma]\!] \notin S$:

$$\left(\mu'^A_{a^0_i}\right)_1 (b) = \mu'_1(b) = \mu_1(b) + \lambda = \left(\mu^A_{a^0_i}\right)_1 (b) + \lambda.$$

By hypotheses, $\mu_2(b) = \mu'_2(b)$, then $\left(\mu'^A_{a^0_i}\right)_2 (b) = \left(\mu^A_{a^0_i}\right)_2 (b)$.

Next, we will provide an extension for the notion of reactivity presented in [13]. Just as it is done for the case of $FRGs$, each active zero-order arrow triggers an aggregation function.

Definition 19 (Reversal Fuzzy Reactive Graphs). *Consider M a $RFSG$, the sets $\Gamma = \{a^0_i \in S^0 : \mu_1(a^0_i) > 0\}$ of zero-order arrows and $A = \{A_1, ..., A_k : [0, 1]^3 \to [0, 1]\}$ of aggregation functions, and a function $A_g : \Gamma \to A$. The pair $M_R = \langle M, A_g \rangle$ is called reversal fuzzy reactive graph (RFRG).*

If $a^0_i \in \Gamma$, the reconfiguration of M_R after crossing a^0_i is the RFRG $M_R^{a^0_i} = \langle M^{a^0_i}, A_g \rangle$, where $M^{a^0_i} = \langle W, \mu^{A_g}_{a^0_i} \rangle$ is a RFSG s.t.

$$\mu^{A_g}_{a^0_i}(b) = \begin{cases} \left(A_g(a^0_i)\left(\mu_1(a^0_i), \mu_1([\![a^0_i, b, \bullet]\!]), \mu_1(b)\right), \text{ON}\right), & if \; [\![a^0_i, b, \bullet]\!] \in S; \\ \left(A_g(a^0_i)\left(\mu_1(a^0_i), \mu_1([\![a^0_i, b, \circ]\!]), \mu_1(b)\right), \text{OFF}\right), & if \; [\![a^0_i, b, \circ]\!] \in S; \\ \mu(b), \; otherwise. \end{cases} \quad (7)$$

Example 12. Let M be the $RFSG$ at Fig. 3, $\Gamma = \{[xy], [xu], [uy], [vy], [yv], [vu]\}$, $A = \{arith, max\}$, $A_g([xy]) = A_g([xu]) = A_g([yv]) = arith$ and $A_g([vy]) = A_g([uy]) = A_g([vu]) = max$. The Fig. 5 contains $M_R^{[xu]}$ and $(M_R^{[xu]})^{[uy]}$, respectively.

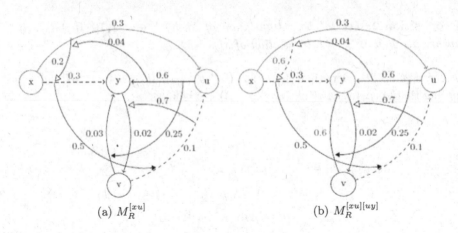

Fig. 5. Reconfiguration of M_R.

3.2   Products of *RFSGs*

In the following, we will consider the *RFSGs* $M = \langle W, \mu : S \to [0,1] \times \{\text{ON}, \text{OFF}\}\rangle$ and $N = \langle V, \delta : T \to [0,1] \times \{\text{ON}, \text{OFF}\}\rangle$ with W and V disjoint sets.

Definition 20 (Product of *RFSGs*). *The **cartesian product** of the RFSGs M and N is the RFSG $M \times N = \langle W \times V , \psi : (W \times T) \cup (S \times V) \to [0,1] \times \{\text{ON}, \text{OFF}\}\rangle$ s.t. $\psi(w,t) = \delta(t)$ and $\psi(s,v) = \mu(s)$.*

Example 13. Consider M and N shown in Fig. 6(a). The product $M \times N$ can be observed at Fig. 6(b).

In order to define the product of *RFRGs*, we consider:

- The *RFRGs* $M_R = \langle M, Ag_M \rangle$ and $N_R = \langle N, Ag_N \rangle$;
- The functions $Ag_M : \Gamma_M \longrightarrow A_M$ and $Ag_N : \Gamma_N \longrightarrow A_N$;
- The sets of aggregations A_M and A_N;
- The sets of zero-order arrows Γ_M and Γ_N.

The aggregations $a_m \in A_M$ and $a_n \in A_N$ will be denoted by $(M, a_m) : [0,1]^3 \to [0,1]$ and $(N, a_n) : [0,1]^3 \to [0,1]$.

Definition 21 (Product de *RFRGs*). *Consider the RFRGs M_R and N_R, the sets $A_M \oplus A_N = \{(M, a_m) : a_m \in A_M\} \cup \{(N, a_n) : a_n \in A_N\}$ and $\Gamma_{M \times N} = \{a_i^0 \in (W \times T) \cup (S \times V) : \psi_1(a_i^0) > 0\}$, and the function $Ag_{M \times N} : \Gamma_{M \times N} \to A_M \oplus A_N$ s.t.*

$$Ag_{M \times N}(a_i^0) = \begin{cases} \left(N, Ag_N(t)\right), & \text{if } a_i^0 = (w,t) \in W \times T; \\ \\ \left(M, Ag_M(s)\right), & \text{if } a_i^0 = (s,v) \in S \times V. \end{cases} \tag{8}$$

*The structure $M_R \times N_R = \langle M \times N, Ag_{M \times N} \rangle$ is the **product** of RFRGs M_R and N_R.*

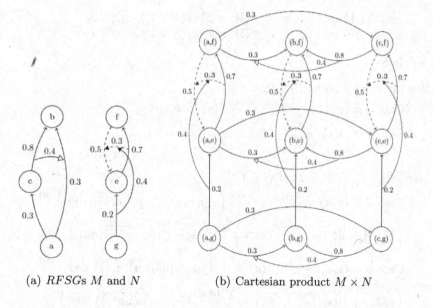

(a) RFSGs M and N (b) Cartesian product $M \times N$

Fig. 6. .

The next proposition ensures that the updated product is obtained from the updated factors.

Proposition 3. *Consider the RFRGs M_R, N_R, the product $M_R \times N_R$, $a_i^0 \in \Gamma_{M_R \times N_R}$ and $a \in (W \times T) \cup (S \times V)$ s.t. $\left(\psi_1(a_i^0), \psi_1(\llbracket a_i^0, a, \circ \rrbracket), \psi_1(a)\right) = \overline{\llbracket a_i^0, a, \circ \rrbracket}$ and $\left(\psi_1(a_i^0), \psi_1(\llbracket a_i^0, a, \bullet \rrbracket), \psi_1(a)\right) = \overline{\llbracket a_i^0, a, \bullet \rrbracket}$. Then,*

$$\psi_{a_i^0}^{Ag_{M \times N}}(a) = \begin{cases} \delta(t), & \text{if } C_1; \\ \mu(s), & \text{if } C_2; \\ \left(Ag_N(t)(\overline{\llbracket a_i^0, a, \circ \rrbracket}), \text{OFF}\right), & \text{if } C_3; \\ \left(Ag_N(t)(\overline{\llbracket a_i^0, a, \bullet \rrbracket}), \text{ON}\right), & \text{if } C_4; \\ \left(Ag_M(s)(\overline{\llbracket a_i^0, a, \circ \rrbracket}), \text{OFF}\right), & \text{if } C_5; \\ \left(Ag_M(s)(\overline{\llbracket a_i^0, a, \bullet \rrbracket}), \text{ON}\right), & \text{if } C_6; \end{cases} \quad (9)$$

For:

- $C_1 : a = (w, t)$ *and* $\llbracket a_i^0, a, \sigma \rrbracket \notin (W \times T) \cup (S \times V)$;
- $C_2 : a = (s, v)$ *and* $\llbracket a_i^0, a, \sigma \rrbracket \notin (W \times T) \cup (S \times V)$;
- $C_3 : a_i^0 = (w, t)$ *and* $\llbracket a_i^0, a, \circ \rrbracket \in (W \times T) \cup (S \times V)$;
- $C_4 : a_i^0 = (w, t)$ *and* $\llbracket a_i^0, a, \bullet \rrbracket \in (W \times T) \cup (S \times V)$;

- $C_5 : a_i^0 = (s,v)$ and $[\![a_i^0, a, \circ]\!] \in (W \times T) \cup (S \times V)$;
- $C_6 : a_i^0 = (s,v)$ and $[\![a_i^0, a, \bullet]\!] \in (W \times T) \cup (S \times V)$.

Proof. Indeed,

* Case $[\![a_i^0, a, \sigma]\!] \notin (W \times T) \cup (S \times V)$,
- Case $a = (w,t)$: $\psi_{a_i^0}^{Ag_M \times N}(a) \overset{\text{def}}{=} \psi(a) \overset{\text{def}}{=} \delta(t)$.
- Case $a = (s,v)$: $\psi_{a_i^0}^{Ag_M \times N}(a) \overset{\text{def}}{=} \psi(a) \overset{\text{def}}{=} \mu(s)$.

* Case $[\![a_i^0, a, \circ]\!] \in (W \times T) \cup (S \times V)$,
- Case $a = (w,t)$: $\psi_{a_i^0}^{Ag_M \times N}(a) \overset{\text{def}}{=} \left(Ag_{M \times N}(a_i^0)(\overline{[\![a_i^0, a, \circ]\!]}), \text{OFF} \right) \overset{\text{def}}{=}$
$\left((N, Ag_N)(t)(\overline{[\![a_i^0, a, \circ]\!]}), \text{OFF} \right) \overset{\text{def}}{=} \left(Ag_N(t)(\overline{[\![a_i^0, a, \circ]\!]}), \text{OFF} \right)$.
- Case $a = (s,v)$: $\psi_{a_i^0}^{Ag_M \times N}(a) \overset{\text{def}}{=} \left(Ag_{M \times N}(a_i^0)(\overline{[\![a_i^0, a, \circ]\!]}), \text{OFF} \right) \overset{\text{def}}{=}$
$\left((M, Ag_M)(s)(\overline{[\![a_i^0, a, \circ]\!]}), \text{OFF} \right) \overset{\text{def}}{=} \left(Ag_M(s)(\overline{[\![a_i^0, a, \circ]\!]}), \text{OFF} \right)$.

* Case $[\![a_i^0, a, \bullet]\!] \in (W \times T) \cup (S \times V)$,
- Case $a = (w,t)$: $\psi_{a_i^0}^{Ag_M \times N}(a) \overset{\text{def}}{=} \left(Ag_{M \times N}(a_i^0)(\overline{[\![a_i^0, a, \bullet]\!]}), \text{ON} \right) \overset{\text{def}}{=}$
$\left((N, Ag_N)(t)(\overline{[\![a_i^0, a, \bullet]\!]}), \text{ON} \right) \overset{\text{def}}{=} \left(Ag_N(t)(\overline{[\![a_i^0, a, \bullet]\!]}), \text{ON} \right)$.
- Case $a = (s,v)$: $\psi_{a_i^0}^{Ag_M \times N}(a) \overset{\text{def}}{=} \left(Ag_{M \times N}(a_i^0)(\overline{[\![a_i^0, a, \bullet]\!]}), \text{ON} \right) \overset{\text{def}}{=}$
$\left((M, Ag_M)(s)(\overline{[\![a_i^0, a, \bullet]\!]}), \text{ON} \right) \overset{\text{def}}{=} \left(Ag_M(s)(\overline{[\![a_i^0, a, \bullet]\!]}), \text{ON} \right)$.

4   A Logic for *RFSG*s

In order to verify a system described by a $RFSG$, we provide a formal language and a fuzzy semantics. We use the sets $S^{0^*} = \{a_i^0 \in S^0 \mid \mu_2(a_i^0) = \text{ON}\}$ and for any $w \in W$, the set $S^{0^*}[w] = \{w' \in W; (w,w') \in S^0\}$.

Definition 22 (Syntax). *Consider AtomProp a set of symbols (called atomic propositions) and $p \in AtomProp$. The set of formulas is generated by the following grammar:* $\varphi :: = p \mid true \mid false \mid (\neg\varphi) \mid (\varphi \wedge \varphi) \mid (\varphi \vee \varphi) \mid (\varphi \rightarrow \varphi) \mid (\varphi \leftrightarrow \varphi) \mid (SNext(\varphi)) \mid (ANext(\varphi))$.

Given the formulas φ and ψ, we interpret:

$(\neg\varphi)$: φ is not true;
$(\varphi \wedge \psi)$: φ and ψ are true;
$(\varphi \vee \psi)$: φ or ψ is true;

$(\varphi \rightarrow \psi)$: If φ is true, then ψ is true;

$\varphi \leftrightarrow \psi$: φ is true if and only if ψ is true;

$SNext(\varphi)$: φ is true in some next state;

$ANext(\varphi)$: φ is true in all next states.

Definition 23. *A **model** over the set AtomProp is a pair $M = (M, V)$, s.t. $M = \langle W, \mu \rangle$ is a RFSG and $V : W \times AtomProp \rightarrow [0, 1]$ is a function called* ***fuzzy valuation***.

Definition 24 (Semantics). *Consider M a model, A an aggregation function, $\mathcal{F} = \langle [0,1], T, S, N, I, B, 0, 1 \rangle$ a fuzzy semantics and $w \in W$ a state. The notation $[\![M, w \models_{\mathcal{F}}^{A} \varphi]\!]$ represents the **grade of uncertainty of a given formula** φ, **at state** w, **taking into account** $M, \mathcal{F}$ and A. The value of $[\![M, w \models_{\mathcal{F}}^{A} \varphi]\!]$ is defined in the following way:*

- $[\![M, w \models_{\mathcal{F}}^{A} p]\!] = V(w, p)$, *for* $p \in AtomProp$.
- $[\![\mathcal{M}, w \models_{\mathcal{F}}^{A} true]\!] = 1$.
- $[\![\mathcal{M}, w \models_{\mathcal{F}}^{A} false]\!] = 0$.
- $[\![\mathcal{M}, w \models_{\mathcal{F}}^{A} (\varphi \wedge \psi)]\!] = \mathbf{T}([\![\mathcal{M}, w \models_{\mathcal{F}}^{A} \varphi]\!], [\![\mathcal{M}, w \models_{\mathcal{F}}^{A} \psi]\!])$.
- $[\![\mathcal{M}, w \models_{\mathcal{F}}^{A} (\varphi \vee \psi)]\!] = \mathbf{S}([\![\mathcal{M}, w \models_{\mathcal{F}}^{A} \varphi]\!], [\![\mathcal{M}, w \models_{\mathcal{F}}^{A} \psi]\!])$.
- $[\![\mathcal{M}, w \models_{\mathcal{F}}^{A} (\varphi \rightarrow \psi)]\!] = \mathbf{I}([\![\mathcal{M}, w \models_{\mathcal{F}}^{A} \varphi]\!], [\![\mathcal{M}, w \models_{\mathcal{F}}^{A} \psi]\!])$.
- $[\![M, w \models_{\mathcal{F}}^{A} ANext(\varphi)]\!] = \displaystyle\mathop{\mathbf{T}}_{w' \in S^{0*}[w]} \left(\mathbf{I}\left(\mu([ww']), [\![M_A^{[ww']}, w' \models_{\mathcal{F}}^{A} \varphi]\!] \right) \right)$ *since* $M_A^{[ww']}$ *means* $\left(M_A^{[ww']}, V \right)$.
- $[\![M, w \models_{\mathcal{F}}^{A} SNext(\varphi)]\!] = \displaystyle\mathop{\mathbf{S}}_{w' \in S^{0*}[w]} \left(\mathbf{T}\left(\mu([ww']), [\![M_A^{[ww']}, w' \models_{\mathcal{F}}^{A} \varphi]\!] \right) \right)$.

The uncertainty degree that "$SNext(\varphi)$" is true at the state w is computed by using the uncertainty degree that φ is true at some state with active relationship to w. On the other hand, the uncertainty degree that "$ANext(\varphi)$" is true at state w is computed by using the uncertainty degree that φ is true at every state with active relationship to w. We must highlight, contrary to what happens in the classic case, the truth of $SNext(\varphi)$ and $ANext(\varphi)$ deal with all active edges in S^0 with source w. The expression: $[\![M_A^{[w,w']}, w' \models \varphi]\!]$, in this case, represents the uncertainty degree of the statement: "φ is true" at state w' after the active zero-order arrow $a_i^0 = [w, w']$ has been crossed and the RFSG M has been updated to $M_{a_i^0}^A$.

Observation: *Observe, according to Notation 2, that the application f in the definition of $ANext(\varphi)$ is a fuzzy implication $\mathbf{I}$. Similarly, in the definition of $SNext(\varphi)$, the application f is a t-norm $\mathbf{T}$.*

Example 14. Consider the Fig. 3 and take the atomic propositions: *High risk of contagion* and *Low risk of contagion*, according to the Table 1. What is the uncertainty degree at state x for the proposition: *"In some next state we have a low risk of contagion with a next state which has a higher risk of contagion?"* The assertion can be expressed as: $SNext(L \wedge SNext(H))$.

Table 1. Truth values of propositions on each state.

	x	y	u	v
H	0.2	0.8	0.3	0.01
L	0.1	0.9	0.15	0.2

Assuming the *arithmetical mean* as the unique aggregation function, the Gödel Semantic $\mathcal{F}_G$ and $\varphi = L \wedge SNext(H)$,

$$[\![M, x \models^A_{\mathcal{F}_G} SNext(\varphi)]\!] \overset{\text{def}}{=} \mathbf{S}_M \left(\mathbf{T}_M \left(0.3, [\![M^{[xu]}_A, u \models^A_{\mathcal{F}_G} \varphi]\!] \right), \right.$$

$$\left. \mathbf{T}_M \left(0.4, [\![M^{[xy]}_A, y \models^A_{\mathcal{F}_G} \varphi]\!] \right) \right) \overset{\text{def}}{=} \mathbf{S}_M \left(\mathbf{T}_M (0.3, 0.15), \mathbf{T}_M (0.4, 0.01) \right) = 0.15$$

Since,

a) $[\![M^{[xu]}_A, u \models^A_{\mathcal{F}_G} \varphi]\!] \overset{\text{def}}{=} \mathbf{T}_M \left([\![M^{[xu]}_A, u \models^A_{\mathcal{F}_G} SNext(H)]\!], [\![M^{[xu]}_A, u \models^A_{\mathcal{F}_G} L]\!] \right) =$

$\mathbf{T}_M (0.6, 0.15) = 0.15$ due to $[\![M^{[xu]}_A, u \models^A_{\mathcal{F}_G} SNext(H)]\!] \overset{\text{def}}{=}$

$\mathbf{S}_M \left(\mathbf{T}_M \left(\mu^A_{[xu]} ([uy]), [\![M^{[xu][uy]}_A, y \models^A_{\mathcal{F}_G} H]\!] \right) \right) = \mathbf{S}_M \left(\mathbf{T}_M (0.6, 0.8) \right) = 0.6;$

b) $[\![M^{[xy]}_A, y \models^A_{\mathcal{F}_G} \varphi]\!] \overset{\text{def}}{=} \mathbf{T}_M \left([\![M^{[xy]}_A, y \models^A_{\mathcal{F}_G} SNext(H)]\!], [\![M^{[xy]}_A, y \models^A_{\mathcal{F}_G} L]\!] \right) =$

$\mathbf{T}_M (0.01, 0.9) = 0.01.$ due to $[\![M^{[xy]}_A, y \models^A_{\mathcal{F}_G} SNext(H)]\!] \overset{\text{def}}{=}$

$\mathbf{S}_M \left(\mathbf{T}_M \left(\mu^A_{[xy]} ([yv]), [\![M^{[xy][yv]}_A, v \models^A_{\mathcal{F}_G} H]\!] \right) \right) = \mathbf{S}_M \left(\mathbf{T}_M (0.02, 0.01) \right) = 0.01$

In this case, in order to calculate the uncertainty degree at state v for the same proposition, we should note that the state v has only one next state y (the inactive arrow $[vu]$ is not considered). Therefore,

$$[\![M, v \models^A_{\mathcal{F}_G} SNext(\varphi)]\!] \overset{\text{def}}{=} \mathbf{S}_M \left(\mathbf{T}_M \left(0.03, [\![M^{[vy]}_A, y \models^A_{\mathcal{F}_G} \varphi]\!] \right) \right) = 0.01.$$

since $[\![M^{[vy]}_A, y \models^A_{\mathcal{F}_G} \varphi]\!] \overset{\text{def}}{=} \mathbf{T}_M \left([\![M^{[vy]}_A, y \models^A_{\mathcal{F}_G} SNext(H)]\!], [\![M^{[vy]}_A, y \models^A_{\mathcal{F}_G} L]\!] \right) =$

$\mathbf{T}_M (0.01, 0.9) = 0.01$ due to

$[\![M^{[vy]}_A, y \models^A_{\mathcal{F}_G} SNext(H)]\!] \overset{\text{def}}{=} \mathbf{S}_M \left(\mathbf{T}_M \left(\mu^A_{[vy]} ([yv]), [\![M^{[vy][yv]}_A, v \models^A_{\mathcal{F}_G} H]\!] \right) \right) =$

$\mathbf{S}_M \left(\mathbf{T}_M (0.02, 0.01) \right) = 0.01.$

5 Modeling a Tank Level Control System

In industrial processes that use tanks, the control of the fluid level is a common practice. Even with a relatively simple structure, logic controllers are often used.

The study and the modeling of tank plants and logic controllers are important because they provide the understanding of the current scenario of the system, causing benefits such as: the increase of productivity and the prevention of accidents [5].

The Fig. 7(a) shows a scheme where a tank control system is built with three signal transmitters $\{ST_1, ST_2, ST_3\}$, two pumps $\{P_1, P_2\}$ and a channel for fluid inlet called $START$. The dynamics of the system works as follows:

- **Fluid level rising**: At $START$ the fluid starts to be inserted into the tank while pumps P_1 and P_2 are on standby receiving a minimum electric current. When the fluid level triggers ST_2, P_1 receives an increment of electric current and is activated. If the fluid level continues to rise and trigger ST_3, the pump P_2 receives an increment of electric current and is also actived.
- **Fluid level decreasing**: When the fluid level is maximum, the pumps P_1 and P_2 are active. When the fluid level decreases, the ST_3 is triggered and P_2 goes to standby with a decrease in its electric current. If the fluid level continues to decrease, ST_2 is triggered and P_1 goes to standby with a decreasing in its electric current.

The signal transmitter receives the difference pressure of two points with different weights and converts it into a proportional electrical signal. This electric signal is sent to pumps [5].

Consider in Fig. 7(b):

- The set of arrows S;
- The set of worlds $W = \{ST_1, ST_2, ST_3, P_1, P_2, START\}$;
- The membership function $\mu : S \rightarrow [0,1] \times \{\text{ON}, \text{OFF}\}$ which assign to each arrow in S, the electric signal generated when they are crossing;
- The function $A_g : S^0 \rightarrow A$, where $A = \{T_L, S_L\}$.

The $RFRG$ $M_R = \langle M, A_g \rangle$ models the system of tank control above. These systems could also be model by using a FSG in which all arrows are active and all high-order arrows are connecting. However, in this case, there would be no possibility of working on deactivation of the pumps.

The reconfiguration of M_R, after crossing the arrows sequence $[ST_1\ ST_2]$, $[ST_1\ ST_2][ST_2\ ST_3]$ and $[ST_1\ ST_2][ST_2\ ST_3][ST_3\ ST_2]$, can be observed in Fig. 8. Assuming:

- $\mu(a_i^0) = 1$, for all $a_i^0 \in S^0 - \{[ST_1\ P_1], [ST_2\ P_2]\}$;
- $A_g([ST_1\ ST_2]) = A_g([ST_2\ ST_3]) = S_L$;
- $A_g([ST_2\ ST_1]) = A_g([ST_3\ ST_2]) = T_L$.

The fuzzy value and the status of the arrow $[ST_1\ P_1]$ after the arrow $[ST_1\ ST_2]$ has been crossed is calculate in the follow way:

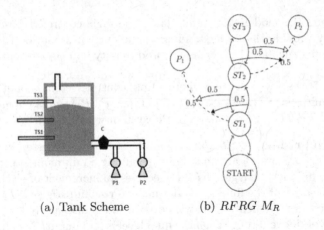

(a) Tank Scheme   (b) $RFRG$ M_R

Fig. 7. Model of tank control system.

$$\mu^{Ag}_{[ST_1\ ST_2]}([ST_1\ P_1]) = \Big(S_L(1, 0.5, 0.5), \text{ON} \Big)$$

$$= \Big(S_L(1, S_L(0.5, 0.5)), \text{ON} \Big)$$

$$= \Big(S_L(1, 1), \text{ON} \Big)$$

$$= \Big(1, \text{ON} \Big)$$

Consider the propositions

$$p: \text{``}P_1 \text{ is active''} \text{ and } q: \text{``}P_2 \text{ is active''}$$

for the model $\mathsf{M} = \langle M, V \rangle$, with $V(ST_1, p) = 0.05$, $V(ST_2, p) = 0.08$, $V(ST_3, p) = 0.6$, $V(ST_1, q) = 0.01$, $V(ST_2, q) = 0.5$ and $V(ST_3, q) = 0.7$. Using the *Gödel Fuzzy Semantics*, we are able to compute the true value of the formula $SNext(p \wedge q)$ to the states ST_2 and ST_3:

$$[\![\mathsf{M}, ST_2 \models^{Ag}_{\mathcal{F}_G} SNext(p \wedge q)]\!] = \mathbf{S}_M\Big(\mathbf{T}_M\big(1, [\![\mathsf{M}^{[ST_2\ ST_1]}_{Ag}, ST_1 \models^{Ag}_{\mathcal{F}_G} (p \wedge q)]\!]\big),$$

$$\mathbf{T}_M\big(1, [\![\mathsf{M}^{[ST_2\ ST_3]}_{Ag}, ST_3 \models^{A_G}_{\mathcal{F}_G} (p \wedge q)]\!]\big) \Big) = 0.01 \text{ and}$$

$$[\![\mathsf{M}, ST_3 \models^{Ag}_{\mathcal{F}_G} SNext(p \wedge q)]\!] = \mathbf{S}_M\Big(\mathbf{T}_M\big(1, [\![\mathsf{M}^{[ST_3\ ST_2]}_{Ag}, ST_2 \models^{Ag}_{\mathcal{F}_G} (p \wedge q)]\!]\big) \Big) =$$

0.08.

So, the degree of the sentence,

"There is a next state in which the pumps P1 and P2 are working"

at the state ST_2 is 0.01 and at the state ST_3 is 0.08.

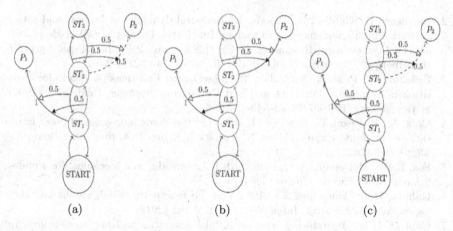

Fig. 8. M_R configuration after: (a) $[ST_1 \ ST_2]$, (b) $[ST_1 \ ST_2][ST_2 \ ST_3]$ and (c) $[ST_1 \ ST_2][ST_2 \ ST_3][ST_3 \ ST_2]$.

6   Final Remarks

This paper introduces a structure called *Reversal Fuzzy Switch Graph* (*RFSG*) which extends the concept of Fuzzy Switch Graph (FSG) introduced by Santiago et al. (2020) [13] by assigning the device to enable/disable arrows. We present the cartesian product of *RFSG*s and produce an application to demonstrate how RFRGs can model dynamic systems. The model is accompanied with a formal logic which enables the verification of properties.

In order to keep the text reduced, further algebraic operators and concepts, like simulation and bisimulations, were not exposed. These constructions as well as the relationship of *RFSG*s with other models that describe reactive systems, other types of logic and other notions of certainty (such as fuzzy interval logic), will be subject of future works.

Acknowledgements. Santiago was supported by National Council for Scientific and Technological Development (CNPq) within the project 312053/2018-5, by Coordination for the Improvement of Higher Education Personnel (CAPES) within the project Capes-Print 88887.363001/2019-00.

Martins and Figueiredo were supported by ERDF, through the COMPETE 2020 Program, and by FCT, within the projects PTDC/CCI-COM/30947/2017, UIDB/ 04106/2020 and UIDP/04106/2020.

References

1. Baczynski, M., Jayaram, B.: Fuzzy Implications. Studies in Fuzziness and Soft Computing. Springer, Heidelberg (2008). https://doi.org/10.1007/978-3-540-69082-5

2. Barringer, H., Gabbay, D., Woods, J.: Temporal dynamics of support and attack networks: from argumentation to zoology. In: Hutter, D., Stephan, W. (eds.) Mechanizing Mathematical Reasoning. LNCS (LNAI), vol. 2605, pp. 59–98. Springer, Heidelberg (2005). https://doi.org/10.1007/978-3-540-32254-2_5

3. Beliakov, G., Pradera, A., Calvo, T.: Aggregation Functions: A Guide for Practitioners. Studies in Fuzziness and Soft Computing. Springer, Heidelberg (2007). https://doi.org/10.1007/978-3-540-73721-6

4. Cruz, A., Bedregal, B., Santiago, R.H.N.: On the characterizations of fuzzy implications satisfying $i(x, i(y, z)) = i(i(x, y), i(x, z))$. Int. J. Approximate Reasoning **93**, 61–276 (2018)

5. Fox, R.W., McDonald, A.T., Pritchard, P.J.: Introdução à Mecânica dos Fluidos, 6th edn. LTC, Rio de Janeiro (2004)

6. Gabbay, D.M., Marcelino, S.: Global view on reactivity: switch graphs and their logics. Ann. Math. Artif. Intell. **66**(1–4), 131–162 (2012)

7. Gabbay, D.M.: Introducing reactive Kripke semantics and arc accessibility. In: Avron, A., Dershowitz, N., Rabinovich, A. (eds.) Pillars of Computer Science. LNCS, vol. 4800, pp. 292–341. Springer, Heidelberg (2008). https://doi.org/10.1007/978-3-540-78127-1_17

8. Gabbay, D.M.: Reactive Kripke semantics and arc accessibility. In: Carnielli, W., Dionisio, F.M., Mateus, P. (eds.) Proceedings of CombLog 2004, pp. 7–20. Centre for Logic and Computation, University of Lisbon (2004)

9. Klement, E.P., Mesiar, R., Pap, E.: Triangular Norms. Trends in Logic. Springer, Cham (2013). https://doi.org/10.1007/978-94-015-9540-7

10. Lee, K.H.: First Course on Fuzzy Theory and Applications. Advances in Intelligent and Soft Computing. Springer, Heidelberg (2006). https://doi.org/10.1007/3-540-32366-X

11. Marcos, J., Bedregal, B., Callejas, C.: Actions of automorphisms on some classes of fuzzy bi-implications. Mathware Softcomput. Mag. **1**(20), 94–114 (2013)

12. Pinheiro, J., Bedregal, B., Santiago, R.H.N., Santos, H.: A study of (t, n)-implications and its use to construct a new class of fuzzy subsethood measure. Int. J. Approximate Reasoning **97**, 1–16 (2018)

13. Santiago, R.H., Martins, A.M., Figueiredo, D.: Introducing fuzzy reactive graphs: a simple application on Biology. Soft Computing (2020)

Separation Logic-Based Verification Atop a Binary-Compatible Filesystem Model

Mihir Parang Mehta[✉] and William R. Cook

University of Texas at Austin, Austin, TX 78712, USA
{mihir,wcook}@cs.utexas.edu

Abstract. Filesystems have held the interest of the formal verification community for a while, with several high-performance filesystems constructed with accompanying proofs of correctness. However, the question of verifying an existing filesystem and incorporating filesystem-specific guarantees remains unexplored, leaving those application developers underserved who need to work with a specific filesystem known to be fit for their purpose. In this work, we present an implementation of a verified filesystem which matches the specification of an existing filesystem, and with our new model AbsFAT tie it to the reasoning framework of separation logic in order to verify properties of programs which use the filesystem. This work is intended to match the target filesystem, FAT32, at a binary level and return the same data and error codes returned by mature FAT32 implementations, considered canonical. We provide a logical framework for reasoning about program behavior when filesystem calls are involved in terms of separation logic, and adapt it to simplify and automate the proof process in ACL2. By providing this framework, we encourage and facilitate greater adoption of software verification by application developers.

Keywords: Filesystems · Theorem proving · Separation logic

1 Introduction

Filesystems have been of interest to the formal verification community for a while. This paper discusses our recent work on supporting code proofs for programs making use of a verified filesystem, using separation logic. Although alternative approaches towards code proofs exist, we find separation logic to be a natural choice for its intuitiveness as well as its easy applicability towards verifying code through term rewriting as implemented in general purpose theorem proving systems.

This work introduces AbsFAT, an axiomatization of a subset of the POSIX system calls offered by filesystems, specifically FAT32. We build on our earlier work [18] developing the FAT32 models HiFAT and LoFAT in the ACL2 general-purpose theorem prover; our axiomatic approach here complements the refinement approach the earlier work advocated. Although refinement remains necessary to keep tractable the problem of verifying the binary compatible model

© Springer Nature Switzerland AG 2020
G. Carvalho and V. Stolz (Eds.): SBMF 2020, LNCS 12475, pp. 155–170, 2020.
https://doi.org/10.1007/978-3-030-63882-5_10

LoFAT, axiomatization is needed in order to prove properties about external programs which are not (and should not be) developed with the details of our formalization in mind, except for the POSIX-like interface that LoFAT offers.

$$\{True\}$$
$$\text{r := mkdir(path); s := stat(path)}$$
$$\{(r \Rightarrow 0) \rightarrow (s \Rightarrow 0)\}$$

Fig. 1. A simple conjecture involving mkdir and stat

Figure 1 is an example of a simple external program that calls mkdir, a system call for creating a directory at the given path, and then stat, a system call for checking the existence of a file at given path and obtaining pertinent metadata (which we overlook for the purposes of this proof). This example conjectures a Hoare triple with the precondition True and the postcondition $(r \Rightarrow 0) \rightarrow (s \Rightarrow 0)$. This conjecture says that stat succeeds when mkdir succeeds, and proving it requires precise specifications of these system calls both in terms of changes in filesystem state and in terms of return values and success/error conditions. AbsFAT provides such specifications, and ACL2 is able to prove this conjecture automatically through rewriting with AbsFAT. Programmers working at this level of abstraction rely on these return values and success/error conditions, around which they build their program logic; this makes the present work valuable.

Our principal contributions are

– the development of AbsFAT on the basis of abstract separation logic;
– the formalization of its connection to the existing models HiFAT and LoFAT, which involves the development of a number of system calls and showing that they are equivalent to the versions of those system calls in HiFAT and in turn in LoFAT;
– the development of a library of lemmas which facilitate a number of Hoare-style code proofs through rewriting, accompanied by examples of such proofs.

We detail these contributions in the rest of the paper, providing necessary background about program reasoning and FAT32 in Sect. 2, detailing our approach towards and implementation of abstract separation logic in Sect. 3, and evaluating our work in Sect. 4.

2   Background

2.1   ACL2

ACL2 [17] is an interactive theorem prover for first-order logic. Prior work on program verification with ACL2 has highlighted its library support for code proofs based on executable models [9] and its support for rewriting-based proofs of separation properties in the context of program verification [22] through the use of proof tactics (i.e. rewrite rules) which act upon a quantifier-free representation of separation predicates.

2.2   Program Logic

Floyd-Hoare logic [7,11], which introduced Hoare triples.

{precondition} statement {postcondition}

for simple and compound statements comprising a program, forms the basis of program verification. In recent years, the logic has been strengthened in many different program verification domains, and been successfully automated for static analysis both at the programming language level and at the machine code level. In this paper, we are interested in Floyd-Hoare logic as applied to linearly addressed memory for storage of fixed-size elements, such as bytes. Such memory models have been developed to model RAM, which usually provides byte- or word-addressing; we find the idea immediately applicable to filesystems, which operate on various kinds of linearly addressed storage media while abstracting away the details of those media to expose a directory tree interface to the user.

One such extension is separation logic [25,26], which was initially developed to address certain *scalability* challenges in reasoning about programs operating on a RAM-like memory model, i.e. the *flat heap* model. Heaps are mappings from locations (*heap cells*) to fixed-size data values; they can be composed using the *separating conjunction* operator $*$. The heap $P * Q$ is defined as the union of the mappings P and Q, along with the assertion that no mappings are common between P and Q which is implicit whenever $P * Q$ appears in a Hoare triple. Yang et al. [30] describe a bargain of sorts: in exchange for using only *tight specifications*, i.e. Hoare triples $\{P\} stmt \{Q\}$ in which the precondition P names all the locations modified by $stmt$, we get a *frame rule* allowing us to infer from this Hoare triple the new Hoare triple $\{P * R\} stmt \{Q * R\}$. This derivation is sound since the formula P * R contains the assertion that locations in P and R are disjoint from each other; and the new Hoare triple preserves tightness.

Structured Separation Logic (SSL) [29], an extension of this theory, replaces the flat heap with a *structured heap*. Here, a heap cell is allowed to be either a flat heap cell containing a fixed-size value, or a structured heap cell containing a rich value such as a linked list or a sublist thereof. The utility in reasoning about filesystems is immediately obvious, when we consider rich values to include the contents of directories.

In SSL, the notion of a structured heap goes together with the notion of an *abstract heap* which helps reason about accesses and updates to substructures of structured data. Like structured heaps, abstract heaps contain flat heap cells and structured heap cells; in addition, they contain *abstract heap cells*, pairs of values each consisting of a substructure of some structured data and the path where the substructure fits in the larger structure. When a substructure is placed in an abstract heap cell, at the same time the structure where it fits is changed to replace the substructure with a *body address* pointing to this heap cell. This process of creating an abstract heap cell is known as *abstract allocation*; it serves to create a new cell in the abstract heap and "separate" a substructure. The converse operation is *abstract deallocation*; it does away with an abstract heap cell by folding its contents back into the larger structure whence they came, in a manner similar to application of functions in lambda calculus. Abstract allocation and abstract deallocation can both be carried out at will depending on the needs of the proof, since neither has any effect on the state of the system. Since Hoare judgments about sequences of commands often require abstract allocations and deallocations to be written out explicitly, we use Hoare triples of the form $\{P\}\,id\,\{Q\}$, to represent them, where id is a vacuous statement (i.e. a no-op).

The path stored in each heap cell is known as a *path promise*, ensuring that the substructure in the first element is identifiable as to its origin in the substructure. In the context of SSL applied to filesystems, this marks a difference in approach from prior work in specifying filesystems [10,20] which choose to index into the heap by file path, making the path of each file its heap address. While a variable may be deallocated and thus removed from the abstract heap, its path promise cannot change as long as it is in the abstract heap.

2.3   FAT32

FAT32 has been widely used, on personal computers where it was for several years the Windows operating system's default, and on removable media and embedded devices where it continues to be ubiquitous. Microsoft provides an authoritative specification [19] which specifies the on-disk layout of the filesystem in terms of file data, directory-level metadata and volume-level metadata. Two pertinent details follow.

- FAT32's data region is indexed by its file allocation table, which holds a linked list for each file called a *clusterchain*. Looking up a file's clusterchain in the data region yields its contents. Clusterchains are not shared between files; thus, there is no hard linking.
- Each directory in FAT32 is explicitly required to include, in addition to directory entries for regular files and subdirectories, an entry for itself (.) and its parent (..).

Our previous work [18] introduced LoFAT and HiFAT, two models at different levels of abstraction. LoFAT is a disk-image level model of FAT32, while HiFAT is a directory tree-based model of FAT32 which abstracts LoFAT. LoFAT includes the capability to read its state from a FAT32 disk image and write back its state to a disk image; efficient implementations of both of these make the model executable. The efficient execution of the model supports a suite of co-simulation tests for programs from the Coreutils and mtools sets of programs; in each of these tests, the canonical program is run with the same input as the ACL2 test program to check that the standard outputs of these two programs, if any, are identical and filesystem states, if changed, are identical as well. The system calls in LoFAT are proved to be refinements of the corresponding system calls in HiFAT, because the latter is an easier model to reason about. These refinement properties rest on transformations between the two models and proofs that these transformations are inverses of each other under appropriate equivalence relations.

$$\{(\text{path} \Mapsto P/b/a) * (\alpha^P \mapsto b[C * can\_create(a)])\}$$
$$r := \text{mkdir(path)}$$
$$\{r \Rightarrow 0 * \alpha^P \mapsto b[C + a[\varnothing]]\}$$

$$\{(\text{path} \Mapsto P/b/a) * (\alpha^P \mapsto b[C + a : s])\} \qquad \{(\text{path} \Mapsto P/b/a) * (\alpha^P \mapsto b[C + a[\beta]])\}$$
$$r := \text{mkdir(path)} \qquad\qquad\qquad r := \text{mkdir(path)}$$
$$\{r \Rightarrow \text{EEXIST}\} \qquad\qquad\qquad\qquad \{r \Rightarrow \text{EEXIST}\}$$

$$\{(\text{path} \Mapsto P/b/a) * (\alpha^P \mapsto b : s)\} \qquad \{(\text{path} \Mapsto P/a) * \text{ENOENT}(P)\}$$
$$r := \text{mkdir(path)} \qquad\qquad\qquad r := \text{mkdir(path)}$$
$$\{r \Rightarrow \text{ENOTDIR}\} \qquad\qquad\qquad\quad \{r \Rightarrow \text{ENOENT}\}$$

Fig. 2. Hoare triples describing the possible behaviors of mkdir

3 Abstract Separation Logic for Filesystem Verification

In AbsFAT, the model for reasoning about filesystem calls in programs, filesystem states are represented as collections of logically separate variables. Maintaining this separation through state changes from applications of system call specifications, abstract allocations, and abstract deallocations is a substantial part of how the proofs are resolved in the theorem prover. This formal development is structured around these principles:

- To profit from separation logic, properties of the filesystem state are represented as local properties where possible, in a way that allows them to be proved by rewriting without induction.
- Global properties, which pertain to the whole system and which have the potential to expand the state space, are packaged into disabled predicates in order to keep the state space manageable (for the prover) and make them more comprehensible (to the user.) This, in turn, leads to the creation of general and reusable lemmas to resolve subgoals involving these predicates which arise from file operation specifications.
- Also in the interest of reducing state space and helping user comprehension, file operation specifications are kept compact.
- Wherever new global properties are required specifically for FAT32, they are distinguished where possible to simplify possible reuse of the proof infrastructure for a future filesystem formalization.
- A completion semantics is used, in which the effect of a system call is deterministically evaluated regardless of whether it returns an error code.

3.1 System Calls and Support for Filesystem Clients

It is illustrative to more closely examine Fig. 1 and its proof, which in turn requires us to consider the specification of mkdir itself. This system call has one success condition and several error conditions, as shown in Fig. 2, where path $\Mapsto$ $P/b/a$ means that path matches a directory P with subdirectory b, which has a component a; $b[C * can\_create(a)]$ describes a directory b in which a can be created; $b[C + a : s]$ describes a directory b where regular file a already exists with contents s, $b[C + a[\beta]]$ describes a directory b where directory a exists with contents β, and $b : s$ describes a regular file b with contents s. In all but the first of these five Hoare triples, mkdir exits returning an error code, as standardized by POSIX which defines the meanings for each one of the errors ENOENT, ENOTDIR, ... and their applicability to a given system call.[1]

The AbsFAT axiomatization works on frames, collections of logically separate abstract variables, and supports claims such as the following which is likely to arise in the context of any proof involving the system call mkdir:

> When a given filesystem state corresponds to a given well-formed separation logic frame, the state after a successful call to mkdir(path) corresponds to a new well-formed frame with all abstract variables unrelated to dirname(path) unchanged, and with a new variable α representing the current state of dirname(path) containing a new empty directory named basename(path).

This claim, expressed in terms of the Linux utility functions basename [13] and dirname [14], is an example of the benefits of local reasoning. It expresses the new state after an operation as a change to the old state that clearly leaves the remainder of the filesystem unchanged and simplifies reasoning about the next operation on the filesystem in both cases, when this next operation affects the directory tree under dirname(path) and when it does not. Since our system makes filesystem operations deterministic, including at the AbsFAT level, we are able to make the stronger claim:

> When a given filesystem state corresponds to a given well-formed separation logic frame, the state after a call to mkdir(path), successful or not, corresponds to a new well-formed frame with all abstract variables unchanged which are logically separate from the contents of basename(path). Further, when dirname(path) exists as a directory and no file exists at path, the frame will have a new variable α representing the current state of dirname(path) containing a new empty directory named basename(path).

The proof of the Fig. 1 conjecture splits into a number of cases, as expected from our understanding of the mkdir specification; Fig. 3 shows these case splits.

---

[1] We use the values ENOENT, ENOTDIR as the return values of system calls, but POSIX enumerates these as values assigned to the global variable errno, which is different from the function's actual return value. Our implementation of each system call must return both these values, in order to capture the entirety of the effect of the system call in ACL2, a functional language lacking global program state. For brevity in this paper, however, we find it convenient to refer to a single return value which is zero in the case of success, and one of the errno values enumerated by POSIX [15] in the case of failure. This is no less informative than providing the return value and the errno value separately, since none of our system calls sets errno to 0 upon success.

$$\begin{array}{c} \{(\text{path} \mapsto P/a) * \text{ENOENT}(P)\} \\ r := \text{mkdir}(\text{path}) \\ \{r \Rrightarrow \text{ENOENT}\} \\ s := \text{stat}(\text{path}) \\ \{(r \Rrightarrow 0) \to (s \Rrightarrow 0)\} \end{array} \qquad \begin{array}{c} \{(\text{path} \mapsto P/a) * (\alpha^P \mapsto a : -)\} \\ r := \text{mkdir}(\text{path}) \\ \{r \Rrightarrow \text{EEXIST}\} \\ s := \text{stat}(\text{path}) \\ \{(r \Rrightarrow 0) \to (s \Rrightarrow 0)\} \end{array}$$

$$\begin{array}{c} \{(\text{path} \mapsto P/a) * (\alpha^P \mapsto a[-])\} \\ r := \text{mkdir}(\text{path}) \\ \{r \Rrightarrow \text{EEXIST}\} \\ s := \text{stat}(\text{path}) \\ \{(r \Rrightarrow 0) \to (s \Rrightarrow 0)\} \end{array} \qquad \begin{array}{c} \{(\text{path} \mapsto P/a) * \text{ENOENT}(P/a)\} \\ r := \text{mkdir}(\text{path}) \\ \{r \Rrightarrow 0\} \\ s := \text{stat}(\text{path}) \\ \{(r \Rrightarrow 0) \to (s \Rrightarrow 0)\} \end{array}$$

$$\begin{array}{c} \{True\} \\ r := \text{mkdir}(\text{path}); \ s := \text{stat}(\text{path}) \\ \{(r \Rrightarrow 0) \to (s \Rrightarrow 0)\} \end{array}$$

Fig. 3. Proof tree for the conjecture in Fig. 1

While all but one of the cases are vacuous, since the postcondition implication $\{(r \Rrightarrow 0) \to (s \Rrightarrow 0)\}$ is vacuously true whenever r is nonzero, the cases still need to be explored for soundness of the proof. The justification for developing the theorem proving infrastructure becomes apparent simply from exploring the number of cases arising in this proof for a trivial sequence of two operations, which is not conducive to hand proofs.

As one might expect, a complementary conjecture that mkdir leaves the filesystem state unchanged in an error condition, i.e. when $\neg(r \Rrightarrow 0)$, is also automatically provable with the help of AbsFAT.

3.2 Rewriting

AbsFAT's abstract separation-logic based formulation of file operations has a logically straightforward representation in the theorem proving environment, which connects neatly with the existing HiFAT directory-tree representation. Thus, a valid filesystem instance can be represented as a *frame*, an association list mapping variables to unrooted trees in which the root is distinguished from the other variables.

The usability of a proof technique depends, to a significant extent, on the degree to which it can be automated by the prover, freeing the user from the manual instantiation of lemmas and other laborious aspects of theorem proving. In ACL2, this is naturally the task of the rewriter, which efficiently completes proofs even when they involve large terms of the kind that show up in code proofs. Accordingly, we look for a method to phrase the separation properties in a way that is palatable to the rewriter, after the fashion of Myreen and Kaufmann's work on code proofs [22] demonstrating a logical workaround for the difficulties of separation logic proofs in the presence of existential quantifiers. The recursive predicate *separate* served to take the place of the conventional separating conjunction operator, which by definition introduces the unwanted existential quantifiers. In proofs, the *separate* predicate under the action of certain rewriting tactics was shown to create those case splits which were necessary to resolve the subgoals and complete the proof. Our formulation of *separate* is similar, and helps us avoid existential quantifiers.

$$\text{old} \Rightarrow P/a * \text{new} \Rightarrow P'/b * \alpha^P \mapsto a[C] * \beta^{P'} \mapsto b[C']$$
$$\text{rename old new}$$
$$\alpha^P \mapsto \phi * \beta^{P'} \mapsto b[C' + a[C]]$$

Fig. 4. An axiom that means different things in the HiFAT and LoFAT contexts

In the general setting where zero or more abstract variables exist at body addresses within the frame frame, and each corresponds to an abstract heap cell in the heap, we can recursively define the predicate separate, in Haskell notation:

$$\text{separate } [] = True$$
$$\text{separate } ((\alpha, entry_\alpha) : frame) = (\text{disjoint } frame \; entry_\alpha) \wedge (\text{separate } frame)$$

This predicate has an analogous effect to Myreen's predicate in the flat memory model, creating case splits which help resolve the subgoals of the proof. This holds true even though the filesystem model is more complex with the abstract variables needing to be maintained in a well-formed state in the sense of collapsibility. Collapsibility, which needs to be maintained as an invariant through various file operations, is necessarily a global property; separate facilitates reasoning about it locally and generally minimizes the need for non-local lemmas.

A choice, here, is whether separate and abstract allocation/deallocation should be implemented at the LoFAT level, or the HiFAT level. At a first glance, it seems useful to reason about clusterchains in LoFAT and declare them disjoint through the separate predicate; however, these disjointness properties are adequately addressed by the definition of lofat-to-hifat, a function which transforms a LoFAT instance to a HiFAT instance and returns an error for ill-formed LoFAT instances, including those with any overlap between clusterchains. The choice is ultimately determined by a FAT32-specific consideration: a subdirectory is not completely independent of its parent directory, because it needs to have an explicit .. directory entry pointing to its parent. Thus, a naïve implementation over LoFAT would cause inconsistencies; one such inconsistency arises in one of the axioms for the system call rename (Fig. 4), which addresses the moving of a subdirectory. This axiom implies that the contents of the subdirectory b are unchanged, which is untrue for LoFAT since the .. directory entry is updated from P to P/b. This axiom holds true for HiFAT though, which has no . or .. entries since it's a directory tree model and doesn't need them. Thus, we opt to implement this logic at the HiFAT level, avoiding inconsistencies such as the above in AbsFAT and generally benefitting from HiFAT's ease of use for reasoning.

AbsFAT deals with filesystems, instrumented with body addresses and accompanied by heaps which bind each abstract variable in some body address to a *partial directory*, i.e. a fragment of a directory, with none, some, or all of that directory's contents. AbsFAT refers to such entities as frames, assisting the intuition that a frame contains some immediately useful information and some less immediately useful information, which the frame rule of separation logic helps in managing.

The well-formedness of such a frame is determined by Gardner et al.'s [8] definition of the one-step collapse relation $\downarrow$, which describes a single context application folding an abstract heap cell into the incomplete directory tree holding the corresponding body address, and its transitive closure $\downarrow^*$. A frame is well-formed if it is related by $\downarrow^*$ to some frame consisting of only the root variable, τ, bound to a *complete directory tree* which contains no body addresses. This definition is, self-evidently, existentially quantified over all frames that the given frame could be related to, and is therefore a difficult definition to work with in ACL2 which has limited support for quantified predicates.

It is intuitive, however, and a fact we prove in ACL2, that if a given frame is related via $\downarrow^*$ to two complete directory trees then these two trees must have the same directory structure and contain the same files modulo rearrangement of files within subdirectories. Thus, AbsFAT opts for an alternative formulation of transitive collapse, iterating over all abstract heap cells until all are folded into the root variable (or until no variable can be folded, which shows the frame to be ill-formed). This iterative formulation simplifies the task of maintaining well-formedness as an invariant across file operations from a reasoning perspective, and also makes the invariant intuitive: the property being preserved is the ability of the frame to be properly collapsed.

An instrumented filesystem consists of a root directory and an association list mapping each numbered variable to:

- a partial directory, possibly containing body addresses itself;
- a path promise; and
- a source pointer to an abstract variable (possibly the root itself) containing a body address for the given variable.

The well-formedness of such an instrumented filesystem becomes the proposition of whether it can be collapsed without errors; i.e. whether every abstract cell corresponds to a body address in some variable, matching its path promise. As a basic property of our formulation, we prove that a successful collapse as described above yields a HiFAT instance with no duplicate filenames in any directory, under the hypotheses of separation between the different variables in the separate sense and the absence of "dangling" body addresses which lack corresponding abstract cells.

The α values are chosen to be natural numbers to simplify the bookkeeping involved in the implementation; and disjointness requires all of them to be distinct from each other. Each $entry_\alpha$ value is a partial directory. These entries match Gardner et al.'s definition of an unrooted tree[2], given by the grammar:

$$ud ::= \phi \mid a : s \mid a[ud] \mid ud + ud \mid x$$

In this grammar, ϕ is the empty tree, $a : s$ is a regular file with name a and contents s, $a[ud]$ is a directory named a and containing unrooted tree ud, $ud + ud$ is composition, and x is a variable. This definition allows for multiple variables in a directory, as does our code, but in practice we find it useful while reasoning about file operations to avoid having more than one variable in a directory. When this property holds, it becomes possible to check the existence of a file at a given path by examining the contents of at most one abstract variable.

It remains to address one point: how are abstract allocations to be done in a proof? In the proof tree in Fig. 3 for instance, the $r \Rightarrow 0$ case assumes the existence of variable α^P with the appropriate path promise and the appropriate contents; in a proof search the variable needs to be allocated procedurally. A naïve answer would be to collapse the entire frame into a single root variable and then allocate a new variable with the desired path promise, creating the corresponding body address in the root. This is undesirable, limiting if not entirely curtailing the local reasoning we hope for by bringing all variables together.

AbsFAT solves this question by implementing a transformation on the frame of abstract variables, called *partial collapse*. For a given path, this operation iteratively deallocates every abstract variable with a path promise prefixed by this path, leaving the frame in a state where the contents of the directory at that path are to be found, without holes, in one variable. All other variables are left as is. This is essential to the specification of almost every one of the system calls we consider, since they require some directory to be brought into a variable for examination, the way α^P in the mkdir(path) specification brings in the contents of basename(path). For instance:

- In the specification of mkdir(path), partially collapsing the frame on dirname(path) allows the contents of the parent directory to be seen, which determines whether the system call will succeed (when no file exists at path) or fail (when a regular or directory file does exist at path.)
- Similarly, in the specification of stat(path), partially collapsing dirname(path) reveals the contents of the parent directory which determines whether the system call will succeed (when a regular or directory file does exist at path) or fail.

Using partial collapse necessitates a somewhat complex proof to show that a partially collapsed frame collapses to the same filesystem as it would have before the partial collapse, modulo rearrangement of files within directories. The payoff for this proof is in the form of clean specifications of system calls, deterministically evaluating the state of the filesystem just like the system call specifications in HiFAT and LoFAT. The specifications capture the read-over-write properties of the implementations of HiFAT and LoFAT, while avoiding

---

[2] We replace inodes in the original grammar with strings. In FAT32, with no hardlinks, it is easier to just represent the contents of regular files as strings.

one of the key problems, namely, the general difficulty of getting read-over-write theorems to apply because of various simplifications in the course of a rewriting proof that keep the left-hand side of the rewrite rule from being unifiable with the target.

$$
\begin{aligned}
&\{ \\
&r := \mathsf{mkdir}(\text{"/tmp/docs"}) \\
&s := \mathsf{mkdir}(\text{"/tmp/docs/pdf-docs"}) \\
&r \Rightarrow 0 * s \Rightarrow - * t \Rightarrow - \\
&t := \mathsf{stat}(\text{"/tmp/docs"}) \\
&r \Rightarrow 0 * t \Rightarrow 0 \\
&\}
\end{aligned}
$$

Fig. 5. Reasoning about longer sequences of system calls

This leads to another example (Fig. 5), which is worked out in ACL2 along the same lines as demonstrated here. This exemplifies the kinds of properties we need to prove across sequences of operations, when sometimes we need to logically disregard the effect of one system call such as the second mkdir in this case.

This example also shows one interesting approach to verifying filesystem properties, in which the precondition for one system call to do the desired thing may be excessively verbose to write out in full, but can be more concisely expressed in terms of the return value of a previous system call.

3.3 LoFAT-HiFAT Correspondence

Many of the system calls in LoFAT are implemented through three primitive operations: lofat-find-file, lofat-remove-file, and lofat-place-file. For instance, the system call mkdir is implemented as a call of lofat-place-file with an empty directory as an argument. Thus, the proofs of specifications for these system calls reduce to proofs about these three primitives.

More precisely, we prove the HiFAT versions of these system calls, respectively hifat-find-file, hifat-remove-file, and hifat-place-file, to have properties as required by the specifications for the system calls. These turn out to be read-over-write properties, adapted as the case may be for "writes" to the filesystem which are file creations, file updates and file deletions. In a general form, these properties state:

1. A read from the filesystem following a write at the same location yields that which was written.
2. A read from the filesystem following a write at a different place yields the same result as a read before the write.

Then, by proving the refinement relationship for each of these three primitives in LoFAT, we are able to much more easily prove that LoFAT meets specifications. LoFAT is a linearly addressed data structure, since it emulates the layout of an actual FAT32 disk image; thus, any proofs regarding operations on LoFAT by necessity involve separation properties between different files. The executable function lofat-to-hifat, which transforms a LoFAT instance to a HiFAT instance, checks whether the clusterchains across all the different files in a filesystem are disjoint from each other. This disjointness is a necessary property for a well-formed FAT32 disk image, and therefore a necessary property of a well-formed LoFAT instance. However, such checks on the disjointness of sets of clusterchains can get expensive in a large filesystem instance, which is why we deem it inadvisable to continue with the earlier implementation of LoFAT which effects one or more transformations between HiFAT and LoFAT for each system call. Therefore, we develop more efficient implementations of the LoFAT primitives lofat-find-file and lofat-remove-file; verify that each refines the respective HiFAT primitive; and adapt the system calls in LoFAT to use the new primitives.

We provide specifications for the system calls in LoFAT, through which programs making use of the filesystem can be reasoned about. LoFAT functions at one level of remove from the disk image, since it is a single-threaded object; however, it replicates the structure of the disk in memory and each system call it offers is an analogue of the system call of the same name, adapted for the use of programs written in the applicative ACL2 language. Some of the system calls implemented in LoFAT involve file descriptors; as a result file descriptor tables and file tables are implemented as part of LoFAT. This means that, viewing the disk image as a linearly addressable entity and disregarding details about caching, each execution of a program using FAT32's POSIX interface is mirrored by an execution of an ACL2 program using LoFAT with the same program logic but making use of LoFAT's system calls; and any proofs carried out on the latter also apply to the former. This correspondence underlies the focus on binary compatibility and efficient execution in the present work.

A significant part of the implementation has been the reworking of the LoFAT primitives lofat-find-file and lofat-remove-file. The latter now guarantees that files not in the path of a file operation will remain unchanged in their placement in the data region, in contrast to the earlier implementation which transformed to HiFAT, performed the removal, and transformed back to HiFAT, effectively reallocating space in the data region for every file in the filesystem. For proving that these functions refine their HiFAT equivalents, respectively hifat-place-file and hifat-remove-file, we opted to simplify the specifications of these functions to make them *no-change losers*[3]: functions which operate on a data structure making sure to return it unchanged if returning an error code indicating failure. This yielded rewrite rules with fewer hypotheses, which made it simpler to prove the lemmas necessary to support our filesystem call specifications.

---

[3] This is a term from ACL2 lore, and often used in the ACL2 source code.

cp, ls, mkdir, mv, rm, rmdir, stat, truncate, wc

Fig. 6. Coreutils programs in the co-simulation test suite

4 Evaluation

In evaluating this system, we account for the ease of writing and verifying programs using LoFAT. To demonstrate that realistic programs can indeed be written, we develop a test suite of programs which emulate existing programs from the Coreutils. Building upon the tests already developed our earlier work on HiFAT and LoFAT, we add support for the system calls readdir, opendir, closedir and truncate; following this, we are able to write a program emulating the Coreutils program truncate. Each of the programs in our test suite is compared in terms of output and filesystem state to the program it emulated in one or more co-simulation tests; programs which write to standard output are tested for character-by-character correspondence to the canonical programs, and programs which change the state of the filesystem are compared for file-by-file correspondence to the state after running the canonical program with the same arguments Fig. 6 summarizes the programs which are tested in the co-simulation test suite.

The proof development for supporting the filesystem proofs demonstrated in this paper is necessarily complex, since AbsFAT needs to abstract HiFAT and in turn LoFAT without loss of information. Examining the code supporting the basic frame operations collapse and partial collapse, the different system calls, the proofs that these system calls abstract the corresponding system calls in HiFAT and the proofs of the examples developed in this paper, we count 33,106 lines of code across 79 function definitions and 1143 lemmas. It remains of interest to check if ACL2's features for automatically generating lemmas [1], already used in LoFAT, could be brought to bear on some of these.

5 Related Work

Much of the prior work has developed new verified filesystems, making crash consistency a priority. Yggdrasil [28], a verification toolkit, employing SMT solving in Z3 [21] but eschewing explicit separation reasoning, delivers the Yxv6 filesystem which has verified crash consistency properties. COGENT [2], a verifying compiler, provides a domain specific language and generates executable filesystem code from a specifications in that language, accompanied by proofs of correctness in Isabelle/HOL [23]. FSCQ [6], which introduces Crash Hoare Logic, is the first in a family of related filesystems verified in Coq [3] which also includes DFSCQ [5], a filesystem providing and adhering to a formal specification for the fdatasync system call, and SFSCQ [12], a filesystem with verified security properties. While separation logic is part of the development of Crash Hoare Logic in FSCQ, that effort does not include reasoning at the file operation level.

The work of Gardner et al. on specifying preconditions and postconditions of POSIX filesystem calls [8] has been extended into a theory of concurrent operation of filesystems [24]. This work, however, has not attempted to deliver an executable filesystem upon which programs could be run.

Two tangentially related systems with similar aims to AbsFAT are the work of Koh et al. [16] towards verifying the operating system components involved in a networked server, and the work of Chajed et al. [4] on Argosy, a verified system for stacking storage layers. While these systems are executable, they do not offer the sort of support for constructing and simplifying proofs about filesystem clients that AbsFAT does.

6   Conclusion

This paper describes AbsFAT, a separation logic model which formally describes the different system calls in LoFAT, a faithful executable model of FAT32. AbsFAT's formal descriptions of these system calls support proofs of correctness for programs which interact with the filesystem. The examples in the paper demonstrate the kinds of Hoare triples that arise in this verification context and how ACL2 completes these proofs by rewriting guided by AbsFAT's separation logic formulation. This application of abstract separation logic to an executable filesystem model is novel and shows several general principles which are applicable to the verification of filesystems other than FAT32 and the programs which make use of them.

An informal survey of filesystem-related bug reports yielded the interesting examples of Shareaza, a file sharing application [27]. A bug in Shareaza caused an infinite loop when files larger than 4 GB were to be saved to a FAT32-formatted partition. Such an operation is disallowed by the published FAT32 specification in the interests of keeping clusterchains to a manageable length and the error code EFBIG is designated for filesystem implementations to indicate an error of this nature. This sort of bug, which could be mitigated by attention to return values and error codes, is our motivation for building the precise filesystem models this paper discusses.

Availability

The proofs and the cosimulation tests discussed in the paper can be found in the books/projects/filesystem subdirectory of the ACL2 distribution, which is available at https://github.com/acl2/acl2/. Instructions for certifying the books in ACL2 are provided in README.md in that subdirectory.

References

1. ACL2 Community: ACL2 documentation for MBE. http://www.cs.utexas.edu/users/moore/acl2/current/manual/index.html?topic=ACL2____MAKE-EVENT

2. Amani, S., et al.: Cogent: verifying high-assurance file system implementations. ACM SIGPLAN Not. **51**(4), 175–188 (2016)
3. Bertot, Y., Castéran, P.: Interactive Theorem Proving and Program Development: Coq'Art: The Calculus of Inductive Constructions. Springer, Heidelberg (2004)
4. Chajed, T., Tassarotti, J., Kaashoek, M.F., Zeldovich, N.: Argosy: verifying layered storage systems with recovery refinement. In: Proceedings of the 40th ACM SIG-PLAN Conference on Programming Language Design and Implementation (PLDI), pp. 1054–1068. ACM (2019)
5. Chen, H., et al.: Verifying a high-performance crash-safe file system using a tree specification. In: Proceedings of the 26th Symposium on Operating Systems Principles (SOSP), pp. 270–286. ACM (2017)
6. Chen, H., Ziegler, D., Chajed, T., Chlipala, A., Kaashoek, M.F., Zeldovich, N.: Using crash Hoare logic for certifying the FSCQ file system. In: USENIX Annual Technical Conference (USENIX ATC 2016). USENIX Association (2016)
7. Floyd, R.W.: Assigning meanings to programs. Proc. Am. Math. Soc. Symp. Appl. Math. **6**, 19–31 (1967)
8. Gardner, P., Ntzik, G., Wright, A.: Local reasoning for the POSIX file system. In: Shao, Z. (ed.) ESOP 2014. LNCS, vol. 8410, pp. 169–188. Springer, Heidelberg (2014). https://doi.org/10.1007/978-3-642-54833-8_10
9. Goel, S.: Formal verification of application and system programs based on a validated x86 ISA model. Ph.D. thesis, Department of Computer Science, The University of Texas at Austin (2016)
10. Hesselink, W.H., Lali, M.: Formalizing a hierarchical file system. Electron. Not. Theoret. Comput. Sci. **259**, 67–85 (2009). Proceedings of the 14th BCS-FACS Refinement Workshop (REFINE)
11. Hoare, C.: An axiomatic basis for computer programming. Commun. ACM **12**(10), 576–580 (1969)
12. Ileri, A., Chajed, T., Chlipala, A., Kaashoek, F., Zeldovich, N.: Proving confidentiality in a file system using DiskSec. In: 13th USENIX Symposium on Operating Systems Design and Implementation (OSDI), pp. 323–338. USENIX Association, October 2018
13. Kerrisk, M.: Basename (3)-Linux manual page. Accessed 01 Aug 2020
14. Kerrisk, M.: Dirname (3)-Linux manual page. Accessed 01 Aug 2020
15. Kerrisk, M.: Errno (3)-Linux manual page. Accessed 01 Oct 2019
16. Koh, N., et al.: From C to interaction trees: specifying, verifying, and testing a networked server. In: Proceedings of the 8th ACM SIGPLAN International Conference on Certified Programs and Proofs (CPP), pp. 234–248. ACM (2019)
17. Kaufmann, M., Manolios, P., Moore, J.S.: Computer-Aided Reasoning: An Approach. Kluwer Academic Publishers, Dordrecht (2000)
18. Mehta, M.P., Cook, W.R.: Binary-compatible verification of filesystems with ACL2. In: 10th International Conference on Interactive Theorem Proving (ITP). Leibniz International Proceedings in Informatics (LIPIcs), vol. 141, pp. 25:1–25:18. Schloss Dagstuhl-Leibniz-Zentrum fuer Informatik (2019)
19. Microsoft: Microsoft extensible firmware initiative FAT32 file system specification, December 2000. https://download.microsoft.com/download/1/6/1/161ba512-40e2-4cc9-843a-923143f3456c/fatgen103.doc
20. Morgan, C., Sufrin, B.: Specification of the UNIX filing system. IEEE Trans. Softw. Eng. **SE-10**(2), 128–142 (1984)
21. de Moura, L., Bjørner, N.: Z3: an efficient SMT solver. In: Ramakrishnan, C.R., Rehof, J. (eds.) TACAS 2008. LNCS, vol. 4963, pp. 337–340. Springer, Heidelberg (2008). https://doi.org/10.1007/978-3-540-78800-3_24

22. Myreen, M.O.: Separation logic adapted for proofs by rewriting. In: Kaufmann, M., Paulson, L.C. (eds.) ITP 2010. LNCS, vol. 6172, pp. 485–489. Springer, Heidelberg (2010). https://doi.org/10.1007/978-3-642-14052-5_34

23. Nipkow, T., Wenzel, M., Paulson, L.C.: Isabelle/HOL: A Proof Assistant for Higher-Order Logic, vol. 2283. Springer, Heidelberg (2002)

24. Ntzik, G., da Rocha Pinto, P., Sutherland, J., Gardner, P.: A concurrent specification of POSIX file systems. In: 32nd European Conference on Object-Oriented Programming (ECOOP). Leibniz International Proceedings in Informatics (LIPIcs), vol. 109, pp. 4:1–4:28. Schloss Dagstuhl-Leibniz-Zentrum fuer Informatik (2018)

25. O'Hearn, P., Reynolds, J., Yang, H.: Local Reasoning about Programs that Alter Data Structures. In: Fribourg, L. (ed.) CSL 2001. LNCS, vol. 2142, pp. 1–19. Springer, Heidelberg (2001). https://doi.org/10.1007/3-540-44802-0_1

26. Reynolds, J.C.: Separation logic: a logic for shared mutable data structures. In: Proceedings of the 17th Annual IEEE Symposium on Logic in Computer Science (LICS), pp. 55–74. IEEE Computer Society (2002)

27. Bug: file-system file-size limit handling (2011). http://shareaza.sourceforge.net/phpbb/viewtopic.php?f=7&t=1118

28. Sigurbjarnarson, H., Bornholt, J., Torlak, E., Wang, X.: Push-button verification of file systems via crash refinement. In: 12th USENIX Symposium on Operating Systems Design and Implementation (OSDI), pp. 1–16. USENIX Association, November 2016

29. Wright, A.: Structural separation logic. Ph.D. thesis, Imperial College London (2013)

30. Yang, H., O'Hearn, P.: A semantic basis for local reasoning. In: Nielsen, M., Engberg, U. (eds.) FoSSaCS 2002. LNCS, vol. 2303, pp. 402–416. Springer, Heidelberg (2002). https://doi.org/10.1007/3-540-45931-6_28

Software Product Lines

Merging Cloned Alloy Models with Colorful Refactorings

Chong Liu[1,2], Nuno Macedo[1,3(✉)], and Alcino Cunha[1,2]

[1] INESC TEC, Porto, Portugal
nuno.m.macedo@inesctec.pt
[2] Universidade do Minho, Braga, Portugal
[3] Faculdade de Engenharia, Universidade do Porto, Porto, Portugal

Abstract. Likewise to code, *clone-and-own* is a common way to create variants of a model, to explore the impact of different features while exploring the design of a software system. Previously, we have introduced *Colorful Alloy*, an extension of the popular Alloy language and toolkit to support feature-oriented design, where model elements can be annotated with feature expressions and further highlighted with different colors to ease understanding. In this paper we propose a catalog of refactorings for Colorful Alloy models, and show how they can be used to iteratively merge cloned Alloy models into a single feature-annotated colorful model, where the commonalities and differences between the different clones are easily perceived, and more efficient aggregated analyses can be performed.

Keywords: Feature-oriented design · Refactoring · Alloy · Model merging · Clone-and-own

1 Introduction

Modern software systems are often highly-configurable, effectively encoding a family of software products, or a *software product line* (SPL). *Feature-oriented software development* [3] is the most successful approach proposed to support the development of such systems, organizing software around the key concept of a *feature*, a unit of functionality that implements some requirements and represents a configuration option. Naturally, software design is also affected by such concerns, and several formal specification languages and analyses have been proposed to support *feature-oriented software design* [4,8,26,31]. In particular, this team has proposed Colorful Alloy [26], a lightweight, annotative approach for Alloy and its Analyzer [17], that allows the introduction of fine-grained variability points without sacrificing the language's flexibility. Although different background colors are used to ease the understanding of variability annotations [18], fine-grained extensions still cause maintainability and obfuscation problems.

Refactorings [12,30] – transformations that change the structure of code but preserve its external behavior – could be employed to address some of those problems and generally improve the quality of variability-annotated formal models.

© Springer Nature Switzerland AG 2020
G. Carvalho and V. Stolz (Eds.): SBMF 2020, LNCS 12475, pp. 173–191, 2020.
https://doi.org/10.1007/978-3-030-63882-5_11

However, classical refactoring is not well-suited for feature-oriented development, since both the set of possible variants and the behavior of each variant must be preserved [36], and refactoring laws are typically too coarse-grained to be applied in this context, focusing on constructs such as entire functions or classes.

One of the standard ways to implement multiple variants is through *clone-and-own*. However, as the cost to maintain the clones and synchronize changes in replicas increases, developers may benefit from migrating (by merging) such variants into a single SPL. Fully-automated approaches for clone merging (e.g., [32]) assume a quantifiable measure of quality that is not easy to define when the goal is to merge code, and even less so when the goal is to merge formal abstract specifications. An alternative approach is to rely on refactoring [11], supporting the user in performing stepwise, semi-automated merge transformations.

In this paper we first propose a catalog of variability-aware refactoring laws for Colorful Alloy, covering all model constructs – from structural declarations to axioms and assertions – and granularity levels – from whole paragraphs to formulas and expressions. Then, we show how these refactorings can be used to migrate a set of legacy Alloy clones into a colorful SPL using an approach similar to [11]. Fine-grained refactoring is particularly relevant in this context: design in Alloy is done at high levels of abstraction and variants often introduce precise changes, and refactoring only at the paragraph level would lead to unnecessary code replication and a difficulty to identify variability points. The individual refactoring laws and some automatic refactoring strategies, that compose together several merge refactorings, have been implemented in the Colorful Analyzer. We evaluate them by merging back Alloy models projected from previously developed Colorful Alloy SPLs, and by merging several variants of plain Alloy models that are packaged in its official release.

The remainder of this paper is organized as follows. Section 2 presents an overview of Colorful Alloy. Section 3 presents some of the proposed variability-aware refactoring laws, and Sect. 4 illustrates how they can be used to refactor a collection of cloned models into an SPL. Section 5 describes the implementation of the technique and its preliminary evaluation. Section 6 discusses related work. Finally, Sect. 7 concludes the paper and discusses some future work.

2   Colorful Alloy

Colorful Alloy [26] is an extension of the popular Alloy [17] specification language and its Analyzer to support feature-oriented software design, where elements of a model can be annotated with feature identifiers – highlighted in the visualizer with different colors to ease understanding – and be analyzed with feature-aware commands. The annotative approach of Colorful Alloy contrasts with compositional approaches to develop feature-oriented languages (either for modeling or for programming), where the elements of each feature are kept separate in different code units (to be composed together before compilation or analysis). We reckon the annotative approach is a better fit for Alloy (and design languages in

```
1   fact FeatureModel {
2     2 1 some none 1 2    // 2 Hierarchical requires 1 Categories
3     3 1 some none 1 3 }  // 3 Multiple requires 1 Categories
4
5   sig Product {
6     images: set Image,
7     1 catalog: one Catalog 1 ,
8     1 3 category: one Category 3 1 ,
9     1 3 category: some Category 3 1 }
10
11  sig Image {}
12  sig Catalog { thumbnails: set Image }
13  fact Thumbnails {
14    1 all c:Catalog | c.thumbnails in (catalog.c).images 1
15    1 all c:Catalog | c.thumbnails in (category.( 2 inside 2 + 2 ^inside 2 ).c).images 1 }
16
17    1 2 sig Category { inside: one Catalog } 2 1
18    1 2 sig Category { inside: one Catalog+Category } 2 1
19    1 2 fact Acyclic { all c:Category | c not in c.^inside } 2 1
20
21  pred Scenario { some Product.images and 1 some Category 1 }
22  run Scenario for 10
23
24  assert AllCataloged { 2 all p:Product | some (p.category.^inside & Catalog) 2 }
25  check AllCataloged with 1 , 2 for 10
```

Fig. 1. E-commerce specification in Colorful Alloy, where background and strike-through colors denote positive and negative annotations, respectively.

general), since changes introduced by a feature are often fine-grained (for example, change part of a constraint) and not easily implemented (nor perceivable) with compositional approaches.

Consider as an example the design of multiple variants of an e-commerce platform, adapted from [9], for which a possible encoding in Colorful Alloy is depicted in Fig. 1. The base model (with no extra feature) simply organizes products into catalogs, illustrated with thumbnail images. Like modeling with regular Alloy, a Colorful Alloy model is defined by declaring *signatures* with *fields* inside (of arbitrary arity), which introduce sets of atoms and relations between them. A signature *hierarchy* can be introduced either by extension (**extends**) (with parent signatures being optionally marked as **abstract**) or inclusion (**in**), and simple *multiplicity* constraints (**some**, **lone** or **one**) can be imposed both on signatures and fields. In Fig. 1 the base model declares the signatures Product (l. 5), Image (l. 11) and Catalog (l. 12). Fields images (l. 6) and catalog (l. 7) associate each product with a *set* of images and exactly *one* catalog, respectively; field thumbnails (l. 12) associates each catalog with a set of images.

Additional model elements are organized as *paragraphs*: *facts* impose axioms while *assertions* specify properties to be checked; *predicates* and *functions* are reusable formulas and expressions, respectively. Atomic formulas are either inclusion (**in**) or multiplicity (**no**, **some**, **lone** or **one**) tests over relational expressions, which can be composed through first-order logic operators, such as universal (**all**) and existential (**some**) quantifiers and Boolean connectives (such as **not**, **and**, **or** or **implies**). Relational expressions combine the declared signatures and fields (and constants such as the empty relation **none** or the universe of

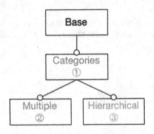

Fig. 2. Feature diagram of the e-commerce specification, where empty bullets denote optional child features.

atoms **univ**) with set operators (such as union **+** or intersection **&**) and relational operators (such as join **.** or transitive closure **^**). For the base e-commerce model all catalog thumbnails are assumed to be images of products that appear in that catalog. This is enforced in fact **Thumbnails** (l. 14), where expression **c.thumbnails** retrieves all thumbnails in catalog **c**, **catalog.c** all products in **c**, and (**catalog.c).images** all images of the products in **c**.

This design of the catalog considers 3 optional features: ① allowing products to be classified in categories; ② allowing hierarchical categories; and ③ allowing products to have multiple categories. Not all combinations of these features are valid, as depicted in the feature diagram [3] from Fig. 2: both hierarchical and multiple categories require the existence of categories. In Colorful Alloy certain elements can be annotated with positive ⓒ or negative ⬤ feature delimiters, determining their presence or absence on variants with or without feature *c*, respectively. Annotations can only be applied to elements of the Alloy AST, either optional elements whose removal does not invalidate the AST – such as declarations and paragraphs – or branches of binary expressions that have a neutral element which can replace the annotated element – such as conjunctions, disjunctions, intersections or unions. Annotations can be nested, which denotes the conjunction of presence conditions. To ease the understanding, and inspired by [18], the Colorful Analyzer employs background colors (for positive annotations) and colored struck-through lines (for negative ones).

In the e-commerce example, feature ① introduces a new signature **Category**, but depending on whether ② is present or not, this signature declares a different field **inside**: without hierarchical categories each category is inside exactly one catalog (l. 17); otherwise, a category can also be inside another category (l. 18). Fields may also be annotated: with categories the **catalog** field of products is removed with a negative annotation ⬤ (l. 7) and products are now assigned a category through **category** which, depending on whether ③ is present, assigns exactly one (l. 8) or multiple (l. 9) categories to a product. Hierarchical categories require an additional fact **Acyclic** (l. 19) that forbids categories from containing themselves, either directly or indirectly. Fact **Thumbnails** must be adapted when categories are introduced, so that products are retrieved indirectly from the categories of the catalog. Since one constraint is negatively annotated with

❶ and the other positively with ①, they are actually exclusive. In the latter, depending on the presence of ② either `inside` or its transitive closure `^inside` is used to retrieve all parent categories of products. This finer variability point is introduced by annotating the branches of a union expression; when a presence condition is not met, that branch is replaced by its neutral element, the empty relation. Colorful Alloy does not explicitly support feature models, but the user can restrict valid variants using normal facts. In Fig. 1 fact `FeatureModel` (ll. 1–3) encodes the restrictions from the feature diagram in Fig. 2, forcing ① to be selected whenever ② or ③ are: otherwise formula **some none** would be introduced in the model creating an inconsistency.

Like in Alloy, *run* commands can be declared to animate the model under certain properties and *check* commands to verify assertions, both within a specified scope (max size) for signatures. In Colorful Alloy, a scope on features may also be provided, to restrict the variants that should be considered by a command. In Fig. 1 a run command is defined (l. 22) to animate predicate `Scenario` (l. 21): show an instance for any variant (no feature scope is defined) where there are products with images assigned (expression `Product.images` retrieves all images of all products), and, if the variant considers categories, some must also exist. Since no feature scope is imposed, the generated scenario may be for any of the 5 valid variants. To verify the correctness of the design for hierarchical categories, an assertion `AllCataloged` is specified (l. 24) to check whether every product is inside a catalog. The feature scope ①,② of the associated check command (l. 25) restricts analysis to the two variants that have those features selected, those for which `AllCataloged` is relevant.

Some typing rules are imposed on Colorful Alloy models. Roughly, annotations may be nested in an arbitrary order but must not be contradictory, and conditional elements may only be used in compatible annotation contexts. Feature constraints are extracted from simple facts such as `FeatureModel` making these rules more flexible. For instance, `AllCataloged` refers to elements only present in ① variants, but since we known that ② implies ①, that redundant annotation may be omitted from its specification. This is actually an enhancement of the type system from the original proposal [26]. Another improvement is the support for duplicated signature and field identifiers as long as their annotation context is disjoint. Such is the case of both `Category` declarations. The rule for calling such elements was also relaxed: they may be used in contexts compatible with the union of all the declaration' annotations. For instance, `Category` can be used in any context annotated with ① since one of the two signatures will necessarily exist.

3 Refactoring Laws for Colorful Alloy

Variability-aware refactorings can promote the maintenance of SPLs while preserving the set of variants and their individual behavior. This section proposes a catalog of such refactorings for Colorful Alloy, which complements non variability-aware ones previously proposed for standard Alloy [13,14]. Due to space limitations, only a sample of this catalog is presented.

The refactoring laws for Colorful Alloy are presented in the form of equations between two templates (with square brackets marking optional elements), following the style from [14], under the context of a feature model F extracted from the colorful model under analysis (as described in Sect. 5). When the preconditions are met and the left or right templates matched, rules can be derived to apply the refactoring in either direction. Throughout the section ⓒ will denote an either positive or negative annotation for c, and Ⓒ a (possibly empty) sequence of positive or negative annotations. Models are assumed to be type-checked when the rules are applied, so without loss of generality, in an expression Ⓒⅇ Ⓒ we assume that the features c in the closing annotations appear in the reverse order as those in the opening annotations, that there are no contradictory annotations, that only supported elements of the AST are annotated, and that duplicated identifiers have disjoint annotation contexts. We use *ann* to refer to any element amenable of being annotated (possibly itself already annotated), *exp* for expressions, *frm* for formulas, *n* for identifiers, *ds* for (possibly-annotated) relation declarations, and *scp* for scopes on atoms. We assume that the extracted feature model F is encoded as a propositional formula over positive or negative feature annotations [10].

The first set of laws concern the feature annotations themselves, and are often useful to align them in a way that enables more advanced refactorings.

Law 1 (Annotation reordering).

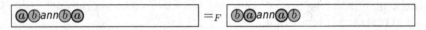

This basic law originates from the commutativity of conjunction, and allows users to reorganize feature annotations.

Law 2 (Redundant annotations).

ⓐⓑ*ann*ⓑⓐ $=_F$ ⓐ*ann*ⓐ

provided $F \models$ ⓐ $\rightarrow$ ⓑ.

This law relies on the feature model to identify redundant annotations that can be removed or introduced. For instance, if F imposes ② $\rightarrow$ ① (as in the e-commerce SPL), then whenever a ② annotation is present ① is superfluous, and vice-versa for ❶ and ❷. Note that it can also be used to remove duplicated annotations. Similar laws are defined to manage the feature scopes of commands.

The next set of refactoring laws concerns declarations. The first removes the **abstract** qualifier from signature declarations.

Law 3 (Remove abstract qualifier).

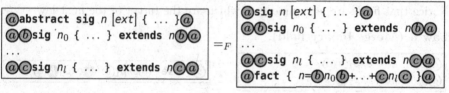

provided $l \geq 0$.

Our catalog contains several similar variability-aware laws, some adapted from [13], to remove syntactic sugar from signature and field declarations (e.g.., multiplicity annotations) while preserving the behavior in all variants. These laws are used as a preparatory step to enable the following merge refactorings.

Law 4 (Merge top-level signature).

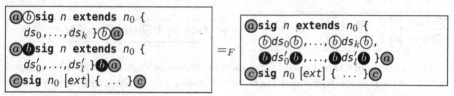

Law 5 (Merge sub-signature).

$$\begin{array}{l}
\text{@⑤sig } n \text{ extends } n_0 \text{ \{} \\
\quad ds_0,\dots,ds_k \text{ \}⑤@} \\
\text{@⑤sig } n \text{ extends } n_0 \text{ \{} \\
\quad ds'_0,\dots,ds'_l \text{ \}⑤@} \\
\text{©sig } n_0 \text{ [ext] \{ \dots \}©}
\end{array}
=_F
\begin{array}{l}
\text{@sig } n \text{ extends } n_0 \text{ \{} \\
\quad \text{⑤}ds_0\text{⑤},\dots,\text{⑤}ds_k\text{⑤}, \\
\quad \text{⑤}ds'_0\text{⑤},\dots,\text{⑤}ds'_l\text{⑤} \text{ \}@} \\
\text{©sig } n_0 \text{ [ext] \{ \dots \}©}
\end{array}$$

provided $F \models @ \rightarrow ©$.

Signatures cannot be freely merged independently of their annotations, since in Colorful Alloy they are not sufficiently expressive to represent the disjunction of presence conditions. Signatures with the same identifier can be merged if they partition a certain annotation context @ on ⑤, in which case the latter can be dropped (but pushed down to the respective field declarations). Due to the opposite ⑤ annotations the two signatures never coexist in a variant, and the merged signature will exist in exactly the same variants, those determined by @. Law 5 considers the merging of the signatures that extend another signature. Here, a precondition guarantees that there are no conflicts after merging: the context © of the parent signature n_0 must be determined solely by the @ portion of the children annotations (i.e., regardless of ⑤ which will be dropped). Thus, the signature n_0 must be merged beforehand. Notice that these laws act on signatures without qualifiers. If qualifiers were compatible between the two signatures, they can be reintroduced after merging by applying the syntactic sugar laws in the opposite direction.

Returning to the e-commerce example, it could be argued that the declaration of two distinct Category signatures under ① depending on whether ② is also selected or not, is not ideal. Since neither signature has other qualifiers, Law 4 can be applied directly from left to right, resulting in the single signature

```
①sig Category { ②inside: one Catalog②, ②inside: one Catalog+Category② }①
```

Notice that fields are left unmerged, which are the target of the next law.

Law 6 (Merge binary field).

$$\begin{array}{l} @ⓑn\text{: set } exp_1 ⓑ@, \\ @ⓑn\text{: set } exp_2 ⓑ@ \end{array} \quad =_F \quad @n\text{: set } ⓑexp_1ⓑ + ⓑexp_2ⓑ@$$

This law allows binary fields with the same identifier to be merged, even when they have different binding expressions, whenever they partition an annotation context @. Similar laws are defined for fields of higher arity. Back to the e-commerce example, the duplicated field `inside` introduced by the merging of signature `Category` could be merged into a single field with Law 6, after applying a syntactic refactoring law to move the **one** multiplicity annotation to a fact.

```
①sig Category { inside: set ②Catalog②+②Catalog+Category② }①
①②fact{ all this:Category | one this.inside }②①
①②fact{ all this:Category | one this.inside }②①
```

Facts can be soundly merged for whatever feature annotations, since they are all just conjuncted when running a command.

Law 7 (Merge fact).

$$\begin{array}{l} @\textbf{fact } [n] \{ frm_1 \}@ \\ ⓑ\textbf{fact } [n] \{ frm_2 \}ⓑ \end{array} \quad =_F \quad \textbf{fact } [n] \{ @frm_1@\textbf{and}ⓑfrm_2ⓑ \}$$

Other elements that can be used in expressions or commands can be merged only when a feature partitions their annotation context. As examples, we show those laws for predicates and assertions.

Law 8 (Merge predicate).

$$\begin{array}{l} @ⓑ\textbf{pred } n[n_0:exp_0,\ldots,n_k:exp_k] \{ \\ \quad frm_1 \}ⓑ@ \\ @ⓑ\textbf{pred } n[n_0:exp_0',\ldots,n_k:exp_k'] \{ \\ \quad frm_2 \}ⓑ@ \end{array} \quad =_F \quad \begin{array}{l} @\textbf{pred } n[\\ \quad n_0:ⓑexp_0ⓑ+ⓑexp_0'ⓑ,\ldots, \\ \quad n_k:ⓑexp_kⓑ+ⓑexp_k'ⓑ] \{ \\ \quad ⓑfrm_1ⓑ\textbf{and}ⓑfrm_2ⓑ \}@ \end{array}$$

Law 9 (Merge assertion).

$$\begin{array}{l} @ⓑ\textbf{assert } n \{ frm_1 \}ⓑ@ \\ @ⓑ\textbf{assert } n \{ frm_2 \}ⓑ@ \end{array} \quad =_F \quad \begin{array}{l} @\textbf{assert } n \{ \\ \quad ⓑfrm_1ⓑ\textbf{and}ⓑfrm_2ⓑ \}@ \end{array}$$

Commands are bounded by the feature scope rather than annotated. If two commands act on a partition of the variants, they can be merged into a command addressing their union. As an example, we show a law for merging run commands.

Law 10 (Merge run command).

$$\begin{array}{l} \textbf{run } n \ scp \ \textbf{with } @,ⓑ \\ \textbf{run } n \ scp \ \textbf{with } @,ⓑ \\ ©\textbf{pred } n[\ldots] \{ \ldots \}© \end{array} \quad =_F \quad \begin{array}{l} \textbf{run } n \ scp \ \textbf{with } @ \\ ©\textbf{pred } n[\ldots] \{ \ldots \}© \end{array}$$

provided $F \models$ ⓐ → ⓒ.

Likewise Law 5, a precondition guarantees that there are no ambiguities after merging, so that the merged annotation ⓐ completely determines the the predicate to be run. Thus, the respective predicates must be merged beforehand.

Lastly, we provide refactoring laws for formulas and expressions. This distinguishes our approach from other works, addressing finer variability annotations.

Law 11 (Merge common expression).

$$\boxed{ⓐ ann\ op'\ ann_1 ⓐ op ⓐ ann\ op'\ ann_2 ⓐ} =_F \boxed{ann\ op'\ (ⓐ ann_1 ⓐ op ⓐ ann_2 ⓐ)}$$

where $op \in \{\text{+}, \&, \textbf{and}, \textbf{or}\}$ *and* op' *is op or its dual.*

This law arises from the distributivity of operators and can be applied to both annotated formulas and expressions. An extreme application is when we have ⓐ*ann*ⓐ*op*ⓐ*ann*ⓐ, which can be refactored into *ann*.

Law 12 (Merge left-side inclusion).

$$\boxed{ⓐ exp\ \textbf{in}\ exp_1 ⓐ \textbf{and} ⓑ exp\ \textbf{in}\ exp_2 ⓑ} =_F \boxed{exp\ \textbf{in}\ (ⓐ exp_1 ⓐ \& ⓑ exp_2 ⓑ)}$$

Law 13 (Merge right-side inclusion).

$$\boxed{ⓐ exp_1\ \textbf{in}\ exp ⓐ \textbf{and} ⓑ exp_2\ \textbf{in}\ exp ⓑ} =_F \boxed{(ⓐ exp_1 ⓐ \text{+} ⓑ exp_2 ⓑ)\ \textbf{in}\ exp}$$

These laws allow the simplification of inclusion tests over the same expression, for whatever annotations, and arise from the properties of intersection and union.

Law 14 (Merge quantification).

$$\boxed{\begin{array}{l} ⓐ ⓑ qnt\ n{:}exp_1\ |\ frm_1 ⓑ ⓐ \textbf{and} \\ ⓐ ⓑ qnt\ n{:}exp_2\ |\ frm_2 ⓑ ⓐ \end{array}} =_F \boxed{\begin{array}{l} ⓐ qnt\ n{:} ⓑ exp_1 ⓑ \text{+} ⓑ exp_2 ⓑ\ | \\ ⓑ frm_1 ⓑ \textbf{and} ⓑ frm_2 ⓑ ⓐ \end{array}}$$

where $qnt \in \{\textbf{all}, \textbf{some}, \textbf{lone}, \textbf{one}, \textbf{no}\}$.

This law is an example of a simple refactoring for formulas. Our catalog includes laws for other operators, such as composition and multiplicity tests. These, together with Law 11, allow us to merge the two facts that resulted from merging field `inside` into a single fact.

```
①fact{ all this:Category | one this.inside }①
```

We can now apply a syntactic sugar law to move this multiplicity constraint back into the field declaration and remove the fact, which, after an application of Law 11, results in

```
①sig Category { inside: one Catalog+②Category② }①
```

This means that each category is inside exactly one element, which can always be a catalog, or another category if hierarchies are supported. As another example, fact `Thumbnails` can be refactored into

```
fact Thumbnails { all c:Catalog | c.thumbnails in
  (①catalog.c①&①category.(②inside②+②^inside②).c①).images
```

The resulting fact is more compact, but whether it improves model comprehension is in the eyes of the designer.

```
sig Product {
  images: set Image, catalog: one Catalog }
sig Image {}
sig Catalog { thumbnails: set Image }
fact Thumbnails { all c:Catalog |
  c.thumbnails in (catalog.c).images }


pred Scenario {
  some Product.images }
run Scenario for 10
```

```
sig Product {
  images: set Image, category: one Category }
sig Image {}
sig Catalog { thumbnails: set Image }
fact Thumbnails { all c:Catalog |
  c.thumbnails in (category.inside.c).images }

sig Category { inside: one Catalog }

pred Scenario {
  some Product.images and some Category }
run Scenario for 10
```

Fig. 3. E-commerce base model ❶❷❸.

Fig. 4. Clone ①❷❸ introducing categories.

4   Migrating Clones into a Colorful Alloy Model

Approaches to SPL engineering can either be *proactive* – where an *a priori* domain analysis establishes the variability points that guide the development of the product family, *reactive* – where an existing product family is extended as new products and functionalities are developed, or *extractive* – where the family is extracted from existing software products with commonalities [21]. Colorful Alloy was initially conceived with the proactive approach in mind, with annotations being used precisely to extend a base model with the variability points addressing each desired feature. The model in Fig. 1 could be the result of a such a proactive approach to the design of the e-commerce platform.

With plain Alloy, to develop this design we would most likely resort to the clone-and-own approach. First, a base model, such as the one in Fig. 3 would be developed. This model would then be cloned and adapted to specify a new variant adding support for categories, as depicted in Fig. 4. This model would in turn be further cloned and adapted twice to support hierarchical or multiple categories. A final clone would then be developed to combine these two features. Due to space restrictions, these last three clones are not depicted, but they would very likely correspond to something like the projections of the colorful model in Fig. 1 over the respective feature combinations. This section first presents an extractive approach that could be used to migrate all such plain Alloy clone variants into a single Colorful Alloy model. Later we will also show how this technique can be adapted for a reactive scenario, where each new clone variant is migrated into a Colorful Alloy model already combining previous clones.

Our technique follows the idea proposed in [11] for migrating Java code clones into an SPL: first combine all the clones in a trivially correct, but verbose, initial SPL, and then improve it with a step-wise process using a catalog of variant-preserving refactorings. Some of the refactorings used in [11] are similar to those introduced in the previous section (e.g., there is a refactoring for pulling up a class to a common feature that behaves similarly to the merge signature refactoring of Law 4), but in the process they also use several preparatory refactorings to deal with alignment issues: sometimes the name of a method or class is changed in a clone, and in order to apply a merging refactoring the name in the clone

```
1   fact FeatureModel { 2 1 some none 1 2 and 3 1 some none 1 3 } .
2
3   1 2 2 sig Product { images: set Image, catalog: one Catalog } 2 2 1
4   ...
5   run Scenario with 1,2,3 for 10
6   1 2 2 sig Product { images: set Image, category: one Category } 2 2 1
7   ...
8   run Scenario with 1,2,3 for 10
9   1 2 3 sig Product { images: set Image, category: one Category } 3 2 1
10  ...
11  run Scenario with 1,2,3 for 10
12  check AllCataloged with 1,2,3 for 10
13  1 2 3 sig Product { images: set Image, category: some Category } 3 2 1
14  ...
15  run Scenario with 1,2,3 for 10
16  1 2 3 sig Product { images: set Image, category: some Category } 3 2 1
17  ...
18  run Scenario with 1,2,3 for 10
19  check AllCataloged with 1,2,3 for 10
```

Fig. 5. Part of the initial migrated e-commerce colorful model.

should first be made equal to the original one. Although we also require preparatory refactorings (e.g., to remove syntactic sugar from declarations), the name alignment problem is orthogonal to the migration problem, and in this paper we will focus solely on the latter, assuming names in different clones were previously aligned.

To obtain the initial Colorful Alloy model it suffices to migrate every clone to a single model, annotating all paragraphs and commands of each clone with the feature expression that exactly describes the respective variant. For example, for the e-commerce example, the base model of Fig. 3 would be annotated with the feature expression ❶❷❸, since this clone does not specify any of the three features, the clone of Fig. 4 would be annotated with the feature expression ①❷❸, since it specifies the variant implementing only simple categories, and so on. If some feature combinations are invalid (there are only clones for some of the combinations), a fact that prevents the forbidden combinations should also be added, similar to the FeatureModel of Fig. 1. For the e-commerce example, part of the initial colorful model with all five variants is depicted in Fig. 5. Notice that, since all of the elements of the different clones are included and annotated with disjoint feature expressions, this Colorful Alloy model trivially and faithfully captures all the variants, although being quite verbose.

After obtaining this initial model, the refactorings presented in the previous section can be repeatedly used in a step-wise fashion to merge common elements, reducing the verbosity (and improving the readability) of the model. For the structural elements the key refactorings are merging signatures (Laws 4 and 5) and fields (Law 6), but, as already explained, some additional preparatory refactorings might be needed to enable those, for example reordering (or removing redundant) feature annotations or removing multiplicity qualifiers.

For example, in the initial model of Fig. 5 we can start by merging signature Product (and the respective fields) from clones ❶❷❸ and ①❷❸ and obtain

```
❷❸sig Product {
    images: set Image, ❸catalog: one Catalog❶, ①category: one Category① }❸❷
```

and then merge this with the definition from clone ①②❸ (by first removing the redundant feature annotation ① to enable the application of Law 4 – notice that from the feature model we can infer that ② implies ①) in order to obtain

```
❸sig Product {
    images: set Image, ❸❸catalog: one Catalog❸❸, ①category: one Category① }❸
```

The same result would be obtained if we first merged the declarations of Product from clones ①❷❸ and ①②❸, and then the one from clone ❶❷❸ (in this case, to apply Law 4 we would first need to remove the redundant annotation ❷, since from the feature model we can also infer that ❶ implies ❷). By repeatedly merging the variants of Product we can eventually get to the ideal (in the sense of having the least duplicate declarations) definition for this signature.

```
sig Product { images: set Image, ❶catalog: one Catalog❶, ①category: set Category① }
①fact { all p:Product | ❸one p.category❸ and ①some p.category① }①
```

If we repeat this process with all other model elements, we eventually get a (slightly optimized) version of the Colorful Alloy model in Fig. 1. This merging process also has an impact on performance: for instance, the merged command AllCataloged with feature scope ①,② and atom scope 10 – which only analyses two variants – takes 13.4 s if run in the clones individually, but after the presented merging process the command is checked 1.5x faster at 8.7 s in Colorful Alloy.

A similar technique can be used to migrate a new clone into an existing colorful model, thus enabling a reactive approach to SPL engineering. Let us suppose we already have the ideal colorful model for e-commerce, but we decide to introduce a new variant to support multiple catalogs when categories are disabled (a new feature ④). The definition of Product for this clone would be

```
sig Product { images: set Image, catalog: some Catalog }
```

To migrate this clone to the existing colorful SPL we would annotate the elements of the new variant with the feature expression that characterizes it, ❶❷❸④, annotate all elements of the existing SPL with ④ (since it does not support this new feature), refine the feature model to forbid invalid variants (adding some none annotated with ①④ to forbid the new feature in the presence of categories), and then restart the refactoring process to improve the obtained model.

5   Implementation and Evaluation

We implemented our catalog of refactorings in the Colorful Alloy Analyzer[1]. Individual refactorings are implemented in a contextual menu, activated by a right-click. The Analyzer automatically detects which refactorings can be applied in a given context. It also scans the model facts to extract feature model constraints

---

[1] https://github.com/chongliujlu/ColorfulAlloy/.

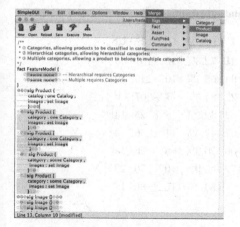

Fig. 6. Automatic merge strategies.

Fig. 7. Contextual refactoring menu.

from statements with the shape @some none@, so that the application of laws with preconditions on feature dependencies (Laws 2, 5 and 10) can be automated. For efficiency reasons, the prototype implements an incomplete decision procedure to check these preconditions, considering only simple implications directly derived from the feature model. This does not affect the soundness of the procedure but may fail to automatically detect some possible rule applications.

To simplify the application of the technique described in the previous section, we also implemented some automatic refactoring strategies to merge signature declarations and other model elements. The strategy to merge signature declarations first applies syntactic sugar refactorings to align the qualifiers of the different declarations. Then, it repeatedly applies Laws 4 and 5 to merge declarations, trying to eliminate features one at a time. Finally, a similar process is applied to merge field declarations with Law 6. To ensure termination, this strategy does not attempt to remove or add redundant features (sometimes it is necessary to add redundant features to enable further merging), being the user responsible for applying that law if necessary (by resorting to the contextual menu). The automatic strategies to merge the remaining paragraphs are similar. The strategy to merge facts essentially attempts to apply laws in the simplification direction (from left to right), until no further law is applicable. Figure 6 shows the menu with the automatic merge refactorings for our running example. If the option to merge signature Product is selected we will get the result in Fig. 7, where we still have three declarations for Product. To merge these, the user must first use the contextual menu to remove the redundant ① from the first two declarations, through right-clicking in Product as shown in Fig. 7. Then, by selecting again the automatic merge signature for Product we would get the single Product declaration (and additional fact) presented in the previous section.

Table 1. Evaluation results.

SPL	NP	LI	LF	R	DL	RS	US
E-commerce	5	112	31	72.3%	15	101	30
Vending	4	269	94	65.1%	10	140	19
Bestiary	16	140	22	84.3%	7	207	9
RingElection	2	91	52	42.9%	8	25	14
Grandpa	3	99	52	47.5%	11	36	9
AddressBook	3	133	106	20.3%	9	26	18
Hotel	4	324	172	46.9%	9	70	22
Average	5	267	76	54.2%	10	86	17

Our evaluation aimed to answer the following research questions: 1) Since in principle smaller specifications are easier to understand, how effective is the clone migration technique at reducing the total size of the models? 2) Is our catalog of refactorings sufficient to reach an ideal colorful model specified by an expert? To this purpose we considered various sets of cloned Alloy models that fall in two categories: three examples previously developed by us using a proactive approach with Colorful Alloy (e-commerce, vending machine, and bestiary) and four examples developed by D. Jackson in [17] and packaged with the standard Alloy Analyzer distribution as sample models (ring election, grandpa, address book, and hotel), for which several plain Alloy variants exist (very likely developed with clone-and-own). For the former examples, we generated the plain Alloy clones by projecting the colorful model over all the valid feature combinations.

To answer question 1) we applied our clone migration techniques to all of the examples, until we reached a point where no more merge refactorings could be applied, and compared the size of the resulting Colorful Alloy model with the combined size of all plain Alloy clones (measured in number of lines). The results are presented in Table 1, where NP denotes the number of product clones in the example, LI the initial number of lines, LF the number of lines after migration, R the achieved reduction in lines, DL the number of distinct refactoring laws that were used in the process, RS the number of individual refactoring steps (including those applied during the automatic strategies), and US the number of actions effectively performed by the user (each either a selection of an automatic refactoring strategy or an individual refactoring from a contextual menu). In average we achieved a reduction of around 54% lines, which is quite substantial: the formal design of the full SPL in the final Colorful Alloy model occupies in average half the size of all the plain Alloy clones combined, which in principle considerably simplifies its understanding. The lowest reduction was for the address book example (around 20%), since some of the clones had a completely different approach to specify the system events. The average number of refactoring steps was 86. This number has a strong correlation with the number of clones, since the proposed merging refactorings operate on two clones at a time – if a common element exists in n clones, we will need at least $n - 1$ rule applications to merge it. The average number of steps required by the user was 17, meaning that the proposed technique is quite usable in practice.

For question 2) we relied on the three examples where the clones were derived from previously developed Colorful Alloy models. For all of them, our catalog of refactorings was sufficient to migrate the clones and obtain the original colorful model from which they were derived. As seen in Table 1, these examples required a wider range of refactoring laws than the ones whose variants were developed with clone-and-own in plain Alloy, because the original Colorful Alloy models were purposely complex and diverse in terms of variability annotations, since they were originally developed to illustrate the potential of the Colorful Alloy language.

6 Related Work

Refactoring of SPLs. Some work has been proposed on behavior-preserving refactorings for systems with variability, although mostly focusing on compositional approaches [6,22,35,36] (even though some of these could be adapted to the annotative context). Refactorings for an annotative approach are proposed in [23] for C/C++ code with #ifdef annotations, which are often used to implicitly encode variability. The AST is enhanced with variability annotations which are considered during variability-aware static analysis to perform transformations that preserve the behavior of all variants. It does not, however, consider the existence of feature models. All these approaches adapt classic refactoring [12] operations, such as renaming or moving functions/fields, while our approach also supports finer-grained refactorings essential to formal software design, including the refactoring of formulas and relational expressions.

Many other refactoring approaches for SPLs have focused only on transforming feature models (e.g., [2]), including some that verify their soundness using Alloy [15,16,39], but without taking into consideration the actual code.

Refactorings have been proposed for formal specification languages such as Alloy [13,14] Object-Z [29,38], OCL-annotated UML [27], Event-B [1] and ASM [37], implementing typical refactorings such as renaming and moving elements, or introducing inheritance. Variability-aware formal specification languages are scarce, and we are not aware of refactorings aimed at them. Our approach relies on the refactorings proposed for normal Alloy [13,14] for the transformations that are not dependent on feature annotations.

Migration into SPLs Since the proactive approach is often infeasible due to the dynamic nature of the software development process, there is extensive work on migrating products into SPLs through extractive approaches, including for clone-and-own scenarios [5]. As detailed in Sect. 4, the approach presented in this paper can be applied for both the extractive and reactive scenarios, since new variants can be introduced to an already existing Colorful Alloy model.

Nonetheless, only some of this work tackles the migration of multiple variants at the source code level – in contrast to those acting at the domain analysis level, focusing on the feature model. Here, the approach most closely related to ours is the one proposed in [11], which builds on the refactoring operations proposed in [36] to handle the step-wise migration of multiple variants into a single software family. It is has been proposed for feature-oriented programming, a compositional approach, unlike our technique that follows an annotative approach. Again, our refactoring operations are also more fine-grained, while [36] focuses mainly on the refactoring of methods and fields, similarly to our merge signature and fields refactorings. Clone detection is used to semi-automate the process, while our approach is currently manual. In [2] refactorings are also proposed to migrate multiple products into an SPL, but focusing mostly on the feature model level.

Some migration approaches have focused on automating the process, which requires the automatic *comparing*, *matching* and *merging* of artifacts [7,32], including n-way merge [33]. However, such approaches are best-suited to deal with structural models, and not Alloy models rich in declarative constraints. They also assume the existence of quality metrics to guide the process, whose shape would be unclear considering the declarative constraints. Other approaches act on source code of cloned variants to extract variability information [25,34] or high-level architectural models with variability [19,20,24,28] but do not effectively transform the code into an SPL.

Among SPL migration techniques for a single legacy product, it is worth mentioning the one proposed in [40] that converts a product into an annotated colorful SPL using CIDE [18], which was the inspiration for Colorful Alloy [26]. Here, the user must initially mark certain elements as the "seeds" of a feature, and annotations are propagated to related elements automatically.

7   Conclusion and Future Work

In this paper we proposed a catalog of variant-preserving refactoring laws for Colorful Alloy, a language for feature-oriented software design. This catalog covers most aspects of the language, from structural elements, such as signature and field declarations, to formulas in facts and assertions, including analysis commands. Using these refactorings, we proposed a technique for migrating sets of plain Alloy clones, specifying different variants of a system, into a single Colorful Alloy SPL. The technique is step-wise and semi-automated, in the sense that the user is responsible for choosing which elements to merge and selecting occasional preparatory refactorings, being the application of the refactorings automated by the Analyzer. We evaluated the effectiveness of this migration technique with several sets of plain Alloy clones and achieved a substantial reduction in the size of the equivalent Colorful Alloy model, with likely gains in terms of maintainability, understandability, and efficiency of analysis.

In the future we intend to conduct a more extensive evaluation, with more examples and measuring other aspects of model quality (besides number of lines), in order to assess if the positive results achieved in the preliminary evaluation still hold. We also intend to implement a full SAT-based decision procedure for checking the preconditions of laws.

Acknowledgments. This work is financed by the ERDF – European Regional Development Fund through the Operational Programme for Competitiveness and Internationalisation – COMPETE 2020 Programme and by National Funds through the Portuguese funding agency, FCT – Fundação para a Ciência e a Tecnologia within project PTDC/CCI-INF/29583/2017 – POCI-01-0145-FEDER-029583.

References

1. Abrial, J., Butler, M.J., Hallerstede, S., Hoang, T.S., Mehta, F., Voisin, L.: Rodin: an open toolset for modelling and reasoning in event-B. Int. J. Softw. Tools Technol. Transf. **12**(6), 447–466 (2010)
2. Alves, V., Gheyi, R., Massoni, T., Kulesza, U., Borba, P., de Lucena, C.J.P.: Refactoring product lines. In: GPCE, pp. 201–210. ACM (2006)
3. Apel, S., Batory, D.S., Kästner, C., Saake, G.: Feature-Oriented Software Product Lines - Concepts and Implementation. Springer, Heidelberg (2013). https://doi.org/10.1007/978-3-642-37521-7
4. Apel, S., Scholz, W., Lengauer, C., Kästner, C.: Detecting dependences and interactions in feature-oriented design. In: ISSRE, pp. 161–170. IEEE Computer Society (2010)
5. Assunção, W.K.G., Lopez-Herrejon, R.E., Linsbauer, L., Vergilio, S.R., Egyed, A.: Reengineering legacy applications into software product lines: a systematic mapping. Empirical Softw. Eng. **22**(6), 2972–3016 (2017)
6. Borba, P., Teixeira, L., Gheyi, R.: A theory of software product line refinement. Theor. Comput. Sci. **455**, 2–30 (2012)
7. Boubakir, M., Chaoui, A.: A pairwise approach for model merging. In: Chikhi, S., Amine, A., Chaoui, A., Kholladi, M.K., Saidouni, D.E. (eds.) Modelling and Implementation of Complex Systems. LNNS, vol. 1, pp. 327–340. Springer, Cham (2016). https://doi.org/10.1007/978-3-319-33410-3_23
8. Classen, A., Cordy, M., Heymans, P., Legay, A., Schobbens, P.: Model checking software product lines with SNIP. Int. J. Softw. Tools Technol. Transf. **14**(5), 589–612 (2012)
9. Czarnecki, K., Pietroszek, K.: Verifying feature-based model templates against well-formedness OCL constraints. In: GPCE, pp. 211–220. ACM (2006)
10. Czarnecki, K., Wasowski, A.: Feature diagrams and logics: there and back again. In: SPLC, pp. 23–34. IEEE (2007)
11. Fenske, W., Meinicke, J., Schulze, S., Schulze, S., Saake, G.: Variant-preserving refactorings for migrating cloned products to a product line. In: SANER, pp. 316–326. IEEE (2017)
12. Fowler, M.: Refactoring - Improving the Design of Existing Code. Addison Wesley object technology series. Addison-Wesley, Boston (1999)
13. Gheyi, R.: A Refinement Theory for Alloy. Ph.D. thesis, Universidade Federal de Pernambuco (2007)
14. Gheyi, R., Borba, P.: Refactoring alloy specifications. Electron. Notes Theor. Comput. Sci. **95**, 227–243 (2004)
15. Gheyi, R., Massoni, T., Borba, P.: A theory for feature models in Alloy. In: Alloy Workshop @ SIGSOFT FSE, pp. 71–80 (2006)
16. Gheyi, R., Massoni, T., Borba, P.: Automatically checking feature model refactorings. J. UCS **17**(5), 684–711 (2011)
17. Jackson, D.: Software Abstractions: Logic, Language, and Analysis, revised edn. MIT Press, Cambridge (2012)

18. Kästner, C., Apel, S., Kuhlemann, M.: Granularity in software product lines. In: ICSE, pp. 311–320. ACM (2008)
19. Klatt, B., Krogmann, K., Seidl, C.: Program dependency analysis for consolidating customized product copies. In: ICSME, pp. 496–500. IEEE (2014)
20. Koschke, R., Frenzel, P., Breu, A.P.J., Angstmann, K.: Extending the reflexion method for consolidating software variants into product lines. Softw. Qual. J. **17**(4), 331–366 (2009)
21. Krueger, C.W.: Easing the transition to software mass customization. In: van der Linden, F. (ed.) PFE 2001. LNCS, vol. 2290, pp. 282–293. Springer, Heidelberg (2002). https://doi.org/10.1007/3-540-47833-7_25
22. Kuhlemann, M., Batory, D., Apel, S.: Refactoring feature modules. In: Edwards, S.H., Kulczycki, G. (eds.) ICSR 2009. LNCS, vol. 5791, pp. 106–115. Springer, Heidelberg (2009). https://doi.org/10.1007/978-3-642-04211-9_11
23. Liebig, J., Janker, A., Garbe, F., Apel, S., Lengauer, C.: Morpheus: variability-aware refactoring in the wild. In: ICSE, vol. 1, pp. 380–391. IEEE (2015)
24. Lima, C., do Carmo Machado, I., de Almeida, E.S., von Flach G. Chavez, C.: Recovering the product line architecture of the Apo-Games. In: SPLC, pp. 289–293. ACM (2018)
25. Linsbauer, L., Lopez-Herrejon, R.E., Egyed, A.: Variability extraction and modeling for product variants. Softw. Syst. Modeling **16**(4), 1179–1199 (2017)
26. Liu, C., Macedo, N., Cunha, A.: Simplifying the analysis of software design variants with a colorful alloy. In: Guan, N., Katoen, J.-P., Sun, J. (eds.) SETTA 2019. LNCS, vol. 11951, pp. 38–55. Springer, Cham (2019). https://doi.org/10.1007/978-3-030-35540-1_3
27. Markovic, S., Baar, T.: Refactoring OCL annotated UML class diagrams. Softw. Syst. Modeling **7**(1), 25–47 (2008)
28. Martinez, J., Thurimella, A.K.: Collaboration and source code driven bottom-up product line engineering. In: SPLC, vol. 2, pp. 196–200. ACM (2012)
29. McComb, T., Smith, G.: A minimal set of refactoring rules for object-Z. In: Barthe, G., de Boer, F.S. (eds.) FMOODS 2008. LNCS, vol. 5051, pp. 170–184. Springer, Heidelberg (2008). https://doi.org/10.1007/978-3-540-68863-1_11
30. Opdyke, W.F.: Refactoring object-oriented frameworks. Ph.D. thesis, University of Illinois at Urbana-Champaign (1992)
31. Plath, M., Ryan, M.: Feature integration using a feature construct. Sci. Comput. Program. **41**(1), 53–84 (2001)
32. Rubin, J., Chechik, M.: Combining related products into product lines. In: de Lara, J., Zisman, A. (eds.) FASE 2012. LNCS, vol. 7212, pp. 285–300. Springer, Heidelberg (2012). https://doi.org/10.1007/978-3-642-28872-2_20
33. Rubin, J., Chechik, M.: N-way model merging. In: ESEC/SIGSOFT FSE, pp. 301–311. ACM (2013)
34. Schlie, A., Schulze, S., Schaefer, I.: Recovering variability information from source code of clone-and-own software systems. In: VaMoS, pp. 19:1–19:9. ACM (2020)
35. Schulze, S., Richers, O., Schaefer, I.: Refactoring delta-oriented software product lines. In: AOSD, pp. 73–84. ACM (2013)
36. Schulze, S., Thüm, T., Kuhlemann, M., Saake, G.: Variant-preserving refactoring in feature-oriented software product lines. In: VaMoS, pp. 73–81. ACM (2012)
37. Yaghoubi Shahir, H., Farahbod, R., Glässer, U.: Refactoring abstract state machine models. In: Derrick, J., et al. (eds.) ABZ 2012. LNCS, vol. 7316, pp. 345–348. Springer, Heidelberg (2012). https://doi.org/10.1007/978-3-642-30885-7_28
38. Stepney, S., Polack, F., Toyn, I.: Refactoring in maintenance and development of Z specifications. Electron. Notes Theor. Comput. Sci. **70**(3), 50–69 (2002)

39. Tanhaei, M., Habibi, J., Mirian-Hosseinabadi, S.: Automating feature model refactoring: a model transformation approach. Inf. Softw. Technol. **80**, 138–157 (2016)
40. Valente, M.T., Borges, V., Passos, L.T.: A semi-automatic approach for extracting software product lines. IEEE Trans. Software Eng. **38**(4), 737–754 (2012)

Porting the Software Product Line Refinement Theory to the Coq Proof Assistant

Thayonara Alves[1], Leopoldo Teixeira[1]([✉]), Vander Alves[2],
and Thiago Castro[3]

[1] Federal University of Pernambuco, Recife, Brazil
{tpa,lmt}@cin.ufpe.br
[2] University of Brasilia, Brasilia, Brazil
valves@unb.br
[3] Systems Development Center - Brazilian Army, Brasilia, Brazil
castro.thiago@eb.mil.br

Abstract. Software product lines are an engineering approach to systematically build similar software products from a common asset base. When evolving such systems, it is important to have assurance that we are not introducing errors or changing the behavior of existing products. The product line refinement theory establishes the necessary conditions for such assurance. This theory has been specified and proved using the PVS proof assistant. However, the Coq proof assistant is increasingly popular among researchers and practitioners, and, given that some programming languages are already formalized into such tool, the refinement theory might benefit from the potential integration. Therefore, in this work we present a case study on porting the PVS specification of the refinement theory to Coq. We compare the proof assistants based on the noted differences between the specifications and proofs of this theory, providing some reflections on the tactics and strategies used to compose the proofs. According to our study, PVS provided more succinct definitions than Coq, in several cases, as well as a greater number of successful automatic commands that resulted in shorter proofs. Despite that, Coq also brought facilities in definitions such as enumerated and recursive types, and features that support developers in their proofs.

Keywords: Software product lines · Theorem provers · Coq · PVS

1 Introduction

Software product lines (SPLs) are sets of related software systems that are systematically generated from reusable assets [1]. SPLs combine the benefits of mass customization and mass production. That is, building individual solutions from a set of reusable parts, while also tackling scale, aiming to reduce development costs and enhancing the quality of the developed products [1,8]. In this context,

© Springer Nature Switzerland AG 2020
G. Carvalho and V. Stolz (Eds.): SBMF 2020, LNCS 12475, pp. 192–209, 2020.
https://doi.org/10.1007/978-3-030-63882-5_12

it is important to take into account that evolving a SPL can be error-prone [10], since a single change might impact a number of products.

Previous works have defined a number of product line refinement theories [3,12,15], which provide a sound and rigorous basis to support SPL evolution, when we need to preserve the behavior of (some of the) existing products after the change. In particular, two concepts are formalized through these theories. The notion of safe evolution [3,10] denotes evolution scenarios where behavior preservation is required for all existing products in the SPL. Partially safe evolution [12], on the other hand, only requires behavior preservation for a subset of the products. In particular, in this work, we focus on the concept of *safe evolution*. These theories have been specified and proven using the *Prototype Verification System* (PVS) [11] proof assistant.

Another widely used proof assistant is *Coq*, with a large user community, which is also reflected by its solid presence in popular websites, such as GitHub repositories; more than 4000 projects returned from our search on the GitHub GraphQL API,[1] and StackOverflow questions.[2] Coq is based on the Calculus of Inductive Constructions (CIC) [14], a higher-order constructive logic. The dependent type system implemented in Coq is able to associate types with values, providing greater control over the data used in these programs.

In this work, we conduct a qualitative study whereby we ported the SPL refinement theory from PVS to Coq. Our goal is twofold: 1) to port the theory to a system used by a wider user community; but more importantly, 2) to provide a case study on this process. This enables us to reflect and investigate the similarities and differences between the two proof assistants in terms of their specification and proofs capabilities, which might be useful for the research community to better understand the strengths and weaknesses of each tool.

To make this comparison, we present some snippets of specifications from both systems, discussing similarities and differences. Moreover, we manually categorized the proof commands, which allow us to compare the proof methods at a higher granularity level. From this study, we can say that we were able to successfully port the theory to Coq, with some advantages from the point of view of usability and definition, but as the refinement theory heavily relies on sets, the PVS version ended up with a more succinct form of specification. PVS proofs also had a greater usage of automated commands than Coq, simplifying their proofs. However, this might be due to previous experience with this particular proof assistant and less experience with Coq by the authors. We have mined data from Github repositories using Coq that suggests that the Coq proofs could have been simplified using specific tactics.

The remainder of this paper is organized as follows. In Sect. 2, we present an overview of SPLs and SPL refinement. In Sects. 3 and 4, we present our comparison between the specifications and proofs in Coq and PVS. In Sect. 5, we present a discussion on lessons learned from our study. Finally, we discuss related work, and conclude pointing out future research directions in Sects. 6 and 7, respectively.

---

[1] https://developer.github.com/v4/explorer/.
[2] https://stackoverflow.com/questions/tagged/coq.

2   Software Product Lines

SPL engineering aims to increase productivity while also reducing costs, since we are not creating products from scratch. Moreover, quality might also be enhanced, since assets are possibly tested a greater number of times [1]. In this work, we adopted an SPL representation consisting of three elements: (i) a feature model that contains features and dependencies among them, (ii) an asset mapping, that contains sets of assets and asset names, (iii) a configuration knowledge, that allows features to be related to assets. In the remainder of this chapter, we introduce these elements in more detail. Variability management is an important aspect, since assets must be developed in a configurable way, to enable generating different products. Therefore, an SPL is typically structured using three different elements that are integrated to derive products.

   We manage variability through features, which are usually organized into *Feature Models* (FM), describing features and their relationships [1,6]. From a particular feature model F, we use $[\![F]\!]$ to denote its semantics, that is, the set of valid configurations, which are used to build SPL products. Additionally, in a SPL, features are implemented by assets, which can be code, documents, configuration files, and any other artifacts that we compose or instantiate to build the different products. Since we might have different versions of the same asset, we use A to refer to the *Asset Mapping* (AM), where asset names are mapped to the real assets [3]. This results in a unique mapping, which can help on eliminating ambiguities. Finally, the *Configuration Knowledge* (CK) maps features to their implementation assets, and guides product derivation. To generate a specific SPL product, given a valid FM configuration c, and the asset mapping A, we use $[\![K]\!]_c^A$ to denote the set of assets that comprise the product generated by processing the CK according to the given configuration.

   Therefore, we establish that an SPL is a triple (F, A, K) of such elements, that jointly generate well-formed products. Well-formedness $(wf())$ might take different meanings depending on the particular languages used for the SPL elements. For instance, it might mean that code is successfully compiling. Since we do not rely on a particular asset language, we just assume the existence of a $wf()$ function that must return a boolean value. Its concrete implementation depends on instantiating the general theory with a particular asset language.

Definition 1. ⟨*Software Product Line*⟩
For a feature model F, an asset mapping A, and a configuration knowledge K, the tuple (F, A, K) is a product line when, $\forall c \in [\![F]\!] \cdot wf([\![K]\!]_c^A)$.

To obtain success with SPL engineering, it is important to understand the impact of changes. Thus, previous works on SPL evolution proposed ways to help developers minimize such impacts [3–5,10,12]. In this work, we deal with the *product line refinement* notion [3,15]. This notion lifts program refinement to product lines, by establishing that an SPL is refined after a change when all of the existing products have their behavior preserved. Since $[\![K]\!]_c^A$ is a well-formed asset set (a program), we use $[\![K]\!]_c^A \sqsubseteq [\![K']\!]_{c'}^{A'}$ to denote the program refinement notion. In what follows we present the main refinement notion, but we provide further details in the following section, as we discuss our formalization.

Definition 2. ⟨*Software Product Line Refinement*⟩
For product lines (F, A, K) and (F', A', K'), the latter refines the former, denoted by $(F, A, K) \sqsubseteq (F', A', K')$, whenever $\forall c \in [\![F]\!] \cdot \exists c' \in [\![F']\!] \cdot [\![K]\!]_c^A \sqsubseteq [\![K']\!]_{c'}^{A'}$.

The refinement theory can be used to reason about changes to an SPL, classifying them as safe evolution, if all products correspond behaviorally to the original products. However, recurring to the formal definition might be burdensome to developers, so we can leverage the theory to support developers by establishing *refinement templates* [10,12]. These templates abstract recurrent evolution scenarios which correspond to the refinement notion, that is, they are an assured way to achieve safe evolution, and they can also help on avoiding errors when evolving the SPL.

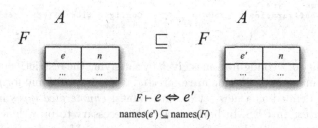

$$F \vdash e \Leftrightarrow e'$$
$$\text{names}(e') \subseteq \text{names}(F)$$

Fig. 1. REPLACE FEATURE EXPRESSION template.

Figure 1 illustrates the REPLACE FEATURE EXPRESSION template. We observe that a template consists of a left-hand side (LHS), corresponding to the original SPL, and a right-hand side (RHS), representing the SPL after the change. We represent the three elements of the SPL, namely the FM (F), AM (A), and CK (K), showing details only when needed. We also use meta-variables to denote their constituent elements. For instance, the CK consists of a feature expression e mapped to an asset name n. If the same meta-variable appears in both LHS and RHS, this means that this element is unchanged. This template establishes that we can replace e by e' whenever they are equivalent according to the feature model F (see condition at the bottom). Moreover, to avoid ill-formed expressions, we demand that any name belonging to e' must be a valid feature name from F. This change can improve the readability of the CK, by replacing complex expressions with simpler ones, if they are equivalent.

3   Coq Formalization

In this section, we present details about our Coq formalization, in parallel with the original PVS specification,[3] when they are different. Otherwise, we only

---

[3] https://github.com/spgroup/theory-pl-refinement.

show the Coq code. For brevity, we are omitting some definitions. The complete formalization is available in the project repository.[4]

3.1   Basic Definitions

A product is described by a valid feature selection, which we call a *configuration*. Listings 3.1 and 3.2 illustrate how we represent a configuration as a set of *feature names*, as given by the Name type. We use *uninterpreted types*, without concrete information about it, which is an important characteristic for reasoning about arbitrary values that satisfy some specifications. The basic Coq library does not include the definition of sets. For this reason, we import the *ListSet* library for finite sets, implemented with lists, to specify sets, as is the case with *Configuration*.

Listing 3.1: Name and Configuration (Coq)

```
Module Name.
Require Import Coq.Lists.ListSet.
Inductive Name : Type.
Definition Configuration : Type :=
    set Name.
End Name.
```

Listing 3.2: Name and Configuration (PVS)

```
Name: THEORY
BEGIN
   Name: TYPE
   Configuration: TYPE = set[Name]
END Name
```

The validity of a configuration is given by satisfying the restrictions among features, which in our specification are expressed using propositional formulae. Such formulas are defined as a new set of data values, *enumerated types* in Coq, and *abstract datatype* in PVS. In both cases, it is necessary to provide a set of constructors that cover the abstract syntax of propositional formulae for the possible values and relations, such as true/false, feature names, negation, conjunction, and implication, which in PVS come along with associated *accessors* and *recognizers*.

Listing 3.3: Formula (Coq)

```
Inductive Formula   : Type :=
  | TRUE_FORMULA    : F
  | FALSE_FORMULA   : F
  | NAME_FORMULA    : Name -> F
  | NOT_FORMULA     : F -> F
  | AND_FORMULA     : F -> F -> F
  | IMPLIES_FORMULA : F -> F -> F.

(*F = Formula*)
```

Listing 3.4: Formula (PVS)

```
Formula_: DATATYPE
BEGIN
   IMPORTING Name
   TRUE_FORMULA: TRUE?: F
   FALSE_FORMULA: FALSE?: F
   NAME_FORMULA(n: Name): NAME?: F
   NOT_FORMULA(f: F): NOT?: F
   AND_FORMULA(f_0, f_1: F): AND?: F
   IMPLIES_FORMULA(f_0, f_1: F):
       IMPLIES?: F
 END Formula_
 % F = Formula_
```

Coq has a small set of built-in features, with only twelve libraries in its Prelude library versus more than one hundred theories in the PVS Prelude. When we define an inductive type, Coq automatically includes theorems, so that it is possible to reason and compute enumerated types. So, for Formula, Coq includes the Formula_ind induction principle, in addition to the Formula_rec and Formula_rect recursion principles. With these implicit definitions, we are able to define a function on the formula type and we can also use Formula_rec to give recursive definitions, without the Fixpoint command, for example.

---

[4] https://github.com/spgroup/theory-pl-refinement-coq.

3.2   Feature Model

Features are used to distinguish SPL products. A feature model is then a set of feature names, together with propositional formulae using such names. As previously mentioned, a configuration is only considered valid if it satisfies the FM formulae. The `satisfies` function is responsible for this check.

Listing 3.5: Valid Configuration (Coq)

```
Fixpoint satisfies (f: Formula)
   (c : Configuration) : Prop :=
match f with
 | TRUE_FORMULA    => True
 | FALSE_FORMULA   => False
 | NAME_FORMULA n => set_In n c
 | NOT_FORMULA f1 =>
    ~(satisfies f1 c)
 | AND_FORMULA f1 f2
    => (satisfies f1 c)
        /\ (satisfies f2 c)
 | IMPLIES_FORMULA f1 f2
    => (satisfies f1 c)
        -> (satisfies f2 c)
   end.
```

Listing 3.6: Valid Configuration (PVS)

```
satisfies(f:Formula_,
      c:Configuration):
   RECURSIVE boolean =
CASES f OF
   TRUE_FORMULA: TRUE,
   FALSE_FORMULA: FALSE,
   NAME_FORMULA(n): (EXISTS
    (n1:Name): c(n1) AND n1=n),
   NOT_FORMULA(f1):
    NOT satisfies(f1,c), AND_
    FORMULA(f1, f2):
      satisfies(f1,c) AND
      satisfies(f2,c),
   IMPLIES_FORMULA(f1, f2):
      satisfies(f1,c) =>
      satisfies(f2,c)
   ENDCASES
MEASURE BY <<
```

To specify a recursive definition in PVS, we need to prove *Type-Correctness Conditions* (TCCs), to guarantee that functions always terminate. This is done by the `MEASURE` keyword that receives a well-founded order relation, to show that the recursive function is total. For recursive datatypes, PVS automatically generates such an structural order relation over `Formula`, which is provided as `<<` in what follows the `BY` keyword. Coq employs conservative syntactic criteria to check termination of all recursive definitions, allowing recursive calls only on syntactic subterms of the original primary argument.

The semantics of the FM is given by the set of all valid configurations. In Coq, following an operational specification, we use the `genConf` function, which generates the powerset of the FM features, that is, it generates all possible configurations from a given set of features. We then use the `filter` function, which takes the FM restrictions into account, to only yield the configurations of interest, that is, the valid ones. Meanwhile, with declarative style of specification, PVS allows subtypes of the form: A = {x: B | P (x)}, which allows a simplified declaration of this function.

Listing 3.7: FM semantics (Coq)

```
Definition semantics (fm : FM)
  : set Configuration :=
   filter fm (genConf (names_ fm)).
```

Listing 3.8: FM semantics (PVS)

```
semantics(fm: FM): set[Configuration]=
 {c:Configuration | satImpConsts(fm,c)
  AND satExpConsts(fm,c)}
```

3.3   Assets and Asset Mapping

A SPL has a set of assets from which products are built. Assets are related to names through the AM. To express this, we created a theory for maps, which are basically key-value pairs, where S represents a key and T the value associated with that key, and both are uninterpreted types. Once we have S and T, we can provide the definition of asset name, asset and map, in the `Asset` module.

Listing 3.9: Asset and Asset Name (Coq)

```
Definition AssetName  : Type := Maps.S.
Definition Asset      : Type := Maps.T.
Definition pair_      : Type := prod S T.
Definition map_       : Type := list pair.
```

The product line refinement notion relies on an asset refinement notion. For generality, we assume this function, as the theory does not depend on a particular asset language. The basic intuition is that it returns True when refinement holds. The constructs of this function are not analogous in the two proof assistants. In Coq, we use global declarations using the `Parameter inline` command to define a function interface.

Listing 3.10: Asset Refinement (Coq)

```
Parameter inline assetRef :
    set Asset -> set Asset -> Prop.
```

Listing 3.11: Asset Refinement (PVS)

```
|- : [set[Asset],set[Asset]->bool]
```

While we do not demand a specific asset refinement notion, we require it to be a preorder. The `Orders` theory in the PVS prelude provides a nice syntactic sugar for specifying this, while we hard-coded this notion in the Coq specification.

Listing 3.12: Refinement is preorder (Coq)

```
Axiom assetRefinement:
    forall x y z:set Asset,
    (*reflexivity*) assetRef x x
    /\ (*transitivity*)
        assetRef x y -> assetRef y z
        -> assetRef x z.
```

Listing 3.13: Refinement is preorder (PVS)

```
assetRefinement: AXIOM
    orders[set[Asset]].preorder?( |- )
```

As mentioned in Sect. 2, the AM is a unique mapping between the asset name and the asset. We also define an AM refinement notion, which is important for establishing compositionality. In this case, the original and modified AM domains must be equivalent. Any asset contained in the original AM must have a corresponding refined version in the modified AM. We observe that the Coq specification is more verbose for dealing with sets, when compared to PVS. Using Coq's dependent typing the definition could have been reduced, since we had to make explicit the `set_In an (dom am1)` premise in aMR

Listing 3.14: AM refinement (Coq)

```
Axiom Asset_dec :
    forall x y: Asset, {x = y} + {x <> y}.

Definition aMR (am1 am2: AM) : Prop :=
    (dom am1 = dom am2) /\
    forall (an : AssetName),
    set_In an (dom am1) ->
    exists (a1 a2: Asset),
    (isMappable am1 an a1) /\
    (isMappable am2 an a2) /\(assetRef
    (set_add Asset_dec a1 nil)
    (set_add Asset_dec a2 nil)).
```

Listing 3.15: AM refinement (PVS)

```
|>(am1,am2): bool =
    (dom(am1)=dom(am2) AND
    (FORALL an: dom(am1)(an) =>
    EXISTS a1,a2: (am1(an,a1))
    AND (am2(an,a2)) AND |-(a1,a2)))
```

Another detail in the Coq definition is that working with lists requires that its element types are *decidable*, due to CIC. A type has decidable equality if any two elements of that type are the same or different. Since ListSet uses lists to implement sets, we need to demand the following predicate $\forall xy : R, \{x = y\} + \{x = y\}$, where R is an arbitrary type for a list element. For this reason, we need to introduce axioms such as Asset_dec to establish that certain types are decidable. Adding axioms is a threat to validity of this study, but these axioms are mostly limited to types belonging to lists, or from things we assume to be true from the SPL refinement theory.

3.4   Configuration Knowledge

The CK relates features to artifacts. One way of doing this is to associate feature expressions to transformations, instead of mere asset selection. In this case, we specify the CK as a list of items, defined as the product of feature expressions and a transformation. For simplicity, we limit one transformation per item, but we could extend the theory to handle an arbitrary number of transformations.

Listing 3.16: CK (Coq)

```
Definition Item : Type := Formula * Transformation .
Definition CK : Type := list Item.
Parameter Inline(40) transform : Transformation -> AM-> AM -> AM.
Fixpoint semanticsCK ( ck : CK ) ( am amt : AM )
    ( c : Configuration ) : set Asset :=
match ck with
| nil = > img amt
| x :: xs = > if is_true ( satisfies ( getExp x ) c )
            then semanticsCK xs am ( transform ( getRS x ) am amt) c
            else semanticsCK xs am amt c
        end.
```

The CK semantics is defined as an interpreter that evaluates transformations to generate products. The Coq version uses pattern-matching to specify the function that runs through the list of items, applying the transformations when the expression is evaluated as true according to the configuration c.

3.5   Software Product Lines

Definition 1 states that an SPL is formed by the FM, AM and CK, jointly generating well-formed products. In PVS, we are able to use predicate subtypes to establish this fact. Using (p) to define a type restricts that all elements of such type satisfy the predicate p. This might result in proof obligations that we might need to satisfy to produce a consistent specification. In Coq, we use records. Record fields are defined with :>, which make that field accessor a coercion. This coercion is automatically created by Coq. Thus, in the definitions that make use of PL, the well-formedness constraint is required, as we see in Listing 3.20.

Listing 3.17: Software product lines (Coq)

```
Record PL: Type := {
        pls:> ArbitrarySPL;
        wfpl:> Prop; }.
```

Listing 3.18: Software product lines (PVS)

```
PL : TYPE = (wfPL)
```

We are then able to formalize the SPL refinement function, as in Definition 2.

Listing 3.19: Software product line refinement (Coq)

```
Definition plRefinement (pl1 pl2: PL): Prop :=
    (forall c1, set_In c1 (FMRef (getFM pl1)) ->
     (exists c2, set_In c2 (FMRef (getFM pl2)) /\
      (assetRef (CKSem (getCK pl1) (getAM pl1) (c1))
        (CKSem (getCK pl2) (getAM pl2) (c2)))))).
```

In practice, it might not be the case that all three elements are changed in an evolution scenario [5, 7]. In this sense, we prove the so-called compositionality theorems, that enable reasoning when a single one of the three elements evolves. The main idea is to establish that safely evolving one of such elements results in safe evolution of the entire SPL. We have compositionality results established for the independent evolution of each element (FM, AM, and CK), and the full compositionality theorem, that enables reasoning when all three of them evolve. It basically states that if we change the FM and CK resulting in equivalent models (this notion is provided in our repository), and the AM is refined as previously described in Listing 3.14, the resulting SPL is a refined version of the original. The formalization in Coq is analogous to that of PVS, except for the use of the *Where* command to define *pl2*, in the PVS theorem.

Listing 3.20: Compositionality (Coq)

```
Theorem fullCompositionality:
 forall pl fm am ck,
  equivalentFMs (getFM pl) fm /\
  equivalentCKs (getCK pl) ck /\
  aMR (getAM pl) am ->
  plRefinement pl
  {| pls:= pl2; wfpl := wfPL pl2|} /\
  wfPL ((fm ,(getAM pl)), (getCK pl)).

(*pl2 = ((fm,(getAM pl)),(getCK pl))*)
```

Listing 3.21: Compositionality (PVS)

```
fullCompositionality: THEOREM
 FORALL(pl,fm,am,ck): (
  equivalentFMs(F(pl),fm) AND
  equivalentCKs(K(pl),ck) AND
  |>(A(pl),am) =>
   plRefinement(pl,pl2) AND wfPL(pl2))
 WHERE pl2=(# F:=fm, A:=am, K:=ck #)
```

3.6   Theory Instantiation and Templates

Even though we present concrete FM and CK languages in the previous section, the SPL refinement theory does not rely on a particular concrete language for FM, CK, or AM. Nonetheless, instantiating the theory with concrete languages enables us to establish refinement templates (see Sect. 2). In PVS, we do this through the theory interpretation mechanism. We use the IMPORTING clause to provide the parameters for the uninterpreted types and functions. PVS then generates proof obligations that we must prove to show that such instantiation is consistent.

Listing 3.22: Theory Interpretation (PVS)

```
IMPORTING SPLrefinement[Configuration,
WFM, Assets.Asset,Assets.
AssetName, CK, semantics, semantics]
```

In Coq, we use typeclasses. We establish the SPL class with interface declarations and required properties. Properties are defined as axioms or theorems. We also specify parameters for instantiating the class. As we import functions from other typeclasses, we need to handle constraints. For instance, the SPL class generates the FeatureModel constraints, due to the typeclass defined earlier. FeatureModel is satisfied by {FM: FeatureModel F Conf}, for example.

Listing 3.23: SPL Class (Coq)

```
Class SPL (A N M Conf F AM CK PL: Type) {FM: FeatureModel F Conf}
{AssetM: AssetMapping Asset AssetName AM} {ckTrans: CKTrans F A AM CK Conf}:
 Type := {
    (*===================functions=====================*)
    plRefinement           : PL -> PL -> Prop;
    products               : PL -> set A
    ...
    (*===========Axioms - Lemmas - Theorems=============*)
    plStrongSubset: forall pl1 pl2: PL,
       strongerPLRefinement pl1 pl2
       -> (forall c: Conf, set_In c (FMRef (getFM pl1))
       -> set_In c (FMRef (getFM pl2)));
    ...
}.
```

We use the Program Instance keyword to provide concrete instance, and we must prove that each parameter satisfies the previously defined properties. Class methods must also be related to their implementation, as is the example of plRefinement. Finally, Coq generates obligations for the remaining fields, which we can prove in the order that they appear, using the Next Obligation keyword.

Listing 3.24: SPL Instance (Coq)

```
Program Instance Ins_SPL: SPL Asset AssetName AM Conf FM AM CK PL:= {
    plRefinement:= plRefinement_func;
    products:= products_func;
    ...
}. Next Obligation. {
    (*plStrong Subset*)
    intros.
    destruct pl1. destruct pl2.
    unfold strongerPLrefinement_func in H. specialize (H c).
    destruct c1, c0. apply H in H0. destruct HO. apply HO.
} Qed.
```

With such instantiation, we are then able to prove soundness of the refinement templates. That is, for each template, we prove that performing the changes as described to the original SPL, results in SPL refinement. The specification and proofs of the templates is a work in progress, so far we have two templates already fully specified and proven, and other templates already specified and with an ongoing proof. For space reasons, we refer the reader to our Github repository.

4   Proofs

In proof assistants, unlike automated theorem provers, we need to interact with the system to prove lemmas and theorems. For this, they provide commands—namely tactics in Coq, and rules or strategies in PVS—that act on the current proof goal, potentially transforming it into subgoals, which might be simpler to prove. Once every subgoal of the proof is dealt with, the task is finished.

Coq offers the Search feature. We use this command to search for previously stated lemmas/theorems that might assist proving the current goal. This prevents us from declaring other lemmas unnecessarily. As Coq's Prelude is smaller, we were unable to obtain much advantage of it, except for the lemmas from ListSet and other results that we had proven. PVS contains a richer Prelude, and we often used available results. For instance, nine existing lemmas were used to prove AM refinement in PVS. Nevertheless, PVS does not provide an easy search feature such as Coq, so the user needs to have prior knowledge of the theories that are in its standard library or integrate PVS with Hypatheon library[5].

Although we are porting an existing PVS specification, the proof methods often differ between the two systems. For example, Listings 4.1 and 4.2 show Coq's and PVS's proofs for the inDom lemma. This lemma belongs to the map theory and states that, if there is a mapping of a key l to any value r, then the domain of that map contains l. In Coq, we prove the lemma by induction. The base case is solved with the HMpb hypothesis simplification and the contradiction tactic, since we obtain False as assumption. In the inductive case, in addition to other tactics, the apply tactic was used to apply the isMappable_elim lemma, to remove a pair from the mapping check. We also use this same tactic to transform the goal from the implications of lemmas *set_add_intro1* and *set_add_intro2*, by *ListSet*.

The intuition tactic was used to complete the last two subgoals. This tactic calls auto, which works by calling reflexivity and assumption, in addition to applying assumptions using hints from all hint databases. These calls generate subgoals that auto tries to solve without error, but limited to five attempts, to ensure that the proof search eventually ends. The prover has the option of increasing this number of attempts in order to increase the chances of success, as well as adding already solved proofs to the hint databases. Both should be used with care due to performance.

---

[5] https://github.com/nasa/pvslib.

Listing 4.1: inDom proof in Coq

```
Lemma inDom :
 forall am (an: AssetName) (a: Asset),
isMappable am an a -> set_In an (dom am).
Proof.
intros am0 an0 a HMpb.
induction am0.
 - simpl in HMpb. contradiction.
 - Search "isMappable".
   apply isMappable_elim in HMpb.
   inversion HMpb. clear HMpb.
   destruct H as [Heql1 Heql2].
  + rewrite Heql1. simpl. Search "set_add".
    apply set_add_intro2. reflexivity.
  + simpl. apply set_add_intro1.
    apply IHam0. apply H.
  + intuition.
  + intuition.
Qed.
```

Listing 4.2: inDom proof in PVS

```
inDom: LEMMA
  FORALL(m,l,r):
    m(l,r) => dom(m)(l)
(inDom 0
  (inDom-1 nil 3498485387
  ("" (skolem 1 (m l r))
  (("" (expand dom)
    (("" (flatten)
     (("" (instantiate 1 r)
      (("" (propax) nil nil))
       nil))
     nil))
    nil))
  nil)
```

The PVS proof, in turn, is simpler. The basis of PVS logic is also based on set theory, which influences in this simplicity. We first perform skolemization, then we expand the definition of dom, which results in the proof goal EXISTS (r: Asset): m(l,r). We instantiate the existential quantifier with r, which concludes the proof.

4.1 Comparing Proof Methods

To compare proof commands of both systems, we have clustered the tactics and proof rules according to their effect on the goals, as follows, with selected examples of Coq tactics and PVS rules or strategies. This is an adaptation of an existing categorization.[6]

- **Category 1 - Proving Simple Goals**: This category groups simple commands that discharge trivial proof goals.
  - **Coq:** assumption, reflexivity, constructor, exact, contradiction;
  - **PVS:** Simple goals are automatically solved.
- **Category 2 - Transforming goals or hypotheses**: These commands change the state of goals through simplification, unfolding definitions, using implications, among others, allowing progress in the proof process.
  - **Coq:** simpl, unfold, rewrite, inversion, replace;
  - **PVS:** replace, replace *, expand, instantiate, use, inst, generalize.
- **Category 3 - Breaking apart goals or hypotheses**: Those that split the goal or hypothesis (antecedent and consequent in PVS) into steps that are easier to prove.
  - **Coq:** split, destruct, induction, case;
  - **PVS:** flatten, case, split, induct.

---

[6] https://www.cs.cornell.edu/courses/cs3110/2018sp/a5/coq-tactics-cheatsheet.html.

- **Category 4 - Managing the local context**: Commands to add hypotheses, rename, introduce terms in the local context. There is no direct progress in the proof, but these commands bring improvements that might facilitate such progress.
  - **Coq**: `intro, intros, clear, clearbody, move, rename`;
  - **PVS**: `skolem!, copy, hide, real, delete`.
- **Category 5 - Powerful Automatic Commands**: Powerful automation tactics and strategies that solve certain types of goals.
  - **Coq**: `ring, tauto, field, auto, trivial, easy, intuition`, `congruence`;
  - **PVS**: `grind, ground, assert, smash`.

We could also establish other categories, but those listed here are sufficient to group all tactics and rules used in our Coq and PVS proofs.

Table 1. Total tactics by category

Proof Assistant	Category 1	Category 2	Category 3	Category 4	Category 5	Total
Coq	25	357	225	120	33	760
PVS	—	209	97	85	126	517

Table 1 presents the numbers for such categories in our specifications. First, we note that the number of tactics in Coq is 47.7% higher than that of PVS, even though we often use sequences of tactics such as `destruct H0, H1`, which breaks hypotheses H0 and H1 into two others in the same step. One possible reason for these differences is the ability of PVS to automatically solve simple goals, which does not happen in Coq. Additionally, the PVS specification has taken more advantage of automatic commands. In these systems, six results are proven using the `grind` rule and, in other six proofs, this command resolved all the subgoals generated by a command of the type **Breaking apart goals and hypotheses**. The PVS documentation recommends automating proofs as much as possible. One reason may be proof brittleness, as on some occasions, updates to PVS have broken existing proofs [9].

A greater number of commands that make changes to goals and hypotheses can also be explained by a greater number of branches generated from the **Managing the local context** category. `induction`, which generates from one to six more subgoals in this formalization, was used 15 times in Coq and only five times in PVS, for example. Also, for each subgoal generated, we mark each one with bullets in Coq, increasing the number of commands in the *Breaking apart goals and hypotheses* category.

Finally, we also notice that we do not use tactics that act on other tactics - which would be a new category - such as `repeat` and `all`, which would simplify the proofs. We intend to do this in the future. We did not find this type of proof rule being used in PVS, but some commands like `skosimp` and `grind` implicitly contain control structures.

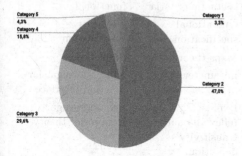

Fig. 2. Tactics from our Coq specification   **Fig. 3.** Tactics from Github

Nonetheless, to provide some external validity for our Coq specification, we also mined Coq repositories from Github using GraphQL API v4 and PyDriller [13]. This resulted in 1.981 projects, with 65.661 .v files. We have also categorized the tactics from these projects, in this case also considering more categories to group a larger number of tactics. Figures 2 and 3 compare the distribution of command among the categories, for both our specification and the aggregated data from the Github projects. The percentage of **Transforming goals or hypotheses** commands is similar, but **Proving Simple Goals** appears more often among Github projects. In addition, automated commands are further explored in these projects. In projects where the `Hint` command was found, 16.43% of the tactics are automated versus 5.38% in projects that have not made such use. This suggests that we could have simplified our proofs using this command.

5 Discussion and Lessons Learned

The general approach of this work was to stay close to the original specification and we were able to successfully port the SPL refinement theory from PVS to Coq. However, Coq posed some difficulties during this process, as well as easing some other tasks. It is important to highlight that authors had a much stronger previous experience in PVS than Coq, so this certainly has an impact in our results. We intend to collect further feedback from experts in Coq to improve the Coq specification. Nevertheless, in general, both specifications are similar for most encodings. Most of the differences noted are presented earlier in this section and their key aspects are summarized in Table 2.

Table 2. Specification summary

Section	Definition	Coq	PVS
Basic definition	Sets	ListSet library	Prelude
	Set of data values	Enumerated type	Abstract datatype
Feature model	Recursive function	Conservative syntactic criteria	TCCs; measure function
	FM semantics	Operational specification	Declarative specification
Asset and AM	AM	Maps theory	Maps theory
	Asset refinement	Parameter inline	Syntactic sugar for function interface
	Refinement is preorder	Explicit reflexivity's and transitivity's definition	Syntactic sugar from order theory
	AM refinement	Axioms of decidability; Explicit definition	Predicative subtype
SPL	PL	Record	Predicative subtype
	Compositionality	PL as a triple	Where command
Theory instantiation	Instances	Typeclasses	Theory Instantiation

A point to be considered in favor of Coq, which contributed to the development of our specification, is its large active community and the vast amount of available information, which provides greater support to its users. There are forums that support Coq developers, as well as an active community in both StackOverflow and Theoretical Computer Science Stack Exchange.[7] We are also aware of *The Coq Consortium*,[8] which provides greater assistance to subscribing members, with direct access to Coq developers, premium bug support, among others.

Regarding the specification, Coq presented an easier way to define recursive functions. It uses a small set of syntactic and conservative criteria to check for termination, where the developer must provide an argument that is decreasing as the calls are made. In fact, there is a way to perform recursive definitions without meeting this requirement. Just specify a well-founded relation or a decreasing measure mapping to a natural number, but it is necessary to prove all obligations to show this function can terminate. On the other hand, PVS generates TCCs to ensure that the function is complete and a measure function to show this.

---

[7] https://cstheory.stackexchange.com/questions/tagged/coq.
[8] https://coq.inria.fr/consortium.

PVS allows partial functions, but only within total logic structures, from predicate subtypes. The definitions that made use of these subtypes made the specifications more succinct and easier to read when compared to the Coq definitions. PVS also provided syntactic sugar throughout its specification, allowing for less coding effort by the developer. We could have further leveraged Coq notations to achieve similar results. Besides that, PVS provides a greater amount of theories in its standard library. However, there is also a wide variety of Coq libraries available on the web.

The proofs are often different between the proof assistants. PVS proofs had a greater usage of automated commands like `grind`, solving some goals with just that command. It was also not necessary to worry about simpler goals. For example, the `flatten` rule not only yields a subgoal in order to simplify the goal, but it also solves simpler goals then, such as when we have `False` in the antecedent. In Coq, except in cases where automated tactics can be used, we need to explicitly use tactics such as `contradiction` to deal with False as assumption, or `reflexivity` to prove goals that are automatically discharged by PVS.

Although the proofs in Coq are longer in our specification, we noticed that important features, which give greater support to the prover, were not used. Tactics like `all` and `repeat` could have been useful to avoid repetition. The use of `Hints` and the increased search depth of the `auto` tactic may increase the chances of automated tactics being successful in their attempts.

From a usability point of view, Coq specifications and their corresponding proofs belong to the same file. In PVS, it is also necessary for the prover to be aware of control rules to go through the .prf file, such as the `undo` rule that undoes commands. In addition, it is common to lose proofs that are in these files, because of automatically renamed TCCs, for example. Finally, Coq also has search commands, either by identifying or by patterns, which might prevent the unnecessary definition of lemmas.

6   Related Work

Wiedijk [16] draws a comparison between 15 formalization systems, including Coq and PVS. In his work, users of each system were asked to formalize the irrationality of $\sqrt{2}$ by reducing it to the absurd. For each system, the author compare the number of lines of the specification, whether it was proven by the irrationality of $\sqrt{2}$ or by an arbitrary prime number, in addition to verifying whether the users proved the statement using their system's library. Despite the breadth of such study, the comparison among the systems is performed against a simple proof problem. This points to the need for comparison on a larger scale, in order to have the possibility to further explore the difference between these systems, specifically. This is what we have attempted to perform in this work, even though we only compare two systems. Moreover, our findings cannot be readily generalized to any mechanization using Coq or PVS, since we have only specified a particular type of theory.

Bodeveix et al. [2] formalized the B-Method using Coq and PVS. The work provides the mechanization of most constructions, showing the main aspects in the coding of the two systems for each stage of formalization. This work is similar to ours, but we also draw a comparison between the tactics and strategies that make up the proof, using data collected from Github projects to strengthen our statements.

7   Conclusions and Future Work

In this work, we port the existing SPL refinement theory mechanized in PVS to Coq. This theory is the basis of previous works [3,5,10,12] related to safe and partially safe evolution of SPLs, although here we only discuss the safe evolution aspect of this theory. We also compared Coq and PVS using the specifications performed on these systems, showing the differences observed in the specifications and proofs.

Through our study, we concluded that Coq's formalism and languages are sufficiently expressive to deal with and represent the different types of definitions found in the PVS mechanization. We have seen, however, that PVS provides ways to simplify most of the formalization presented, as well as proof rules that reduce the proof effort by the user. Nevertheless, we also need to emphasize that Coq brings features, such as *Hint*, tactical commands, dependent typing and advanced notations in which users of this tool can overcome this difference. Its larger community and documentation availability might provide greater support for this purpose. In addition, we must take the constant improvements made to the systems into account.

This is an initial case study on a specific project and we would benefit from conducting similar analyses on other projects. For future work, we intend to complete the proofs of the remaining SPL safe evolution templates, as well as extend our formalization to consider partially safe evolution as formalized through partial SPL refinement [12], since they are threats to the validity of this study. Besides, as mentioned earlier, the fact that the authors have more experience with PVS affects our results, being a threat to the validity of our comparison. We intend to collect feedback from Coq experts to improve our formalization. Nonetheless, our initial focus was to have a Coq specification closer to the previously proposed PVS specification. Additionally, we plan to address simplification of proofs, taking important Coq features presented in Sect. 5 into account, which was not our focus in this work.

Acknowledgments. This work was partially supported by CNPq (grant 409335/ 2016-9) and FACEPE (APQ-0570-1.03/14), as well as INES 2.0 (http://www.ines. org.br), FACEPE grants PRONEX APQ-0388-1.03/14 and APQ-0399-1.03/17, and CNPq grant 465614/2014-0. Thayonara Alves is supported by FACEPE (grant IBPG-0749-1.03/18). Vander Alves was partially supported by CNPq (grant 310757/2018-5), FAPDF (grant SEI 00193-00000926/2019-67), and the Alexander von Humboldt Foundation.

References

1. Apel, S., Batory, D., Kästner, C., Saake, G.: Feature-Oriented Software Product Lines. Springer, Heidelberg (2013). https://doi.org/10.1007/978-3-642-37521-7
2. Bodeveix, J.P., Filali, M., Munõz, C.: A formalization of the B method in Coq and PVS. In: FM'99 - B Users Group Meeting - Applying B in An Industrial Context: Tools, Lessons and Techniques, pp. 32–48. Springer, Cham (1999)
3. Borba, P., Teixeira, L., Gheyi, R.: A theory of software product line refinement. Theoret. Comput. Sci. **455**, 2–30 (2012)
4. Bürdek, J., Kehrer, T., Lochau, M., Reuling, D., Kelter, U., Schürr, A.: Reasoning about product-line evolution using complex feature model differences. Autom. Softw. Eng. **23**(4), 687–733 (2015). https://doi.org/10.1007/s10515-015-0185-3
5. Gomes, K., Teixeira, L., Alves, T., Ribeiro, M., Gheyi, R.: Characterizing safe and partially safe evolution scenarios in product lines: an empirical study. In: VaMoS. Association for Computing Machinery (2019)
6. Kang, K., Cohen, S., Hess, J., Novak, W., Peterson, S.: Feature-oriented domain analysis (foda) feasibility study. Technical report. CMU/SEI-90-TR-21, Software Engineering Institute, Carnegie Mellon University, November 1990
7. Kröher, C., Gerling, L., Schmid, K.: Identifying the intensity of variability changes in software product line evolution. In: SPLC, p. 54–64. Association for Computing Machinery (2018)
8. Van der Linden, F., Schmid, K., Rommes, E.: Software Product Lines in Action: the Best Industrial Practice in Product Line Engineering. Springer, Heidelberg (2007). https://doi.org/10.1007/978-3-540-71437-8
9. Miller, S., Greve, D., Wilding, M., Srivas, M.: Formal verification of the Aamp-Fv microcode. Technical report (1999)
10. Neves, L., et al.: Safe evolution templates for software product lines. J. Syst. Softw. **106**(C), 42–58 (2015)
11. Owre, S., Shankar, N., Rushby, J.M., Stringer-Calvert, D.W.J.: PVS Language Reference. SRI International (2001). http://pvs.csl.sri.com/doc/pvs-language-reference.pdf, version 2.4
12. Sampaio, G., Borba, P., Teixeira, L.: Partially safe evolution of software product lines. J. Syst. Softw. **155**, 17–42 (2019)
13. Spadini, D., Aniche, M., Bacchelli, A.: PyDriller: Python framework for mining software repositories. In: ESEC/FSE, pp. 908–911. Association for Computing Machinery (2018)
14. Team, T.C.D.: The COQ proof assistant reference manual. Technical report, INRIA (2020). https://coq.inria.fr/distrib/current/refman/
15. Teixeira, L., Alves, V., Borba, P., Gheyi, R.: A product line of theories for reasoning about safe evolution of product lines. In: SPLC, pp. 161–170. Association for Computing Machinery (2015)
16. Wiedijk, F.: Comparing mathematical provers. In: Asperti, A., Buchberger, B., Davenport, J.H. (eds.) MKM 2003. LNCS, vol. 2594, pp. 188–202. Springer, Heidelberg (2003). https://doi.org/10.1007/3-540-36469-2_15

Safe Evolution of Product Lines Using Configuration Knowledge Laws

Leopoldo Teixeira[1]([✉])(iD), Rohit Gheyi[2](iD), and Paulo Borba[1](iD)

[1] Federal University of Pernambuco, Recife, Brazil
{lmt,phmb}@cin.ufpe.br
[2] Federal University of Campina Grande, Campina Grande, Brazil
rohit@dsc.ufcg.edu.br

Abstract. When evolving a software product line, it is often important to ensure that we do it in a safe way, ensuring that the resulting product line remains well-formed and that the behavior of existing products is not affected. To ensure this, one usually has to analyze the different artifacts that constitute a product line, like feature models, configuration knowledge and assets. Manually analyzing these artifacts can be time-consuming and error prone, since a product line might consist of thousands of products. Existing works show that a non-negligible number of changes performed in commits deal only with the configuration knowledge, that is, the mapping between features and assets. This way, in this paper, we propose a set of algebraic laws, which correspond to bi-directional transformations for configuration knowledge models, that we can use to justify safe evolution of product lines, when only the configuration knowledge model changes. Using a theorem prover, we proved all laws sound with respect to a formal semantics. We also present a case study, where we use these laws to justify safe evolution scenarios of a non trivial industrial software product line.

Keywords: Safe evolution · Software product lines · Theorem proving

1 Introduction

A Software Product Line (SPL) is defined as a set of software systems built from a common asset base, that share common characteristics, but are sufficiently distinct from each other in terms of features [2,23]. SPLs can bring significant productivity and time to market improvements [23]. Besides code and other kinds of assets, an SPL consists of different artifacts, such as Feature Models (FMs) [18] and Configuration Knowledge (CK) [11]. We use FMs to characterize products, defining what is common and variable through features, which are reusable requirements and characteristics [11]. We establish the relationship between features and concrete assets through the CK. Given a valid feature selection, CK evaluation yields the assets that build a product. When evolving an SPL, for example, to improve its design, it is important to make sure that

© Springer Nature Switzerland AG 2020
G. Carvalho and V. Stolz (Eds.): SBMF 2020, LNCS 12475, pp. 210–227, 2020.
https://doi.org/10.1007/978-3-030-63882-5_13

it remains well-formed, in the sense that it generates valid products, and that behavior of existing products is not affected.

Manually changing different parts to evolve an SPL requires effort, especially for checking necessary conditions to make sure the change is performed without impact to existing products, such as introducing bugs or changing behavior. Moreover, this process is time-consuming and can also introduce defects, compromising the promised benefits on other dimensions of cost and risk. Recent works investigating the evolution of highly configurable systems through their commit history show that the mapping between features and assets evolves independently [17,21] of changes to the variability model or code. For instance, Gomes et al. [17] found that 122 out of 500 commits from the highly configurable system Soletta, only changed the CK, besides other commits that involve changes to multiple elements at the same time. In our earlier work, we formalized general theories for SPL refinement [8,28,33], that take into account FM, CK, and assets (Sect. 3), capturing the informal notions of safe and partially safe SPL evolution. Safe evolution states that the resulting SPL must be able to generate products that behaviorally match all of the original SPL products, while partially safe relates to preserving behavior of only a subset of the original products. Safe evolution, which is our focus in this work, even allows adding new products, as long as we maintain the behavior of the original products. Although formalized, these notions can also be costly to check, since it can be time consuming, besides error-prone, to reason over the semantics of all SPL products.

This way, in this paper, we propose a set of bi-directional, semantics-preserving transformations for compositional CK models, that associate enabling conditions to asset names (Sect. 2). We use such transformations to ease the reasoning over SPL maintenance when only the CK changes, justifying safe evolution. Therefore, there is no need for developers to do semantic reasoning, making their task more productive. We use the Prototype Verification System (PVS) [27] to specify and prove soundness of the transformations. We also use them to justify safe evolution scenarios of a non trivial industrial product line for automated test generation tools with approximately 32 KLOC. The formalization we present here not only avoid errors when manipulating these models, but also contributes towards the general SPL refinement theory [8], providing transformations that work with an instance of the concrete CK language previously defined.

The main contributions of this work are the following:

- We present a new CK equivalence notion and its associated compositionality results for the SPL refinement theory previously proposed [8] (Sect. 3);
- A set of transformations for compositional CK models associating feature expressions to asset names (Sect. 4);
- Soundness proofs for all laws using the formalized semantics (Sect. 5);
- A case study illustrating the applicability of the laws using evolution scenarios from a real SPL (Sect. 6).

The remainder of this work is organized as follows: In Sect. 2.1, we informally discuss the CK model used in this work, and in Sect. 2.2 we present its formalization. In Sect. 7 we discuss related work, and we present conclusions and future work in Sect. 8.

2 Background

In this section, we explain the compositional CK model used in this work. Since its main purpose is to map features to assets, we first discuss FMs. FMs describe commonalities and variabilities in an SPL [18]. For instance, the FM in Fig. 1 describes a simplified mobile game SPL.[1] The root feature is **Rain of Fire**. Every product has an image loading policy, that depends on the memory size, so **Image Load Policy** is a mandatory feature. The loading policy is then either **On Demand** or during **Startup**, but not both. This denotes the mutually-exclusive relationship of *alternative* features. The game might also show clouds or not, so **Clouds** is an optional feature. Moreover, we can state cross-tree constraints over an FM using propositional logic. In this example, the formula below the FM states that whenever we select **Startup**, we must select **Clouds** as well. The FM describes product configurations, that is, valid feature selections that define different SPL products. So, the semantics of an FM denotes the set of SPL products. Formal representations of the semantics of an FM have been previously proposed [4,29].

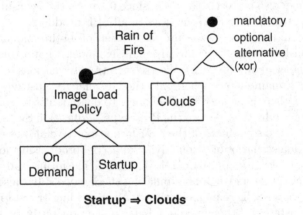

Startup ⇒ Clouds

Fig. 1. FM of a simplified mobile game SPL.

2.1 Overview

The CK establishes the mapping between features and assets [11]. This knowledge can be mixed with implementation [3,5], as in feature-oriented programming and preprocessing directives, or explicitly separated into a dedicated model [6]. In this work, we consider the latter: an artifact consisting on a list of configuration items, relating feature expressions to assets. These expressions, also

---

[1] Rain of fire mobile game, developed by *Meantime mobile creations*.

known as presence conditions, are propositional formulae, and enable expressive mappings of features into assets, instead of 1:1 mapping. The dedicated model also allows to be independent of the variability implementation language, so assets correspond to any kind of artifact.

Figure 2 illustrates the CK for the simplified mobile game SPL described by the FM in Fig. 1. Each row represents a configuration item, associating feature expressions with assets used to build products. In this example, assets are classes and aspects. For example, the second row establishes that if we select **Startup** or **On demand**, then **CommonImgLoad.java** should be part of the product. This class contains behavior shared by both image loading policies. So, we use an *or* feature expression to avoid repeating asset names in different rows.

Feature Expression	Assets
Rain of Fire	Game.java, GameScreen.java
On demand ∨ Startup	CommonImgLoad.java
On demand	OnDemand.aj
Startup	StartUp.aj
Clouds	Clouds.java

Fig. 2. CK for the simplified mobile game SPL.

CK evaluation against a configuration yields the assets needed to build the corresponding product. For example, evaluating the CK of Fig. 2 against {Rain of Fire, Image Load Policy, Startup, Clouds} yields the following set of assets: {Game.java, StartUp.aj, GameScreen.java, CommonImgLoad.java, Clouds.java}. This gives the basic intuition of the semantics of a CK [7,8].

As an SPL evolves, whether with new features and assets or with changes to existing assets, the internal structure of a CK might present problems. For example, in the CK of Fig. 2, we could replace the expression **Startup ∨ On demand** with **Image Load Policy**. This way, if we add a new image loading policy, we do not need to change the expression in the CK. Duplication could also happen. For example, if we had used two rows, one for **Startup** and other for **On demand**, both associated to the same asset name **CommonImgLoad.java**. These issues, akin to bad smells [15], among others, can difficult the understanding of the model and its evolution.

2.2 Formalization

In this section, we present the formalization of CK models we have previously proposed [8] for models such as the one we present in the previous section. We use PVS [27] to specify this theory. Hereafter, we use well-known mathematical symbols instead of PVS keywords, such as SET, AND, EXISTS, and FORALL, for improving readability.

We define the configuration knowledge (CK) as a finite set of items. Items contain a feature expression and a set of assets. We specify them with *record type* declarations, enclosed in angle brackets. The following fragment specifies these and other types such as `FeatureName` and `AssetName`, which are *uninterpreted types*. This means that they only assume that they are disjoint from all other types. We define the `Configuration` type to represent product configurations as a set of feature names, representing the selected features.

```
FeatureName: TYPE
AssetName: TYPE
Configuration: TYPE = P[FeatureName]
Item: TYPE= < exp:Formula, assets:F[AssetName] >
CK: TYPE= F[Item]
```

Each CK item contains a feature expression, which is a propositional formula. Possible formulae are: feature name, negation, conjunction and implication. Other kinds can be derived from these. We represent these with PVS abstract datatypes [27], which we omit here for brevity.

To enable unambiguous references to assets, instead of considering that a SPL contains a set of assets, we assume a mapping from asset names to actual assets. Such an Asset Mapping (AM) corresponds to an environment of asset declarations. This allows conflicting assets in an SPL, for instance, two versions of the same class, that implement mutually exclusive features. The semantics of a given configuration knowledge K is a function that maps AMs and product configurations into finite sets (represented by $\mathcal{F}$) of assets. We define that using the auxiliary `eval` function, which maps configurations into sets of asset names—for a configuration c, the set that *eval* yields contain an asset name n iff there is a row in K that contains n and its expression evaluates to true according to c. We use the notation $A\langle \_ \rangle$ for the relational image [30] of an asset mapping A, and $\exists\ i \in K \cdot p(i)$ as an abbreviation for the PVS notation $\exists\ i:Item \cdot i \in K \land p(i)$.

```
eval(K:CK, c:Configuration) : F[AssetName] =
{an | ∃ i ∈ K · satisfies(exp(i),c) ∧ an ∈ assets(i)}

semantics(K:CK, A:AM, c:Configuration) :  F[Asset] =
A⟨eval(K,c)⟩
```

To evaluate the CK, we need to check, for each item, if the feature expression is satisfied against the product configuration. We do this through the `satisfies` function. It evaluates a propositional formula against a configuration. For instance, feature expression A ∧ B evaluates to true when we select both A and B in a product configuration. More importantly, a configuration c satisfies the feature name formula n if n is a value in c. For conciseness, we do not present here the complete PVS formalization, which is available in our online appendix [32].

3   Safe Evolution of Product Lines

In this section we introduce the necessary concepts about SPL refinement and CK equivalence to understand the algebraic laws presented in this work. We first present a formal definition for SPLs and the refinement notion previously defined [8]. We then present a novel CK equivalence notion, different than the one from previous works, as it is indexed by the FM, and it is necessary for some of the laws we propose.

To guide our SPL evolution analysis, we rely on the SPL refinement theory [8]. Such theory is based on an asset refinement notion, which is useful for comparing assets with respect to behavior preservation. For our purposes, an SPL consists of an FM, a CK, and an AM that jointly generate products, that is, well-formed asset sets in their target languages. Although we use the term FM, this theory is defined in a general way as to avoid depending on particular FM, CK, and asset languages. Thus, we do not depend on a particular FM notation, and could use alternatives such as decision models [36]. The theory just assumes a generic function, represented as $[\![F]\!]$, to obtain its semantics as a set of configurations. Hereafter, for making the discussion less abstract, we use FM terminology. The theory specifies AMs as a finite function from asset names to assets. Finally, it also abstracts the details for CK, representing its semantics as $[\![K]\!]_c^A$—a function that receives a configuration knowledge K, an asset mapping A, and a product configuration c, to yield a finite set of assets that corresponds to a product from the SPL. The definition for SPLs given in what follows establishes that these three elements (FM, CK, AM) must jointly generate well-formed products. We use wf to represent the well-formedness constraint. It is necessary because missing an entry on a CK might lead to asset sets that do not correspond to valid products. Similarly, a mistake when writing a CK or AM entry might yield an invalid asset set due to conflicting assets. Since the theory does not depend on a particular asset language, wf might have different forms, depending on the particular asset language used. For instance, it might mean simply that the code compiles without errors.

Definition 1 ⟨Product line⟩
For a feature model F, an asset mapping A, and a configuration knowledge K, we say that tuple (F, A, K) is a product line when, for all $c \in [\![F]\!]$, $wf([\![K]\!]_c^A)$.

□

Similar to program refinement, SPL refinement is concerned with behavior preservation. However, it goes beyond code and other kinds of reusable assets, considering also FM and CK. In an SPL refinement, the resulting SPL should be able to generate products that behaviorally match the original SPL products. So users of an original product cannot observe behavior differences when using the corresponding product of the new SPL. This is exactly what guarantees safety when improving the SPL design.

In most SPL refinement scenarios, many changes need to be applied to code assets, FMs and CK, which often leads the refactored SPL to generate more products than before [22]. As long as it generates enough products to match the original SPL, users have no reason to complain. We extend the SPL, not arbitrarily, but in a safe way. Figure 3, illustrates this by showing two SPLs, PL and PL'. In this example, PL is refined by PL' because for each product in PL (represented by a star), there is a corresponding product in PL' that refines it (represented by a square). As explained before, PL' can have new products and still preserve the refinement relation. This ensures that the transformation is safe; we extend the SPL without impacting existing users. We formalize these ideas in terms of asset set refinement. Basically, each product generated by the original SPL must be refined by some product of the new, improved, SPL.

Definition 2 ⟨Product line refinement⟩
For product lines (F, A, K) and (F', A', K'), the second refines the first, denoted $(F, A, K) \sqsubseteq (F', A', K')$, whenever $\forall c \in [\![F]\!] \cdot \exists c' \in [\![F']\!] \cdot [\![K]\!]_c^A \sqsubseteq [\![K']\!]_{c'}^{A'}$.   □

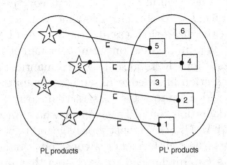

Fig. 3. Software product line refinement notion

Remember that, for a configuration c, a configuration knowledge K, and an asset mapping A related to a given SPL, $[\![K]\!]_c^A$ is a well-formed set of assets. Therefore, $[\![K]\!]_c^A \sqsubseteq [\![K']\!]_{c'}^{A'}$ refers to asset set refinement. Again, as the general theory does not rely on a particular asset language, asset refinement is just assumed as a pre-order. The definition just mentioned relates two SPLs, therefore, all products in the target SPL should be well-formed. The $\sqsubseteq$ symbol is used for SPLs as a relation that says when the transformation is safe. It does not mean functional equivalence because the refinement notion is a pre-order. It can reduce non-determinism, for example. The definition is also compositional, in the sense that refining an FM, AM, or CK that are part of a valid SPL yields a refined valid SPL. Such property is essential to guarantee independent development of these artifacts in an SPL. However, the CK equivalence previously defined [8] states that two CK models K and K' are equivalent, denoted $K \cong K'$, whenever $[\![K]\!] = [\![K']\!]$. Notice that this definition demands equality of functions. The equivalence must hold for any asset mapping and configuration.

However, in some occasions, it is important to have a weaker CK equivalence definition, that is restricted by a particular FM, instead of demanding equality of functions for any FM. In this work, we present a weaker equivalence notion, that is indexed by the FM, since the CK is used in conjunction with such artifact. For example, we can replace **On Demand** ∨ **Startup** with **Image Load Policy** on the CK of Fig. 2. Even though these are not propositionally equivalent, we can do so because selecting **Image Load Policy** implies in selecting one of the two child features. We have proved this equivalence notion to be reflexive, symmetric, and transitive.

Definition 3 ⟨Configuration Knowledge Equivalence⟩
For a feature model F, and configuration knowledge K and K', we say that $K \cong_F K'$ when, for all asset mapping A and $c \in \llbracket F \rrbracket$, $\llbracket K \rrbracket_c^A = \llbracket K' \rrbracket_c^A$. □

Since SPL refinement is reflexive [8], and the CK equivalence defined above ensures that all products remain the same, we can use this notion to justify safe evolution of SPLs when only the CK changes. The following theorem states this.

Theorem 1 ⟨CK equivalence compositionality⟩
For product lines (F, A, K) and (F, A, K'), if $K \cong_F K'$ then $(F, A, K) \sqsubseteq (F, A, K')$. □

Based on these properties, we can propose transformations to avoid reasoning over the semantics of CK models, which might be complex, by specifying syntactic conditions where we can guarantee that the equivalence holds. If the transformations have conditions that depend on reasoning about the FM, we need to use the weaker equivalence notion. Otherwise, we can use the previously proposed stronger equivalence notion [8].

4 Configuration Knowledge Laws

In this section, we propose primitive laws, that is, transformations that fix some of the problems we mention in Sect. 2, while preserving the behavior of the SPL products [8]. Although primitive, we can compose them to derive coarse-grained transformations.

A law consists of two templates (patterns) of equivalent CK models, on the Left-Hand Side (LHS) and Right-Hand Side (RHS). For example, Law 1 establishes that we can replace a feature expression by another whenever their evaluation is equivalent by the FM. Therefore, we use the equivalence notion indexed by the FM, thus the *fm* symbol in the equality. A law may declare meta-variables. For instance, in Law 1, we use *exp* to denote a feature expression and *n* to denote an asset name. For simplicity we use a single asset name in the law, but the proof can handle any set of assets associated with *exp*. The dots represent other CK items that remain unaltered. We can specify a condition below the template. Since each law defines two semantics-preserving CK transformations, the condition holds for both directions of the transformations. The condition for Law 1 states that we can apply this law when, according to *fm*, *exp* is equivalent to *exp'*. A special case of this law is the case where expressions are equivalent by propositional reasoning only, and we would not need to check expressions against the FM.

Law 1 ⟨*Simplify Feature Expression*⟩

Feature Expression	Assets		Feature Expression	Assets
...	...		...	...
exp	*n*	$\stackrel{=}{fm}$	*exp'*	*n*

$$fm \vdash (exp \Leftrightarrow exp')$$

We apply a law whenever the CK matches a template and satisfy its conditions. A matching is an assignment of all variables occurring in LHS/RHS models to concrete values. There are occasions where it might be better to apply a law from left to right, whereas in other situation, it is better to apply it from right to left. Applying Law 1 can be useful to improve CK readability. It might also be useful to improve maintainability. For example, in Fig. 2, we can replace the feature expression OnDemand ∨ Startup with Image Loading Policy, as they are equivalent by the FM, since both form an alternative group, therefore, whenever we select Image Loading Policy, we must select either OnDemand or Startup. If we add another image loading policy, we do not need to update the changed CK, while in the original, we would have to modify the feature expression.

Law 2 establishes that we can merge two CK items whenever their feature expressions are equivalent, according to the FM. We see that we merge *n* and *n'* into the same CK item, when applying the law from left to right. When applying from right to left, it also states that a CK item with multiple asset names can be splitted into items that have equivalent feature expressions. Application of this law from left to right can be useful in the context of improving long CK models, so we can reduce its size, thus, reducing cost for maintenance. However, it can also compromise readability.

Law 2 ⟨*Merge items with equivalent feature expressions*⟩

Feature Expression	Assets		Feature Expression	Assets
...	...		...	...
exp	*n*	$\stackrel{=}{fm}$	*exp*	*n, n'*
exp'	*n'*			

$$fm \vdash (exp \Leftrightarrow exp')$$

Duplicated assets can happen in the CK. Law 3 states that we can merge CK items with duplicated assets. It establishes that, from left to right, we can merge two CK items into a single item, creating a new feature expression. The new expression is the disjunction of the previous feature expressions. Applying the law from right to left, we can split an *or* feature expression into CK items containing duplicated assets. Notice that there is no *fm* in the equality. Therefore, we use the stronger equivalence notion, which is not indexed by the FM, since we do not need it in this case. When applying from left to right, this law improves readability of CK models, since we avoid duplication of assets names in the CK.

Law 3 ⟨*Duplicated Assets*⟩

Feature Expression	Assets
...	...
exp	n
exp'	n

$=$

Feature Expression	Assets
...	...
exp ∨ exp'	n

A dead feature is a feature that does not appear in any product configuration from the FM [34]. During SPL evolution, modifications to the FM can result in dead feature expressions. That is, no product configurations can satisfy them. This might be the result of changing feature relationships. Law 4 establishes that we can remove a feature expression *exp* from the LHS CK, when we deduce from *fm* that it is never evaluated as true. Since we can represent FMs as logical propositions, we can efficiently check this [25]. This law also states that, when applying it from right to left, we can add a line with a dead feature expression to our CK, without changing the semantics.

Law 4 ⟨*Dead Feature Expression*⟩

Feature Expression	Assets
...	...
exp'	n
exp	n'

$\underset{fm}{=}$

Feature Expression	Assets
...	...
exp'	n

$$fm \vdash \neg\, exp$$

Law 5 states that the order in which we write the CK has no effect on its semantics. We can change the order of any item in the CK. This holds since we are dealing with assets selection only, not with complex transformations that might need some sort of ordering among them. This law is useful to generalize application of all other laws. Since we do not modify anything in the CK except for the order, it is straightforward to understand why this transformation preserves semantics. Evaluation of the CK for all product configurations yields the same set of assets in both LHS and RHS CK models.

Law 5 ⟨*Change Order*⟩

Feature Expression	Assets
...	...
exp	*n*
exp'	*n'*

=

Feature Expression	Assets
...	...
exp'	*n'*
exp	*n*

5   Soundness

We also used PVS to prove all laws sound according to the CK equivalence notion (Definition 3). We use a similar approach as the one used for proving FM laws [16] and SPL refinement templates [8, 26, 28]. We structure each law as a theorem ensuring that it preserves the semantics of the CK, as follows. We represent the LHS and RHS CK models with the `ck1` and `ck2` variables, respectively. We represent FMs (`fm`) and AM (`am`) likewise. The `syntax` and `conditions` predicates describe syntactic similarities and differences between the LHS and RHS CK models in the law, and transformation conditions, respectively. The equivalence notion we use depends on the law we want to prove. When the law depends on the FM, we use the equivalence notion indexed by the FM ($\cong_F$). Otherwise, we use the stronger notion.

```
law: THEOREM
  ∀ fm:FM, ck1,ck2:CK ... ·
    syntax(...) ∧ conditions(...)
    ⇒ ck1 ≅ ck2
```

Next we specify these predicates for Law 1—Simplify Feature Expression. For each element in the template, we declare a variable for it in our PVS theory. For instance, the items which we refer to on Law 1 are represented by the PVS variables `it1` and `it2`, respectively. Aside from the item we are interested in changing, all other items from both CK models remain the same—`its`. For the item we are modifying, we are only changing the feature expression. Therefore, the asset set remains the same for `it1` and `it2`.

```
syntax(it1,it2:Item,its:P[Item],ck1,ck2:CK):boolean =
  ck1 = {it1} ∪ its ∧ ck2 = {it2} ∪ its ∧ assets(it1) = assets(it2)
```

We specify the `conditions` predicate as follows. The `sat` function specifies that, for all product configurations that can be derived from `fm`, evaluation of the feature expression (`satisfies`) for both items must be equivalent.

```
conditions(it1,it2:Item,fm:FM) = sat(fm,exp(it1),exp(it2))
```

We now detail the proof for Law 1. For arbitrary `fm`, `ck1`, `ck2`, `it1` and `it2`, assume that the `syntax` and `conditions` predicates hold. Therefore, since we want to prove that $ck1 \cong_{fm} ck2$ we need to prove, for an arbitrary `am` and a $c \in$ `semantics(fm)`, that

```
semantics(ck1,am,c) = semantics(ck2,am,c)
```

Fully expanding the definition of semantics and replacing `ck1` and `ck2` with their respective values from the syntax predicate, we have to prove that

```
{a:Asset |
 ∃ (an:AssetName) ·
  (∃ (i:Item) · item = it1 ∨ item ∈ its ∧ satisfies(exp(i),c)
                ∧ an ∈ assets(i)) ∧ (an,a) ∈ am)}
=
{a:Asset |
 ∃ (an:AssetName) ·
  (∃ (i:Item) · item = it2 ∨ item ∈ its ∧ satisfies(exp(i),c)
                ∧ an ∈ assets(i)) ∧ (an,a) ∈ am)}
```

For items in `its`, it is straightforward to prove that the yielded assets are the same in both models. The only distinct items are `it1` and `it2`. Using the `conditions` predicate, we have that `eval(exp(it1),c)` $\Leftrightarrow$ `eval(exp(it2),c)` for all $c \in$ `semantics(fm)`. This way, we are able to prove that the assets set yielded for `ck1` is equal to the assets set yielded for `ck2`, since we have that `assets(it1) = assets(it2)` in the syntax predicate.

Using similar reasoning, we can prove that Law 2 is sound, since we have the same condition for both laws. For Law 3, we prove soundness by demonstrating that the merging preserves semantics, since the RHS model yields *a* whether *exp* or *exp'* evaluates to true, according to a product configuration. Therefore, the assets set yielded remain the same as in the LHS model. Law 4 also preserves semantics, since we are introducing or removing an item whose feature expression is dead, meaning that it is not evaluated true for any product configuration. Therefore, it has no effect in the assets yielded when evaluating the CK. Finally, in Law 5, all items of both LHS and RHS CK models are the same, except for the order in which we write them. Therefore, it preserves semantics. Formal proofs and all PVS specification files are available at our online appendix [32].

6 Case Study

In this section, we analyze the evolution of a real SPL and evaluate how the laws can be used to evolve the CK during its development and maintenance. We analyzed TaRGeT [14], an SPL of tools that automatically generate functional tests from use case documents written in natural language. This SPL has been used by a mobile phone company to generate tests for its devices. It has six releases and over 32 KLOC on the latest. We manually analyzed CK transformations in commits of its last three versioned releases, looking for scenarios where only the CK was changed. Moreover, after this evaluation, we have extended a toolset for checking SPL refinements [13] to include the automated checking for all of these laws.

We found four scenarios where we could justify safe evolution of the SPL applying the laws presented in this work. In the first one, the developer team replaced the feature expression **TC 3** ∨ **TC 4** with **Output**, to improve CK readability and maintainability. Figure 4 depicts this transformation, presenting the CK before and after the transformation, as well as part of the FM that is of interest for this transformation, represented by *fm* in the equality. After performing this transformation, if we add a new child for **Output**, we do not need to update the feature expression in the CK anymore. We can justify safe evolution in this transformation applying Law 1, from left to right.

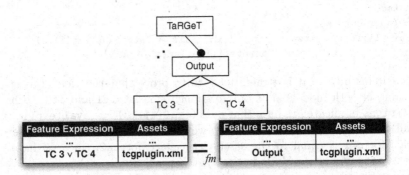

Fig. 4. Usage of Law 1 in TaRGeT SPL to simplify the feature expression.

In the second scenario, the developers merged the **TC 3** and **TC 4** feature expressions into a single item with the **TC 3** ∨ **TC 4** expression, associated to the same asset. This improved CK readability, avoiding duplicated asset names. Figure 5 illustrates this transformation, with the CK models and part of the FM. We apply Law 3 from left to right to justify safe evolution.

In the third and fourth scenarios, developers merged duplicated feature expressions, to improve CK maintainability, reducing its size and removing duplicated feature expressions. Figure 6 presents the third scenario. They merged five items with the repeated **Interruption** expression into just one item and their associated assets. Similarly, Fig. 7 depicts the fourth transformation where they replaced repetitions of **Company 1** and **Company 2**. In both cases, we can use Law 2 from left to right to justify safe evolution. Additionally, in the fourth scenario, the developer team changed the order of the transformations, as presented in Law 5, to apply the previous transformation.

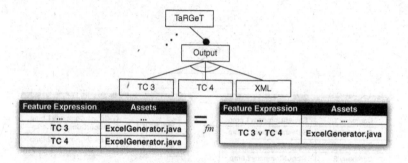

Fig. 5. Usage of Law 3 in TaRGeT SPL to remove assets duplication.

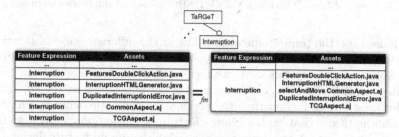

Fig. 6. Usage of Law 2 in TaRGeT SPL to remove duplicated expression.

The commits in TaRGeT consisted of many changes to different assets, instead of commits performed often, with small and localized changes. Therefore, it is possible that other scenarios where only the CK changed were not captured by the SPL version history. A manual analysis of 500 commits from the highly configurable system Soletta identified that 122 commits (24.4%) only change the Makefile [17], which would be analogous to the CK, for Kconfig-based systems. Moreover, 241 out of the 500 commits change the CK in conjunction with FM or code. Therefore, it is possible that changes to the CK are followed by changes to other SPL elements, and could benefit from the transformations proposed here.

7   Related Work

Several approaches [19,20,24,35] focus on refactoring a single product into a SPL. Kolb et al. [20] discuss a case study in refactoring legacy code components into a product line implementation. They define a systematic process for refactoring products to obtain product lines assets. There is no discussion about feature models and configuration knowledge. Moreover, behavior preservation is only checked by testing. Similarly, Kästner et al. [19] focus only on transforming code assets, implicitly relying on refinement notions for aspect-oriented programs [10]. As discussed elsewhere [7] these are not adequate for justifying SPL refinement. Trujillo et al. [35] go beyond code assets, but do not explicitly consider CK transformations. They also do not consider behavior preservation;

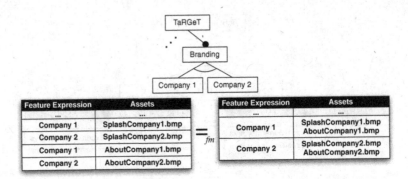

Fig. 7. Usage of Laws 2 and 5 in TaRGeT SPL to remove duplicated expressions.

they indeed use the term "refinement", but in the different sense of overriding or adding extra behavior to assets. Moreover, all of these works focus on whole SPL evolution, while in this work, we focus on CK changes.

Liu et al. [24] also focus on the process of decomposing a legacy application into features, but go further than the previously cited approaches by proposing a refactoring theory that explains how a feature can be automatically associated to a code asset and related derivative assets, which contain feature declarations appropriate for different product configurations. Contrasting with our CK model, this theory assumes an implicit notion of CK based on the idea of derivatives. So it does not consider explicit CK transformations as we do here. In this work, we focus on refinements at a different level—models instead of programs.

Alves et al. extend the traditional notion of refactoring to SPLs [1]. Besides traditional program refactoring, they refactor FMs in order to improve configurability. They present and evaluate a set of sound FM refactorings in a real case study in the mobile domain. In an extension of this work, Gheyi et al. propose a sound, complete and minimal catalog of algebraic laws for FMs [16]. Moreover, they mechanized a theory for FMs in PVS, which we reuse in our theory for CK models in PVS. Nevertheless, these notions are not concerned with CK transformations, they only consider FM transformations.

An informal discussion of the CK semantics discussed here first appeared in a product line refactoring tutorial [7]. Besides talking about SPL and population refactoring, this tutorial illustrates different kinds of refactoring transformation templates that can be useful for deriving and evolving SPLs, including CK transformations. Later, the refinement theory was formalized [8], making clear the interface between the theory and languages used to describe SPL artifacts. Our work is complementary, since we use the CK language that instantiates the interface proposed, proposing individual CK transformations that adhere to the SPL refinement notion. Sampaio et al. extends the theory with a partial refinement notion, which formalizes the concept of partially safe evolution [28]—that is, evolution scenarios where only a subset of products from the original SPL has their behavior preserved. To use such notion we would need to propose transformations that are not behavior-preserving.

Recent works investigating the evolution characteristics of highly configurable systems show that evolving only the mapping between features and assets is not uncommon [12,17,21]. Kröher et al. evaluates the intensity of variability-related changes in the Linux kernel [21]. They measured how often changes occur in FM, AM, and CK, and how do those changes relate to variability information inside these artifacts. Our work could use theirs as input to identify potential instances where only the CK has been changed and investigate the use of the laws, if we adapted our model to comply with the one used by the Linux kernel. A tool with the same purpose is FEVER [12], which allows analysing Kconfig-based systems to extract feature-oriented change information. It is used in the work of Gomes et al. [17] to classifying evolution scenarios into safe or partially safe. Moreover, Gomes et al. also manually evaluated 500 commits from a system, showing that in 122 cases, only the CK has been changed by a commit. Again, this information provides evidence that changing only the CK is not uncommon.

8 Conclusions

In this work, we propose a set of laws for transforming CK models, that justify safe SPL evolution. We ensure this using the SPL refinement theory [8]. We propose a weaker equivalence notion and its associated compositionality result. We can apply these laws to fix problems such as duplicated assets and dead feature expressions. We use PVS to specify and prove soundness of the proposed laws. Therefore, developers do not need to reason based on semantics in order to refactor a CK, as the catalog can be directly applied. Thus, since SPL refinement is a pre-order, we can compose them with laws for FMs [16] and other SPL refinement templates [26] to derive elaborate transformations with the guarantee that we do not change behavior of existing products in the SPL.

As future work, we intend to investigate the completeness and minimality of our laws, proposing a CK normalization algorithm. Even though we did not achieve this result, we observed from our preliminary results, that the laws could justify safe evolution scenarios of a real SPL. We also intend to adapt our model and laws to consider KBuild notation, so we can evaluate it in other highly configurable systems that have been previously investigated in the context of safe and partially safe evolution [17,28]. Moreover, we also intend to implement automated tool support for checking the conditions to apply the laws in this context. As the transformations precisely specify the mechanics and preconditions, their soundness is specially useful for correctly implementing the transformations and avoiding typical problems with current program refactoring tools [31]. Finally, the theory we present in this work formalizes part of the concepts and processes from tools [9,24] and practical experience [1,19,20,35] on SPL refactoring.

Acknowledgments. This work was partially supported by CAPES (grants 117875 and 175956), CNPq (grants 409335/2016-9, 426005/2018-0, and 311442/2019-6) and FACEPE (APQ-0570-1.03/14), as well as INES 2.0, (http://www.ines.org.br) FACEPE grants PRONEX APQ-0388-1.03/14 and APQ-0399-1.03/17, and CNPq grant 465614/2014-0.

References

1. Alves, V., Gheyi, R., Massoni, T., Kulesza, U., Borba, P., Lucena, C.: Refactoring product lines. In: GPCE 2006, pp. 201–210 (2006)
2. Apel, S., Batory, D., Kstner, C., Saake, G.: Feature-Oriented Software Product-Lines: Concepts and Implementation. Springer, Heidelberg (2013). https://doi.org/10.1007/978-3-642-37521-7
3. Batory, D.S.: Feature-oriented programming and the AHEAD tool suite. In: ICSE 2004, pp. 702–703 (2004)
4. Batory, D.: Feature models, grammars, and propositional formulas. In: Obbink, H., Pohl, K. (eds.) SPLC 2005. LNCS, vol. 3714, pp. 7–20. Springer, Heidelberg (2005). https://doi.org/10.1007/11554844_3
5. Berger, T., She, S., Lotufo, R., Wasowski, A., Czarnecki, K.: Variability modeling in the real: a perspective from the operating systems domain. In: ASE 2010, pp. 73–82 (2010)
6. Bonifácio, R., Borba, P.: Modeling scenario variability as crosscutting mechanisms. In: AOSD 2009, pp. 125–136 (2009)
7. Borba, P.: An introduction to software product line refactoring. In: Fernandes, J.M., Lämmel, R., Visser, J., Saraiva, J. (eds.) GTTSE 2009. LNCS, vol. 6491, pp. 1–26. Springer, Heidelberg (2011). https://doi.org/10.1007/978-3-642-18023-1_1
8. Borba, P., Teixeira, L., Gheyi, R.: A theory of software product line refinement. Theoret. Comput. Sci. **455**, 2–30 (2012)
9. Calheiros, F., Borba, P., Soares, S., Nepomuceno, V., Alves, V.: Product line variability refactoring tool. In: WRT 2007 at ECOOP 2007, pp. 33–34 (2007)
10. Cole, L., Borba, P.: Deriving refactorings for AspectJ. In: AOSD 2005, pp. 123–134. ACM (2005)
11. Czarnecki, K., Eisenecker, U.W.: Generative Programming: Methods, Tools, and Applications. ACM Press/Addison-Wesley, New York (2000)
12. Dintzner, N., van Deursen, A., Pinzger, M.: FEVER: an approach to analyze feature-oriented changes and artefact co-evolution in highly configurable systems. Empirical Softw. Eng. **23**(2), 905–952 (2017). https://doi.org/10.1007/s10664-017-9557-6
13. Ferreira, F., Gheyi, R., Borba, P., Soares, G.: A toolset for checking SPL refinements. J. Univ. Comput. Sci. **20**(5), 587–614 (2014)
14. Ferreira, F., Neves, L., Silva, M., Borba, P.: Target: a model based product line testing tool. In: Tools Session at CBSoft 2010, pp. 67–72 (2010)
15. Fowler, M.: Refactoring: Improving the Design of Existing Code. Addison-Wesley, New York (1999)
16. Gheyi, R., Massoni, T., Borba, P.: Algebraic laws for feature models. J. Univ. Comput. Sci. **14**(21), 3573–3591 (2008)
17. Gomes, K., Teixeira, L., Alves, T., Ribeiro, M., Gheyi, R.: Characterizing safe and partially safe evolution scenarios in product lines: An empirical study. In: VaMoS 2019 (2019)
18. Kang, K., Cohen, S., Hess, J., Novak, W., Peterson, A.S.: Feature-oriented domain analysis (FODA) feasibility study. Technical report, CMU Software Engineering Institute (1990)
19. Kastner, C., Apel, S., Batory, D.: A case study implementing features using AspectJ. In: SPLC 2007, pp. 223–232. IEEE (2007)
20. Kolb, R., Muthig, D., Patzke, T., Yamauchi, K.: A case study in refactoring a legacy component for reuse in a product line. In: ICSM 2005, pp. 369–378 (2005)

21. Kröher, C., Gerling, L., Schmid, K.: Identifying the intensity of variability changes in software product line evolution. In: SPLC, pp. 54–64 (2018)
22. Krueger, C.W.: Easing the transition to software mass customization. In: van der Linden, F. (ed.) PFE 2001. LNCS, vol. 2290, pp. 282–293. Springer, Heidelberg (2002). https://doi.org/10.1007/3-540-47833-7_25
23. Van der Linden, F., Schmid, K., Rommes, E.: Software Product Lines in Action: the Best Industrial Practice in Product Line Engineering. Springer, Heidelberg (2007). https://doi.org/10.1007/978-3-540-71437-8
24. Liu, J., Batory, D., Lengauer, C.: Feature oriented refactoring of legacy applications. In: ICSE 2006, pp. 112–121 (2006)
25. Mendonca, M., Wasowski, A., Czarnecki, K.: Sat-based analysis of feature models is easy. In: SPLC 2009, pp. 231–240 (2009)
26. Neves, L., Borba, P., Alves, V., Turnes, L., Teixeira, L., Sena, D., Kulesza, U.: Safe evolution templates for software product lines. JSS **106**(C), 42–58 (2015)
27. Owre, S., Shankar, N., Rushby, J.M., Stringer-Calvert, D.W.J.: PVS Language Reference. SRI International (2001). http://pvs.csl.sri.com/doc/pvs-language-reference.pdf, version 2.4
28. Sampaio, G., Borba, P., Teixeira, L.: Partially safe evolution of software product lines. J. Syst. Softw. **155**, 17–42 (2019)
29. Schobbens, P.Y., Heymans, P., Trigaux, J.C., Bontemps, Y.: Generic semantics of feature diagrams. Comput. Netw. **51**(2), 456–479 (2007)
30. Spivey: The Z Notation: A Reference Manual. Prentice Hall (1987)
31. Steimann, F., Thies, A.: From public to private to absent: refactoring JAVA programs under constrained accessibility. In: Drossopoulou, S. (ed.) ECOOP 2009. LNCS, vol. 5653, pp. 419–443. Springer, Heidelberg (2009). https://doi.org/10.1007/978-3-642-03013-0_19
32. Teixeira, L., Gheyi, R., Borba, P.: Online appendix (2020). http://www.cin.ufpe.br/~lmt/sbmf2020/
33. Teixeira, L., Alves, V., Borba, P., Gheyi, R.: A product line of theories for reasoning about safe evolution of product lines. In: SPLC 2015, pp. 161–170 (2015)
34. Trinidad, P., Benavides, D., Durán, A., Cortés, A.R., Toro, M.: Automated error analysis for the agilization of feature modeling. JSS **81**(6), 883–896 (2008)
35. Trujillo, S., Batory, D., Diaz, O.: Feature refactoring a multi-representation program into a product line. In: GPCE 2006, pp. 191–200 (2006)
36. Weiss, D.M., Li, J.J., Slye, J.H., Dinh-Trong, T.T., Sun, H.: Decision-model-based code generation for SPLE. In: SPLC 2008, pp. 129–138 (2008)

Author Index

Printed in the United States
By Bookmasters

Printed in the United States
By Bookmasters